ENVIRONMENTAL HUMAN RIGHTS

This book is dedicated to my grandparents, James and Audrey Hancock, Lisa Misch and to the memory of Walter Misch.

Environmental Human Rights

Power, ethics and law

JAN HANCOCK
Birkbeck College, University of London

ASHGATE

Published by
Ashgate Publishing Limited
Gower House
Croft Road
Aldershot
Hants GU11 3HR
England

Ashgate Publishing Company
Suite 420
101 Cherry Street
Burlington, VT 05401-4405
USA

Ashgate website: http://www.ashgate.com

British Library Cataloguing in Publication Data
Hancock, Jan
    Environmental human rights : power, ethics and law. -
    (Critical security series)
    1.Human rights 2.Environmental law 3.Environmental
    responsibility 4.Natural resources - Management
    5.Environmental policy - Citizen participation 6.Corporate
    power
    I.Title
    323

Library of Congress Cataloging-in-Publication Data
Hancock, Jan.
    Environmental human rights : power, ethics and law / Jan Hancock.
        p. cm. -- (Critical security series)
    Includes bibliographical references and index.
    ISBN 0-7546-1986-9
        1. Environmental justice. 2. Environmental ethics. I. Title. II. Series.

GE220.H36 2003
363.7--dc21

2002043973

ISBN 0 7546 1986 9

Printed and bound in Great Britain by MPG Books Ltd, Bodmin, Cornwall.

Contents

List of Tables

Acknowledgements

Thanks to all staff and students at Birkbeck College for a great end to 2002. Many thanks also to members of the politics department at Southampton University, especially Tony Evans, Nana Poku, Caroline Thomas, Tony McGrew, Graham Smith, Russell Bentley, David Owen and Andy Mason, for all the discussions that inspired the development of many of the thoughts that find expression in the following pages. Many thanks also to Neil Stammers for both his constructive criticism and insightful comments.

ESRC grant R00429924183 is acknowledged for providing funding for part of this research.

Many thanks to my mother, father and grandparents for all their support and encouragement over the years. Thanks to Dan, Simon and Steph for being such great friends. Thanks also to my friends in Victoria, BC, Laura, Kim, Anne, Elizabeth, Tony and Sarah for a fantastic 1999. Thanks to all the mountains in British Colombia upon whose slopes a great number of the ideas in this research were first considered. Still in Canada, thanks to the Greater Victoria Cycling Coalition for the anti-car stickers and for all their great work on the cycle network in Victoria that kept this author fit and happy during the writing of the first draft.

Thanks to the Southampton triathlon club for the Saturday races in the New Forest and to the Southampton University cycling club for the training runs in the South Downs.

Special thanks to Earth First!ers everywhere for their dedication in raging against the dying of the light.

Most importantly, many, many thanks to Morwenna for everything, for all the hard work, for being a constant source of energy and inspiration and most of all thanks for making me so happy.

List of Abbreviations

AMA	Automobile Manufacturers Association
AWA	Antarctic Wilderness Area
CAFOD	Catholic Fund for Overseas Development
CAMPFIRE	Communal Areas Management Program for Indigenous Resources
CEO	Chief Executive Officer
CHEER	Coalition for Health, Environmental and Economic Rights
CODEH	Committee for the Defense of Human Rights in Honduras
CoP	Conference of Parties
CPR	Common Property Resources
DNA	Deoxyribonucleic Acid
DSS	Dispute Settlement System
EPA	Environmental Protection Agency
EPZ	Export Processing Zone
ERT	European Roundtable of Industrialists
EU	European Union
EUROPABIO	European Association for Bio-industries
EZLN	Zapatista Army of National Liberation
FAO	Food and Agriculture Organization
FDI	Foreign Direct Investment
GAO	General Accounting Office
GATT	General Agreement on Tariffs and Trade
GCIP	Global Climate Information Project
GDP	Gross Domestic Product
GEF	Global Environmental Facility
GEI	Global Economic Institutions
ICCPR	International Covenant on Civil and Political Rights
ICESCR	International Covenant on Economic, Social and Cultural Rights
ILO	International Labor Organization
IMF	International Monetary Fund
IPCC	Intergovernmental Panel on Climate Change
MMT	Methylcyclopentadienyl Manganese Tricarbonyl
MNC	Multi National Corporation
MST	Movement for Landless People
NAFTA	North American Free Trade Agreement
NGO	Non-governmental Organization
OECD	Organization for Economic Co-operation and Development
PCB	Poly Chlorinated Biphenyl
PM10	Particulate pollutant

ppb	parts per billion
RTZ	Rio Tinto Zinc
SAP	Structural Adjustment Policy
SLORC	State Law and Order Restoration Council
SPDC	Shell Petroleum Development Company
TNC	Trans National Corporation
UBBWU	United Banners Banana Workers Union
UK	United Kingdom
UN	United Nations
UNCED	United Nations Conference on Environment and Development
UNCTC	United Nations Center on Trans National Corporations
UNDP	United Nations Development Program
UNESCO	United Nations Economic, Social and Cultural Organization
UNFCCC	United Nations Framework Convention on Climate Change
UNICE	European Employers Confederation
US	United States
WBCSD	World Business Council for Sustainable Development
WHO	World Health Organization
WTO	World Trade Organization

Introduction

Key Conceptual Questions

All the major environmental problems presently confronting the world are ultimately derived from four general patterns characterizing modern societies, (i) pollution, (ii) overuse or misuse of resources, (iii) biodiversity reduction and (iv) habitat destruction. The research presented here suggests that these environmental problems could be in part addressed through respecting the following two universal human rights; (i) to an environment free from toxic pollution and (ii) to ownership rights of natural resources.

Demonstrating environmental benefits is, of course, insufficient grounds for claiming new human rights. Indeed, post-modernists and relativists remind us that the philosophical grounds upon which foundational claims to any human rights can be substantiated is a contestable issue, with the specified criteria typically reflecting the political predilections of the author (Brown, 1992; Ashley, 1996). The criterion utilized in this research to investigate the existence of environmental human rights will be restricted to existing legal human rights stipulations. It will be demonstrated that the two universal environmental human rights claimed above can be imputed from the existing international law on human rights. This legalistic approach is not without either epistemological problems or political bias and it is appropriate to explain these at the outset of the inquiry.

What is the Efficacy of International Law to Implement Environmental Human Rights?

There exists widespread belief that revising and updating either domestic or international law is sufficient to realize social change in the area covered by legislation (Evans and Hancock, 1998). Altering legislation can have a noticeable impact on society. In his study of environmental rights, Hayward for example demonstrates a role for legal developments in initiating (i) an upward ratcheting effect on political expectations, (ii) the fostering of a publicly recognized environmental ethic and (iii) a more comprehensive set of social values rather than a narrow focus on private interest (Hayward, 2000).

However, law does not implement a set of rules in an impartial manner, but is instead an instrument of hegemonic power. It is therefore important to differentiate between (i) the values inherent to the stipulations of international human rights law and (ii) the actual implementation thereof. Whereas the stipulated wording of international human rights law expresses a focus on social provisions for the basic needs of all, law has been implemented in ways that tolerate systematic violations to accommodate the interests of the capitalist economy. This paradox leads to an ambiguous and even contradictory role for international human rights law. On a superficial analysis international human rights law appears to be the rules based mechanism required to protect the vulnerable and marginalized from being exploited or otherwise made to suffer under the self-interested politics of the powerful. Yet the actual implementation of law tends inexorably to reflect existent power relations in society. In the contemporary political economy, this service to power translates into the legalistic prioritization of corporate interests over the social values implied in human rights stipulations where social values are defined as the defense of the otherwise vulnerable (Goodin, 1985). For example it will be demonstrated in the following chapters that the actual implementation of existing international human rights law would require implementation of the two environmental human rights claimed above. The present neglect of the claimed environmental human rights reflects the selective implementation of legal stipulations to serve existing economic processes of consumption, production and exchange. Legal stipulations to the contrary notwithstanding, environmental human rights will remain unimplemented whilst social power relations favor capitalism and processes of economic accumulation that are predicated upon the systematic violation of those rights.

Why Extend Environmental Considerations Beyond Environmental Law and to Human Rights?

This research will argue that the explicit inclusion of environmental factors in human rights legislation is a necessary requirement for existing legal rights to be realized. The history of environmental law has evidenced compromise between environmental and commercial considerations that has consistently prioritized the interests of the latter over the former. In the case of toxic pollutants, for example, environmental laws currently permit emissions at levels that can physically harm individuals (chapter 5). New human rights would therefore be more helpful than revised environmental laws in dealing with environmental problems since the rights discourse could provide environmental legislation with a heightened status which would reflect the importance of environmental concerns (Hayward, 2000). A heightened status accompanies human rights since these are inalienable and can be codified in legislation with established mechanisms of enforcement (Hayward, 2000).

Finally, linking the environmental and human rights discourses can be illuminating since this introduces an alternative conceptualization of both subjects that can facilitate new ways of questioning existing political terms of reference. The value of introducing alternative conceptualizations of political themes resides in understanding how academic discourse has developed not along objective or value neutral lines but rather by focusing on one particular agenda that serves particular social interests at the expense of marginalizing other possibilities. For example, a discourse of human rights that downplays questions of access to food and clean water neglects the principal concerns of those presently denied access to such resources. The agenda that increasingly monopolizes intergovernmental discussions views human rights in terms of state abstention from intervention with individual autonomy, a definition that benefits powerful social elements whose interests are best served through the maintenance of a capitalist political economy (Evans, 2000).

Why a Rights Based Approach Rather Than One of Duties?

Notions of duties or obligations are socially constructed products of the societies whose political culture they embody and whose values they express (Renteln, 1990). According to legal analysis, individuals are duty bound to respect the rights of others and to abstain from disobeying those social customs codified in laws. Duties are therefore derived from, and a reflection of, rights and other laws. Rights can subsequently be identified as the primary focus for attention since they stand logically prior to duties. Rights are also more tangible than duties since they benefit from a higher degree of public visibility, understanding and support than a parallel discourse of duties (Feinberg, 1988).

Of course, duties could be conceptualized in ethical terms based upon arguments of political philosophy rather than upon legal stipulations, but such a project would be susceptible to the same criticisms that beset attempts to establish a philosophical basis for human rights. In particular, claims to duties can be expected to act as a veneer for the political inclinations of the author and are therefore of limited value for epistemological investigation, that is in relation to the claims to truth that are made through such an inquiry. For these reasons, this research is explicitly focused on the discourse of human rights rather than that of duties.

Would Environmental Arguments Not Stand Independently of Being Linked to Human Rights?

The validity or importance ascribed to environmental arguments is a function of the relative weighting of competing values and political positions by the observer. Whereas environmental arguments alone could indeed determine policy in a political culture predicated upon environmental values, this in no sense applies to a capitalist system (Daly and Cobb, 1994). In capitalist politics, environmental arguments have conspicuously failed to subordinate economic considerations to those of ecological protection (chapter 1). Drawing environmental concerns into the remit of human rights offers a further mechanism for the articulation of ecological values.

What Grounds Justify the Investigation of Environmental Human Rights?

Existing legally recognized human rights presuppose a certain environmental quality and distribution of environmental resources (Smith, 1996). Yet this assumption is rarely explicitly stated. A discourse of human rights that focuses on fundamental environmental factors is therefore highlighting an important variable that is typically overlooked by the existing literature.

Conceptual Definitions

To clarify the research to follow, it is appropriate to define and to briefly introduce the concepts used in subsequent chapters.

Environment

The environment is defined as the constitutive components of the biosphere of the planet Earth. Included in this definition are flora, fauna and natural resources such as the atmosphere, land, sub soil resources and water. The environmental perspective refers to the political approach that uses as its central decision making criterion the long term interests of the biosphere as a whole. This definition of environmentalism must be differentiated from the common use of the term in modern political discourse that, as an example of an oxymoron, refers to an agenda that rarely prioritizes ecological over economic values.

Environmentalism as defined in this research is therefore interchangeable with what others have termed deep ecology (Naess, 1973). Ecology is the scientific study of interactions that determine the distribution and numbers of biological organisms in a given area (Marshall, 1998). The ecological perspective, deep ecology, denotes the political approach centered on an ethic of concern for the well-being of biodiversity and habitats (Caldwell, 1971; Naess, 1973; Dryzek, 1983; Tarlock, 1988). Deep ecology is predicated upon an entirely different value system and epistemology from mainstream political and economic theory and can therefore be said to constitute a different form of rationality (chapter 1). Aldo Leopold asserted the fundamental criterion of ecological rationality when he claimed that, 'a thing is right when it tends to preserve the integrity, stability, and beauty of the biotic community. It is wrong when it tends otherwise' (Leopold, 1949).

The overriding importance of ecological considerations is rejected by the second system of rationality discussed in this book, that of neo-liberal economic rationality, hereafter termed economic rationality, which dominates the discipline of economics. Economic rationality defines the policy making process in capitalist states and has considerations of economic growth and the efficient allocation of resources as its central imperatives (chapter 1). Economic rationality reflects materialistic values, advancing the view that human society and the wider environment should be put to work for the benefit of the economy, rather than that the economy should be organized to work for the benefit of the people and the environment. The importance of the biotic community highlighted above by Leopold is excluded from the ethical formula provided by economic rationality to evaluate political policies. Environmental human rights may simultaneously appear self-evident to the environmentalist and nonsensical to the economist because of the incommensurate values and conceptualizations of rationality employed by each theorist. Epistemological claims to human rights on the basis of what is said to be 'rational' will therefore be identified as relative or contingent, rather than as universal in character.

This research does not seek to explicitly contribute to the existing debate between social ecologists and deep ecologists. Instead, basic human needs are identified together with the needs of environmental protection in opposition to economic rationality. Economic rationality validates as allocatively efficient the exploitation of resources for the benefit of luxury markets at the expense of the needs of the impoverished, of future generations and of non-human life (chapter 1). Subsequently, this research argues that it is not the existence of human life but is rather the capitalist configuration of the political economy that is threatening the sustainability of eco-systems. The lament that human life *per se* leads to environmental degradation often begins from the mistaken assumption that human nature can only be defined in terms of egotistical consumerism. One alternative characterization of human nature, prominent in indigenous cultures, identifies the self and other members of human society as a part of a wider ecosystem (chapters 1 and 3).

It is useful to conceptualize incommensurate forms of rationality in terms of distinct paradigms. A paradigm can be defined as a fundamental frame of reference, that is a particular set of models and values that characterize and define both the methodology and epistemology of 'normal' inquiry (Kuhn, 1962; Drengson, 1980). Assertions of a single, objective rational paradigm are epistemologically arbitrary and intellectually oppressive since this falsely universalizes a contingent system of values, standards and practices (that of the dominant model) and denies the validity of truth claims made by alternative paradigms or cultures (Dryzek, 1990).

One environmental issue perceived in different terms by ecological and economic rationality is that of toxic pollution. Toxic pollution can be defined as the anthropogenic introduction into the environment of substances or energy known to harm either human health or ecological systems (Byrne, 1997). Under this definition, toxic pollution is restricted to substances produced by human societies rather than harmful chemicals existing in the environment *per se*. This distinction is made since, unlike anthropogenic activities, the production of chemicals by such natural occurrences as volcanic eruptions cannot be addressed by human notions of justice, social organizations or legal institutions. The production of pollution benefits the polluter at the expense of other individuals and at the expense of the environment and thereby constitutes what economists refer to as an externality (Gowdy, 1999). An externality exists whenever the utility of an individual is diminished by choices made by others in ways that are not recorded through the market mechanism (Bojo, Maler and Unemo, 1990).

Human Rights

The meaning of human rights has been defined in a number of distinct forms by different political theorists. Most important amongst these are concepts of negative, positive and basic rights. Negative rights endow the individual with the right against any form of arbitrary interference from another party that would prejudice their interests (Goodin, 1985). Positive rights conversely require others to take positive action to benefit the rights holder (Goodin, 1985). The central point of tension between these two contending conceptualizations of rights is therefore the issue of interference. Whereas negative rights are premised upon the predominance of liberalism and individual independence, positive rights stress social values and require collective action to aid the otherwise vulnerable. The concept of basic human rights introduced by Shue rejects attempts to differentiate positive from negative rights and instead defines human rights in terms of those goods required for human survival (Shue, 1980; Shue, 1981; Vincent, 1986; Freeden, 1991; Donnelly, 1993; Jones, 1994). In particular, physical needs have been identified by Shue as conferring basic rights to subsistence and security (Shue, 1980).

The differing conceptual foundations of human rights have, however unsatisfactorily, been formally resolved in the inter-governmental forums through a precise listing of rights in the Universal Declaration of Human Rights (Council of Europe Press, 1995). This non-legally binding declaration has subsequently been legally codified in the International Covenant on Economic, Social and Cultural Rights (ICESCR) and the International Covenant on Civil and Political Rights (ICCPR). Together, these documents form the cornerstone of international human rights law. None of the provisions contained in any of these three documents explicitly guarantee entitlements that all people possess, that are principally concerned with environmental conditions although as chapter six discusses, both the ICESCR and the ICCPR do mention rights to natural resources in terms of self-determination.

It will be argued in this research that to guarantee the environmental conditions required for the enjoyment of existing legally stipulated human rights, it is necessary to adopt only two environmental human rights. Based upon philosophical, rather than legal claims, other theorists have advocated an approach of formulating an entirely new generation of human rights to specify a more extensive list of environmental human rights (Shelton, 1991; Waks, 1996). Such an approach could be expected to enhance the profile and priority assigned to environmental values. However, such a project falls outside the remit of this research where the focus is instead placed upon identifying those environmental human rights that are required to realize existing legal rights. Following from this explicit focus, this research examines only anthropocentric rights and does not look at rights of the environment in general or those of non-human animals. However, the absence of a discussion of such rights in this thesis in no sense implies that non-human agents cannot possess rights (Singer, 1990).

The relation between environmental human rights and other categories of human rights eludes simple definition. There are a number of ways in which the environmental human rights claimed above support existing human rights. As chapters five and six explain, it is, for instance, necessary to guarantee a minimum set of environmental conditions to implement universal human rights to life, health, self-determination, freedom from hunger and individual liberty.

However, it is also possible to identify a contradiction between the claimed environmental human rights and the right to economic development. The ICESCR stipulates that:

> the State parties to the present Covenant recognize the right of everyone to an adequate standard of living for himself (sic) and his family, including adequate food, clothing and housing, and to the continuous improvement of living conditions (article 11).

The right to continuous improvement of living conditions can be seen as problematic from an environmental perspective when it is interpreted in such a way as to justify opulent patterns of consumerism that require unsustainable economic growth through the overuse or misuse of natural resources and widespread pollution. Conflicts between human rights are of course nothing new to the rights discourse. The resolution of conflicting rights must be addressed through a process of balancing those different rights, rather than the conflict provided as an excuse for not recognizing rights in the first place (Hayward, 2000). Basic needs offer one coherent criterion for adjudicating between mutually exclusive rights claims (Shue, 1980; Shue, 1981; Vincent, 1986; Freeden, 1991; Donnelly, 1993; Jones, 1994). Under this criterion the environmental human rights to natural resources and to an environment free from toxic pollution would be prioritized over a lifestyle of superfluous consumption for the opulent.

Social Power

This research acknowledges the importance of social power considerations for examining the politics of human rights (Stammers, 1983). Social power exists in a multiformity of aspects, an attribute that problematizes any succinct definition and contributes to the enigmatic nature of the term as an essentially contested concept (Gallie, 1956; Lukes, 1986). In general terms, power is the property exercised over others to affect social activities (Olsen, 1970). More specifically, this research draws upon a Gramscian interpretation of power. Under this conceptualization, social classes employ power to advance their own interests and governments serve the interests of the social class powerful enough to dictate political policy (Olsen, 1970). Social power is thereby exercised in the routine operations of civil society (Hoare and Smith, 1971). Gramsci observed a mutually supportive relation between civil society and the state, resonating the Marxist perception that the state acts on behalf of the dominant group in society (Cox, 1983).

Civil society contains a vast array of divergent groups with competing social and political interests, values and aspirations. Of these various groups, this research differentiates between systemic and anti-systemic forces. Systemic forces refer to groups advocating the capitalist model of political economy. In Gramscian political discourse, the systemic forces constitute a hegemonic bloc that represents an alliance of social interests dedicated to the preservation of capitalism in world politics (Cox, 1983).

Anti-systemic forces are those groups rejecting the capitalist political system in favor of an alternative that is typically tasked with prioritizing social and environmental values over the interests of capital accumulation. Anti-systemic forces therefore deny the validity of the capitalist global economy (Brown, 1997). Anti-systemic groups that challenge the fundamental basis of the capitalist political economy constitute a counter hegemonic bloc that demands, if only in general terms, an alternative political model. Systemic and anti-systemic forces themselves contain a broad range of positions and interests and are clearly not monolithic entities. Thus usage of such terms may appear to generalize the nuance of positions within each movement. Yet such categorizations are methodologically useful for identifying broad trends in the overall political system and are furthermore common terms in the academic literature (Wagar, 1996; Chase-Dunn and Hall, 1997).

Structure

This research employs a structural analysis to contextualize the possibilities and the constraints on environmental human rights by considering how power operates to produce or prevent political change. Structures are referred to in the sense that Rosenberg employs the term. Under this approach, structures denote 'a regularized relation between social positions which places individuals with respect to determinate resources' (Rosenberg, 1994).

Engaging in a structural analysis is validated by Foucault's research on the subject of power that stresses the importance of heteronomy (Hoy, 1986). Heteronomy is the propensity of individuals to internalize, or to assume as normal, the structures typifying the society within which they have been conditioned (Brown, 1991). Giddens also advocates the conceptual use of structures in political discourse as a necessary tool to connect the actions of individuals to the exercise of social power (Giddens, 1981).

The influence of structures over individuals is never absolute because social control can never completely eradicate dissent and resistance and herein lies a potential for systemic challenges and political change (Giddens, 1981; Kelly, 1994). The relation between structure and individual agency is explained in chapter 2 in terms of constructivism. Under this approach, agency and structure interact to constitute the other, suggesting a potential for presently marginalized political interests to effect structural change.

This research identifies capitalism as the dominant structure in the global political economy. Capitalism is defined here as the application of economic rationality through a political economy that co-opts or represses opposition. Thus, capitalism is defined by the values upon which it is predicated and by the social interests that it serves. This definition also accounts for apparent internal contradictions evident in capitalist societies. For example, state subsidies for powerful industries exist alongside an ideology of economic neo-liberalism since both benefit powerful social groups and can be justified as beneficial for economic growth. Similarly, welfare states exist in capitalist systems as a means of social control, to prevent extremes of inequality that would otherwise threaten the social and economic order (chapter 2).

Capitalism thus defined is a broad and diffuse process, rather than a monolithic entity. References to 'capitalism' may appear clumsy and lacking in analytical precision given the different forms of capitalism evident around the world. However, focusing on the nuances that separate the different manifestations of capitalism can lead to the neglect of the equally important assumptions that underpin all variants of capitalism. Subsequently, possible alternatives to capitalism can be arbitrarily excluded by an agenda which is restricted to analyzing differences between variants of capitalism.

The use of capitalism as a reference tool also has advantages over contending descriptive concepts. The notion of modernity for example tends to obfuscate both the specific values upon which the contemporary political economy is predicated and the interests that it serves. Both capitalism and modernity relate to a complex process of interaction amongst social and economic forces and as such it is simplistic to view the two as mutually exclusive. Although appropriate reference to modernity is not avoided in this research, capitalism is preferred as a descriptive tool since this highlights the basis of decision-making in economic rationality. For example in the case of energy production, a technologically 'modern' society based on ecological values would invest in non-polluting forms of energy production rather than fossil fuel or nuclear energy. Such investment is conspicuously absent in the modern capitalist economy because economic cost benefit analysis concludes that such an outcome is allocatively inefficient, irrespective of the ecological consequences (chapter 1).

Globalization is defined as the recreation on a global scale of the capitalist political economy (Gill, 1995). Such a definition reflects the centrality of economic rationality and capitalism as terms of reference adopted in this research. According to this characterization, globalization is primarily a product of interest-based capitalism and the universalization of economic rationality rather than any form of political theory such as liberalism (Chomsky 1992a; Gill, 1995). The political influence held by global economic investors constitutes a formidable bulwark that prevents the realization of the claimed environmental human rights.

Campaigning for human rights and environmental protection over the economic focus of the capitalist system are a number of Non-governmental Organizations (NGOs). NGOs are 'any non-profit-making, non-violent, organized group of people who are not seeking government office' (Willetts, 1996; Taylor, 1998). Social movements are composed of campaign oriented NGOs. Social movements, like NGOs, can be differentiated from political parties since they reject attaining power through the electoral process and typically seek broader social change (O'Brien, 1997). This research is interested in those NGOs and social movements campaigning for environmental and human rights protection.

Social movements are composed of a vast array of NGOs evidencing a multiformity of political strategies and ideologies (Willetts, 1996). Some analysts have therefore differentiated between distinct categories of NGOs that together constitute social movements. Willetts identifies the following categories of NGOs; (i) groups of government employees, such as the International Union of Police Federations, (ii) NGOs welcoming government funding, such as the International Planned Parenthood Federation, and (iii) NGOs not welcoming governmental funding, such as Amnesty International (Willetts, 1996). As an alternative framework, Taylor suggests differentiating between (i) mainstream, (ii) co-opted and (iii) radical NGOs. Mainstream NGOs advocate limited structural reforms to mitigate the worst manifestations of environmental degradation or human rights abuses while upholding the dominant values on which the capitalist order is based. Co-opted NGOs rhetorically question capitalism but compromise this opposition so as to be included in the decision-making process, undergoing a process of co-option that abrogates their formal position. Radical NGOs do not compromise their opposition to capitalism in rhetoric or tactics and are subsequently marginalized in the formal political discussions (Taylor, 1998). Of these two models, the framework suggested by Taylor is adopted in this research since it benefits from using the operations of social power to differentiate between NGOs. In particular, the framework conceptualizes the importance of co-option in explaining the relation between NGOs, social power and why certain ideas attain dominance over others in the formal political forum (Taylor, 1998).

Chapter Outlines

This research claims two universal environmental human rights; (i) to an environment free from toxic pollution, and (ii) to natural resources. The central theme of this research identifies the power dynamics inherent to capitalism as the barrier to the realization of the two claimed environmental human rights. The first four chapters expand on this argument through examination of the epistemological, structural, tactical and legal contexts of the claimed environmental human rights.

Deciding which human rights claims are justified on epistemological grounds is a product of the particular paradigm of rationality adopted by the analyst. Claims to environmental human rights are predicated upon ecological values and are typically rejected by practitioners of economic rationality (Bartlett, 1986). It is therefore important to understand how specific paradigms of rationality are elevated or marginalized in the policy-making forum. Chapter 1 investigates this process and argues that the present dominance of economic rationality over other possibilities is explained by the operations of social power interests that seek to legitimize capitalism.

Chapter 2 investigates possibilities for the realization of the claimed environmental human rights given the limitations imposed by structural power relations. The concept of hegemony is used to explain the nature of the capitalist political economy as an instrument of power. Hegemony is the presentation of dominant interests as universal interests (Hoare and Smith, 1971). Hegemony is moreover an expression of power not through the overt use of force, but by civil society and the state combining to establish and maintain approval, tacit consent or political apathy amongst the oppressed (Chomsky, 1996).

To suggest moral leadership, hegemonic systems must promote a veneer of justice and inclusiveness. In practice, states and corporations use the rhetoric of human rights and, more recently, of environmental protection by engaging in gesture politics, tinkering at the margins of capitalism to create this veneer (Hoare and Smith, 1971). Induced by rhetorical statements and symbolic concessions, anti-systemic forces are encouraged to campaign within the formal political forum, rather than challenge the validity of the capitalist political economy (Taylor, 1998). The key feature of hegemonic politics to be discussed in chapter two is subsequently that of co-option. Co-option will be demonstrated to act as a structural mechanism to negate anti-systemic challenges to capitalism through assimilating minor aspects of critical approaches without altering fundamental systemic conditions. This conceptual framework will be applied to an analysis of the environmental and human rights politics where co-option is evident in both cases. The analysis in chapter two will conclude that the effectiveness of co-operating with formal political structures is limited to addressing the worst excesses of capitalism and affecting political change only at the margins. To achieve extensive social change, realize human rights and prioritize environmental protection over commercial considerations, the efforts of anti-systemic forces must first challenge formal hegemonic politics. Only through the promotion of an alternative vision, that is a counter hegemonic bloc, can the environmental and human rights movements mount such a challenge of capitalism (Hoare and Smith, 1971).

Social demands for environmental human rights in campaigns conducted by environmental and human rights NGOs are examined in chapter 3. This evaluation is based upon analysis of responses to a questionnaire circulated to NGOs. The questionnaire results reveal three findings. Firstly, the responses indicate a consensus endorsing environmental human rights. With only three exceptions, all the NGOs who stated a preference replied that they recognized environmental human rights. Most popular amongst the environmental human rights advocated were variants of the two rights claimed in this research. Secondly, the questionnaire responses revealed that campaigns are being conducted both for the formal recognition of environmental human rights and through demanding environmental protection based on claims to human rights irrespective of their current legal status. Thirdly, a significant number of NGOs operationalized ecological rationality by defending their advocacy of environmental human rights on the premise of interconnectedness between all elements of the biosphere, including human societies. There were no significant differences between the responses from mainstream, co-opted and radical NGOs since the questionnaire focused specifically on recognition of environmental human rights, rather than on the broader questions of power upon which grounds NGOs can be differentiated.

The legal status of environmental human rights is critically evaluated in chapter four to understand how the formal political institutions of law and politics have addressed the demands for environmental human rights made by NGOs. A trend towards the legal recognition of environmental human rights will be described. However, legal recognition is argued to be only a necessary, rather than a sufficient, condition for the actual implementation of environmental human rights since many legally stipulated environmental rights are violated in actual social practice. This paradox will be explained by examining the influence of social power on legal efficacy. Refuting legalistic claims to neutrality, impartiality and political independence, law will be argued to be itself a manifestation of hegemonic power, complimenting other institutions of political and economic power. This politicized function means that law tends to reflect existent power relations in society, rather than determine those relations, problematizing its use as a vehicle for social change in general and for the realization of environmental human rights in particular. The relation between social power and legal efficacy is argued to apply to international as well as to domestic law.

Chapters 5 and 6 suggest two universal environmental human rights as alternatives through which to contrast the formal response to environmental human rights claims. Methodologically, this examination is predicated upon analysis of existing human rights texts rather than upon philosophical grounds because of the ontologically contested nature of philosophical claims to human rights. Chapter 5 derives the universal environmental human right to an environment free from toxic pollution from the existing human rights to life, security of the person and health. The centrality of capitalism, rather than liberalism or any other theory of justice, to the present political economy is then established by looking at the accommodation of toxic pollution. Whereas capitalism normalizes the social and ecological damage incurred by toxic pollution as conducive to the realization of allocative efficiency, political liberalism must prohibit the production of such pollutants for it to remain internally coherent as a theory of justice. The discussion identifies capitalism as an interest-based system of politics where questions of justice, human rights and environmental protection are subordinated to considerations of allocative efficiency and economic growth. The universal environmental human right to environmental resources is claimed in chapter 6 to be a necessary requirement for existing legal human rights to cultural self-determination and for the right to be free from hunger to be realized. The implementation of the claimed human right to natural resources will furthermore be recommended on a group, rather than an individual, basis.

Methodology

This research investigates the conceptual linkages between environmental protection, resource ownership and human rights as explained in the above sections. A series of questionnaires compliments the theoretical focus of inquiry. To ascertain the social demands made for environmental human rights and the degree of recognition of such rights, four questionnaires were devised and circulated to different organizations. The main questionnaire was targeted at NGOs to evaluate the extent to which advocacy groups in civil society were campaigning for environmental human rights, or using human rights claims to campaign for environmental protection.

Three further questionnaires were circulated to (i) departments for the environment of selected states, (ii) corporations and corporate lobbying groups, (iii) Global Economic Institutions (GEIs) and United Nations (UN) departments.

The purpose of the questionnaire survey was to gain qualitative, rather than quantitative, data, to understand how environmental human rights are perceived and utilized by the key groups in world politics identified in the theoretical analysis. Specifically, the survey sought to elicit information on (i) how environmental human rights are perceived by different groups, (ii) which environmental human rights were recognized and upon what basis, (iii) what action has been undertaken to promote or implement environmental human rights and (iv) the potential and actual role of environmental human rights in implementing social change. The questionnaires were formulated to avoid providing any leading questions. Specifically, no environmental rights were suggested in the questionnaire. Instead, the concept had to be interpreted by the responding organizations.

A total of 196 NGOs were selected for inclusion in the main questionnaire. These were identified through an internet search of political groups campaigning for environmental or human rights protection. Departments for the environment of 41 states were selected for inclusion in the second survey constituency. The questionnaire was sent via e-mail to the address of the department for the environment given on the chosen state's official web site. Identified states were selected to represent a variety of cultures, geographical locations and levels of economic development.

Eleven corporations were selected for inclusion in the third questionnaire survey through the criteria of (i) prominence, (ii) market size and (iii) relevance to the subject of environmental resources, such as mining, oil and forestry sector based companies. The suitability of specific corporations under these criteria was established from an examination of corporate internet web sites. Also included in this survey were corporate lobbying groups since these specifically exist to communicate the corporate viewpoint to the wider political community. A number of GEIs and UN departments were included in the final survey.

The questionnaire was delivered to each organization via an e-mail that also explained the purpose of the questionnaire as part of a thesis to be made public knowledge. Organizations not responding to the first e-mail were sent two further e-mails repeating the questionnaire and its purpose. Organizations failing to answer any of the three e-mails were deemed non-respondents. NGO response rates (47 per cent) were notably higher than the response rates from states (27 per cent), corporations (36 per cent) and UN/GEIs (30 per cent). These figures cover all responses, including those organizations not completing the questionnaire but replying with other information. The results of the questionnaire responses will be discussed throughout the following chapters, dependent upon the relevance of the response to the subject matter, although most of the analysis will be conducted in chapter 3.

Table 1   Questionnaire e-mail dates

E-mail	NGOs	States	TNCs	UN/GEIs
1	8 Jun 1998	29 Apr 1999	28 Apr 1999	28 Apr 1999
2	22 Oct 1998	5 Aug 1999	5 Aug 1999	5 Aug 1999
3	26 Nov 1998	30 Sep 1999	30 Sep 1999	30 Sep 1999

Table 2   NGO questionnaire response summary

Total number of NGOs contacted	196
NGOs providing no response	103
NGOs providing a response	93
NGOs completing the questionnaire	64
NGOs not completing the questionnaire but sending subject related information	29

Table 3   State questionnaire response summary

Total number of states contacted	41
States providing no response	30
States providing a response	11
States completing the questionnaire	3
States not completing the questionnaire but sending subject related information	8

Table 4   Corporate questionnaire response summary

Total number of corporations and lobby groups contacted	11
Corporations providing no response	7
Corporations providing a response	4
Corporations completing the questionnaire	2
Corporations not completing the questionnaire but sending other relevant information	2

Table 5   GEIs and UN questionnaire response summary

Total number of GEIs and UN bodies contacted	10
Organizations providing no response	7
Organizations providing a response	3
Organizations completing the questionnaire	1
Organizations not completing the questionnaire but sending other relevant information	2

Chapter 1

Rationality, Epistemology and Environmental Human Rights

Capitalism has been the expression of economic rationality finally set free of all restraint.
– Andre Gorz

Introduction

Different forms of rationality are analyzed in this chapter since these constitute the epistemological frameworks within which all political claims are evaluated, including claims to environmental human rights. The singular faculty of reason is thereby differentiated from plural conceptualizations of rationality. In particular, this chapter juxtaposes ecological with economic rationality to illustrate (i) that the criterion constituting what is deemed rational is fundamentally disputed rather than being universally accepted and (ii) how the particular epistemological assumptions of the analyst either justifies or rejects the existence of environmental human rights. Whereas ecological rationality will be argued to approve of the human rights to an environment free of toxic pollution and to environmental resources, the logic of economic rationality will be demonstrated to reject these same rights.

Attention then turns to examine the process by which specific forms of rationality become dominant or subjugated in society. Specifically, the dominance of a form of rationality is argued to be a function of power relations. Power operates in part through the normalization, legitimization and institutionalization of the interests of powerful social groups in political and economic structures (Schaap, 2000). The dominance of economic rationality in world politics will be argued to normalize the systematic violation of the claimed environmental human rights. Corporations and the beneficiaries of global capitalism will be identified as constituting the powerful social group whose commercial interests are served by current patterns of environmental human rights violations. This conclusion is made through a method of analyzing trends in corporate production techniques and lobbying records that provides evidence for both the continued tolerance of toxic pollution and unregulated access to natural resources.

The Philosophy of Human Rights

The question 'are environmental human rights justifiable in political philosophy?' can be answered either affirmatively or negatively, depending upon the epistemological position adopted by the analyst. For example, basic rights theorists such as Shue, Vincent and Galtung justify human rights in terms of the conditions required for biological survival (Shue, 1980; Vincent, 1986; Galtung, 1994). From this basis, there is a logical compulsion to recognize environmental conditions as a component of human rights. Galtung acknowledges this claim in explaining that 'there is a high need for livelihood, for which an ecologically stable environment with a high level of biodiversity is a necessary condition' (Galtung, 1994).

The notion that all humans have rights to the requirements of survival has been questioned by negative rights theorists who argue, typically on the basis of liberal political theory, that human rights must instead reflect autonomy values, allowing the individual to be free of interference from others. Ingram typifies this approach with the claim that 'the best scheme of rights, is one that protects the autonomy interests of citizens' (Ingram, 1994). This approach views the arbitrary interference with the individual by a third party as a violation of the rights of that individual since the individual is considered to be the subject, source and the object of ethical considerations. Forms of social relations must therefore be consented to by individuals, or else will constitute arbitrariness and an unjust intervention of privacy and personal rights to liberty, with liberty being defined in terms of autonomy (Cranston, 1967; Hart, 1984; Merrills, 1996).

Numerous other methods of conceptualizing human rights have been suggested. Campbell for example defines rights in terms of contract, power and interest theories (Campbell, 1983). Some political analysts question the existence of any human rights because rights are seen as culturally specific and socially constructed rather than universal in character (Kausican, 1993). Marxists typically deny that human nature can be identified and abstracted into a universal or essential form since human nature is instead perceived as a structural function of historical processes and social conditioning (McLellan, 1977). A notion of rights derived solely from the fact that people are human is problematic for Marxists since, for such theorists, the economic relations of the societies within which they have been conditioned construct the consciousness of human beings. Utilitarian and consequentialist theorists question the ontological primacy of a political focus on rights, instead suggesting aggregate good as the central criteria of justice (Parekh, 1973; Long, 1977). Still other theorists claim a mutual compatibility between utilitarianism and human rights by arguing that overall social happiness is best achieved through the recognition of individual or group rights (Gray, 1983).

Bauer argues that to validate human rights it is not necessary to agree on their foundation so long as the constitutive norms of the rights can be established (Bauer, 1995). Through a consequentialist focus, Kuhonta claims that human rights are justified in Asia not because of their intrinsic self evidence, but because they promote positive and beneficial values such as public spiritedness (Kuhonta, 1995). For these two theorists, the apparent absence of any philosophical basis for universal rights therefore poses no real problems for recognizing human rights, since rights can be validated by criterion independent of their intrinsic self-evidence.

The Multiformity of Rationality

The philosophical argument as to the existence or otherwise of a basis for human rights has been extensively discussed, reflecting the nature of human rights as an essentially contested concept (Gallie, 1956). The purpose of this chapter is neither to advance nor refute claims to environmental human rights on grounds of political philosophy, since such an endeavor is necessarily a reflection of the particular philosophical paradigm utilized by the author. Instead, the purpose is to understand how separate forms of rationality suggest different criterion by which to evaluate rights claims.

The argument presented in this chapter is that the criterion of rationality is not a universal constant, but rather that it can assume a multiplicity of forms, only one of which constitutes the assumptions of the epistemological paradigm finally employed by an individual to make judgments. The discussion is therefore moved beyond the question of 'can environmental human rights be philosophically justified?' onto the more fundamental level of 'what criterion of different manifestations of rationality support environmental human rights and which condone violations of environmental human rights?'. An epistemological analysis of competing theories of rationality is useful since these conceptualizations provide the criterion by which claims to universal human rights are understood and evaluated.

Bartlett explains that the concept of rationality is multi-dimensional. Each manifestation of rationality has its own order of measurement and comparison of values that are made intelligible through the presence of a central governing principle (Bartlett, 1986). Gorz and Dryzek accompany Bartlett in re-interpreting environmental politics to identify separate manifestations of rationality (Gorz, 1988; Dryzek, 1990). These aforementioned theorists bring their own nuanced perspectives to the topic of understanding the construction of paradigms of rationality. It is not the purpose here to critique or evaluate the points of contention raised by these theorists. Rather the endeavor is more focused. It is to introduce and differentiate two particular forms of rationality, (i) economic rationality and (ii) ecological rationality. Judgments regarding the justification of environmental human rights will then be demonstrated to be a function of the particular epistemological paradigm assumed by the analyst. These two particular manifestations of rationality have been chosen since economic rationality constitutes the dominant form of rationality in the capitalist political economy and ecological rationality constitutes an alternative epistemological paradigm by which to make critical comparisons. Ecological rationality is used in this research to refer to a type of rationality based upon a central concern for all forms of life. It is a rationality that assumes the interconnectedness of all living systems within a wider cosmology centered on respect for life as the unifying underlying principle (Naess, 1973; Bartlett, 1986). This underlying principle determines that 'a thing is right when it tends to preserve the integrity, stability, and beauty of the biotic community. It is wrong when it tends otherwise' (Leopold, 1949; Sessions and Naess, 1991).

There is an array of approaches within the subject of economics, with evident nuances between the contending perspectives. Economic rationality is therefore defined here as the dominant neo-classical model that broadly advocates the market as a method to achieve the desired goal of allocative efficiency (Gorz, 1973; Gorz,

1988; Gowdy, 1999). Allocative efficiency is the allocation of resources to maximize Gross Domestic Product (GDP) respecting conditions of Pareto efficiency (Gowdy, 1999). An allocation is Pareto-efficient 'if it is impossible to move to another allocation which would make some people better off and nobody worse off' (Begg et al, 1987). Allocative efficiency therefore articulates the interests of the opulent, since the market mechanism is endorsed as providing entitlement to resources irrespective of need. The market mechanism makes no differentiation between consumption of luxury and essential goods, since allocation is decided by monetary transactions alone. That is to say, paying for a good provides both sufficient and necessary grounds for entitlement to that resource.[1] Pareto-efficiency furthermore benefits the opulent since redistributive policies that make the rich worse off are deemed illegitimate, even though they could benefit a majority.

Following from the centrality of the market, value is defined in monetary terms according to the logic of economic rationality. Economic rationality relies upon a methodology of positivism, empiricism and cost-benefit analysis to commodify products (including natural resources) and to leave it to the market to determine the subsequent value and allocation of goods. In terms of the individual, a lifestyle of possessive individualism and consumerism is presumed to be an axiomatic and universal feature of human nature. Modern polities promote the desire to consume since people tend to be accorded social status by virtue of the products that they possess (Daly and Cobb, 1994; Edwards, 2000). Rational decisions are largely reduced to instrumental tasks of maximizing personal wealth, private possessions and the consumption of goods and services. This conception of individual identity is typically universalized or 'normalized' and vital processes of identity formation and of becoming an individual are subsequently omitted as useful issues to be researched (Penttinen, 2000). The definition of economic rationality given above necessarily excludes marginalized approaches within the discipline of economics such as ecological and Marxist economists, who reject the centrality of the market principle and the values of possessive individualism upon which it is predicated (Deane, 1978).

Paradigms of rationality have associated value systems. Value systems refer to the relative importance assigned to competing and conflicting values such as ecological protection, care for the vulnerable, human rights, economic growth and materialistic desires. Individuals use value systems to make judgments and calculate rational actions. The prioritization of materialistic values over ecological integrity in capitalist societies is incomprehensible to cultures whose value systems are instead based upon a paradigm of ecological rationality. For example the indigenous U'wa nation in Colombia, fighting corporate plans to drill oil on their traditional lands, declared that:

> we are left with no alternative other than to continue fighting on the side of the sky and earth and spirits or else disappear when the irrationality of the invader violates the most sacred of our laws .... . Our words should be a warning that reunites us again as one family in order to ensure our future in harmony with the whole universe, or they will be one more voice that prophesises the destruction of life because of the absurd disposition of the white man (Cobaria *et al.*, 1998).

Here the decision to drill for oil is seen as 'irrational' because the form of rationality employed by the U'wa interprets the incommensurate value system of economic rationality as an 'absurd disposition' in much the same way that most neo-classical economists would dismiss the stated cosmology of the U'wa nation. This conflict between economic and ecological rationality was expressed by the native American leader, Rolling Thunder, who explained to non-native Americans that:

> Too many people don't know that when they harm the earth they harm themselves, nor do they realize that when they harm themselves they harm the earth ... . It's not very easy for you people to understand these things because understanding is not knowing the kind of facts that your books and teachers talk about. I can tell you that understanding begins with love and respect ... . Such respect means that we never stop realizing and never neglect to carry out our obligations to ourselves and our environment (quoted in Drengson, 1980, p. 236).

This quote demonstrates notions of respect, tolerance and obligations to otherness that would be discredited as unquantifiable, normative and, for both of these reasons, as irrational from the perspective of economic rationality. Ecological rationality conflicts with economic rationality since harmony with nature is contrasted with dominance over nature; nature is imbued with intrinsic worth rather than valued in monetary terms specified by the market and basic limited material goals are contrasted with the twin aspirations of luxury consumption and unlimited economic growth (Naess, 1997). Whereas human and non-human animals alike have, according to the paradigm of ecological rationality, axiomatic rights to an environment free of toxic pollution and to the environmental resources required to satisfy basic needs, these same rights are dismissed as irrelevant by the focus of economic rationality on allocative efficiency.

Economic rationality dominates and underpins the capitalist world order. Sagoff observes that pronouncements that nature is sacred or that greed is detrimental to the individual and society appear judgmental and even embarrassing in modern societies (Sagoff, 1997). In order to influence the policy making process it is necessary to use prudential or economic reasons, rather than ethical or spiritual arguments (Sagoff, 1997). For environmental protection policies to be implemented in a capitalist system it is therefore necessary to rationalize such projects in economic terms, for example, that greater energy efficiency reduces production costs, and it is this agenda that environmental economics now covers as an academic discipline. Possible measures to protect the environment that conflict with efficiency are invariably rejected by policy-makers as too costly or impractical. Most devastating from the ecological focus on habitat preservation is the continued reliance on fossil fuels as an energy source supported by a focus on economic efficiency. Economic rationality dictates it inefficient to invest in non-polluting forms of energy and deems it appropriate to instead risk long-term climatic instability and the resultant habitat changes and threats to biodiversity because of a singular focus on economic criteria. Continuing reliance on fossil fuels reflects not only the supremacy of economic rationality in policy-making circles but also the unlimited ecological damage that the modern discipline of economics is willing to endorse when such destruction leads to the efficient allocation of resources.

Social Power and the Construction of Rationality

Dominant forms of rationality are therefore more a reflection of the culture within which they are constructed, rather than being universal in character. To account for the dominance of economic rationality and to refute its claims to objectivity or neutrality it is necessary to investigate the process by which this particular manifestation of rationality became established.

Dominant epistemological paradigms have a propensity to be both self-legitimizing and self-perpetuating (Foucault, 1994a). The appropriateness of academic questions and agendas are invariably judged according to criteria specified by the dominant epistemological paradigm that have been internalized and normalized by the theorists educated and conditioned within that framework. Applying this process to economic rationality operating in a capitalist world, Opschoor points out that:

> Present day economic science is busy meticulously researching the way that markets work, and the situations in which they maximize individuals' satisfaction of needs, given their incomes and preferences. Economic science – at least the neo-classical mainstream – has thus developed itself into a theory which confirms the system and legitimizes the market mechanism (Opschoor, 1994, p. 195).

The assumptions of neo-classical economics therefore constitute the criteria for the validification of its own form of rationality and the criteria by which subjugated epistemological paradigms are simultaneously discredited. Such criteria relate, for example, to the desired values of positivism, empiricism and a self-legitimizing definition of objectivity as the search for allocative efficiency and economic growth. The outcome of this process of epistemological agenda setting is to limit mainstream academic discourse within the increasingly narrow confines specified by the logic of economic rationality. This logic, along with its associated values, has been elevated to the highest status, while alternatives are viewed as either inferior forms of knowledge or as non-knowledge (Banuri and Marglin, 1993). Through this process, reason itself has become the mere instrument of an all-inclusive economic apparatus (Horkheimer and Adorno, 1972).

Dominance of an epistemological paradigm is typically explained by post-modern political theorists in terms of social power relations, reflecting and legitimizing the interests of powerful groups in society (Hoffman, 1998). This was already noted in 1907 by the biologist Hugo de Vries, who stated that economic interests took precedence over scientific facts in the applied sciences because of the interests and agendas of those making funding decisions. As Berlan and Lewontin report, 'he understood what Monsanto and its ally-competitors use as a guiding principle today: what is profitable affects, or even determines, what is scientifically true' (Berlan and Lewontin, 1999).

Kuhn has argued that the process of knowledge construction and evolution is characterized by power relations affecting what is to be considered as normal science, thereby establishing the boundaries of a paradigm that then authorizes or dismisses specific knowledge claims (Kuhn, 1962). Furthermore, Kuhn contends that the dominant epistemological paradigm reflects the interests of specific social forces through resisting change and to be therefore self-perpetuating, even when a more coherent epistemological model emerges (Kuhn, 1962).

During his academic life, Foucault was prominent at the vanguard of attacks on the autonomy of forms of knowledge. He instead insisted upon a genealogical focus of explaining the emergence of knowledge from structures of power (Foucault, 1994a). This position effectively re-conceptualizes cause and effect in the politics of power. Rather than focusing on traditional subjects of how political philosophy can limit the rights of the powerful, the question was inverted by Foucault to examine how forms of knowledge, such as rules of justice, are devised and implemented by the relations of power (Kelly, 1994). Although the view of power promoted by Foucault has been criticized as being socially ubiquitous and thereby neglecting its more specific concentration in identifiable social groups, his analysis of power and epistemology provides unparalleled insights into the subject matter (Taylor, 1986). In particular, according to Foucault, meaningful and nonsensical claims are adjudicated by a regime of truth that is created by the dominant epistemological model or what Foucault refers to as the hegemonic discourse (Foucault, 1994b; Brown, 1997). The hegemonic discourse marginalizes and discredits subjugated forms of knowledge through insisting on a particular agenda, highlighting specific problems over others, legitimizing desired solutions to the presented problems and by dismissing the alternative agendas, questions and solutions given by subjugated epistemological paradigms (Brown, 1997).

The power to define important questions, topics, agendas and desired solutions is an inherent attribute of the hegemonic discourse since this is where all the experts reside and recreate the dominance of the paradigm in the manner described by Kuhn (Kuhn, 1962). Irrespective of his well publicized disagreements with Foucault's ideas, Jürgen Habermas has extensively documented the role of technical experts who monopolize epistemological claims to legitimate knowledge in the service of private profit and political power at the expense of a more socially inclusive discourse (Dryzek, 1990; Habermas, 1994). This observation highlights the mutual legitimization evident between the experts of the hegemonic discourse and dominant social interests.

The practical application of this argument has been comprehensively explored by Noam Chomsky (Chomsky, 1986; 1987; 1988; 1992a; 1992b; 1993a; 1993b; 1993c; 1993d; 1994; 1995; 1996a; 1996b; 1997a; 1997b; 1998a; 1998b; 1999). Within totalitarian states such as Stalinist Russia, the task of the intellectual to serve dominant power interests is relatively obvious, since the oppressive forces of state systematically eliminate dissenting voices. Thus, intellectuals are openly coerced to 'record with a show of horror the terrible deeds (real or alleged) of designated enemies, and to conceal or prettify the crimes of the state and its agents' (Chomsky, 1996a). Chomsky goes on to document how the same outcome is obtained in capitalist states through the use of more subtle, and therefore also more effective, techniques that give the author the illusion of freedom. Paraphrasing Orwell's introduction to *Animal Farm*, Chomsky argues that:

> The sinister fact about literary censorship in England ... is that it is largely voluntary. Unpopular ideas can be silenced, and inconvenient facts kept dark, without any need for any official ban. Without the exercise of force anyone who challenges the prevailing

orthodoxy finds himself silenced with surprising effectiveness thanks to the internalization of the values of subordination and conformity, and the control of the press by wealthy men who have every motive to be dishonest on certain topics (Chomsky, 1996a, p. 67).

The dominant paradigm espoused by technical experts subsequently influences the opinions of all individuals in a society since, as Drengson reminds us, we interpret the world through the lens of the paradigms that are in dominant use (Drengson, 1980). Russell draws proper attention to the process of manufacturing social conformity by demonstrating that all other forms of power ultimately rest upon the power of opinion and in particular upon those forces that influence and construct public opinion (Russell, 1948). The promotion of alternative opinions and expressions of subjugated forms of knowledge that threaten dominant social interests are prevented by processes of discreditation and marginalization that have been documented by political theorists as diverse as Foucault, Habermas, Kuhn and Chomsky as outlined above. The two findings of this analysis establish (i) the contentious, diverse and disputed nature of the criteria for rationality and (ii) the legitimization or the subjugation of forms of rationality on the basis of the service thereby rendered to dominant social interests. These findings contest the claims made in defense of economic rationality that it is objective, value neutral or in any meaningful sense superior or more indicative of truth than any other form. Establishing the relative, subjective and contingent nature of economic rationality can thereby question the legitimacy of the hegemonic discourse.

Economic Rationality and Environmental Human Rights Violations

The subsequent aspects of economic rationality in particular justify the violations of the environmental human rights claimed in chapters 5 and 6.

The Value of Nature

The paradigm of economic rationality assumes the Greco-Christian position that everything on earth is for the sole use of humankind and that that species is at liberty to modify the environment as it will (Tarlock, 1988). Claims to the intrinsic value of nature, to the existence of values derived from a non-human source, are dismissed by economic rationality as normative and non-quantifiable (Gowdy, 1999). Instead, the value of the environment is determined by economic rationality as a monetary price reflecting market forces of supply and demand. The environment is therefore essentially perceived as a commodity within this paradigm. Following from the separation of human society from ecological systems, the environment is only valued within a framework of economic rationality to the extent that the market mechanism specifies prices for natural resources. Such an interpretation is circumscribed in the extreme. Bartlett and Opschoor draw attention to the fact that crucial elements in ecological systems cannot be expressed in monetary terms and are consequently disregarded in the formula promoted by economic rationality (Bartlett, 1986; Opschoor, 1994). In the case of energy policy for instance, market forces rationalize continuing dependence on fossil fuels with environmental consequences of increasing pollution, acid rain, climate change and degradation of the areas where mining occurs. Environmental degradation is determined, encouraged and legitimized by the subordination of eco-system requirements to the logic of capital and consumption (Saurin, 1993).

In contrast, the paradigm of deep ecology attributes intrinsic value to non-human life, independent of its economic or anthropocentric worth. This sentiment has been articulated through the claim that 'everything has some value for itself, for others, and for the whole' (Drengson, 1980). Sessions and Naess similarly contend that:

> the well being and flourishing of human and non-human life on Earth have value in themselves. These values are independent of the use of the non-human world for human purposes (Sessions and Naess, 1991, p. 157).

Recognition of the intrinsic value of all forms of life is reflected in the characteristic imperatives of ecological rationality to preserve biodiversity and habitats as the highest political priorities and to acknowledge the right of all living beings to unfold (Rolston, 1981; Chew, 1997). Although Kant was in no sense an advocate of ecological rationality, in the *Critique of Judgement* he distinguished between an argument according to truth and an argument according to man. The first considers its object as it is in itself, the second what that object is for us (Lewis, 1995). This Kantian observation is pertinent to considerations of ascribing value to non-human life since living beings, regardless of whether or not they are sentient, and regardless of whether they are plants or animals, have their own projects inherent to the phenomenon of life as experienced by them, independent of any contact with humans. For humans to decide that such factors construe no value is to utilize instrumental rationality to establish what that life is for us and to value it accordingly. This violates the requirement identified by Kant that in order to establish an argument according to truth, we must instead consider the value of the thing, life and nature in this case, as it is in itself. According to such reasoning, it would be logically coercive to recognize a value in nature, independent of human concerns, derived from the phenomenon of the natural unfolding of non-human life.

Rolston points out that life is only treated as devoid of intrinsic value by economists because nature is taken for granted since, he argues, the discovery of life elsewhere in the universe would be recognized by the scientific community as of tremendous value (Rolston, 1981). It should also be noted that Western political philosophy has traditionally used claims to nature to validate notions of justice, as exemplified in discussions over natural justice and natural rights. Such arguments necessarily presuppose some sort of value in nature, since without such value, claims to legitimacy derived from a natural status would be nonsensical.

The denial of intrinsic value has led some theorists to condemn economic rationality as a manifestation of speciesism for making decisions on morally arbitrary grounds that prejudice otherness (Hayward, 1997). One manifestation of speciesism is arbitrarily limiting the rights discourse to humans. Naess, for example, argues that:

> to the ecological field-worker, the equal right to live and blossom is an intuitively clear and obvious value axiom. Its restriction to humans is an anthropocentrism (Naess, 1973, p. 96).

Demonstrating the intrinsic value of non-human life has been comprehensively achieved elsewhere (Agar, 2001). It is not the purpose of this study to repeat the arguments for and against recognizing the intrinsic value of nature. Rather, the purpose is to establish the link between the epistemological dominance of economic rationality in valuing nature solely as a resource for humans and the service thereby provided to the corporate sector to utilize natural resources as they see fit, regardless of the implications for non-human life. The brief juxtaposition of economic and ecological rationality on the subject of the value of nature demonstrates two incommensurate methods of conceptualizing value. Under the ecological model, the intrinsic value of all life is axiomatic. In contrast, economic rationality interprets nature and non-human life forms in instrumental terms of environmental resources to be utilized in the service of economic ends. Subsequently, forests and minerals are viewed by the dominant paradigm of economic rationality as exploitable resources to be utilized as market factors dictate and in such a manner as to minimize private costs. In terms of environmental human rights, the paradigm of economic rationality legitimizes iniquitous environmental resource ownership predicated upon ability to pay rather than considerations of either human or ecological needs.[2] The right to an environment free from toxic pollution is similarly discredited through a methodological focus on efficiency that advocates an optimal level of toxic pollution determined by market forces. For example, one economics textbook explains that:

> the efficient quantity of pollution is not zero but rather the level at which the social marginal cost of cutting back pollution equals its social marginal benefit. The fact that pollution still exists is not sufficient to establish that policy has not been tough enough (Begg *et al.*, 1987, pp. 327–8).

The political implications of accepting an efficient quantity of pollution are revealed by an internal memo written by Lawrence Summers, then chief economist of the World Bank. In this exposition of economic rationality he inquired, 'shouldn't the World Bank be encouraging more migration of the dirty industries to the less developed countries?'. Due to 'under pollution' and lower income levels, developing states were calculated to have lower marginal costs of pollution. Since the economic costs of pollution are calculated through a methodology of income lost through premature death or illness, Summers correctly concluded that, 'the economic logic behind dumping a load of toxic waste in the lowest wage country is impeccable' (quoted in Rich, 1994). It is precisely because of this logic that economic rationality is incompatible with the realization of the claimed environmental human right to an environment free from toxic pollution.

The Value of People

Despite its anthropocentrism, economic rationality is dismissive of the intrinsic value of people (Gorz, 1988). Economic rationality is fundamentally misanthropic since human needs provide no legitimizing basis for resource entitlement. Such entitlement is the sole remit of the market mechanisms of supply and demand. The reality of economic rationality for the poorest in the world who lack sufficient income is continuing starvation and poverty. Quoting United Nations Economic Social and Cultural Organization (UNESCO) figures, Chomsky observes that:

> it's becoming more difficult to tell the difference between economists and Nazi doctors [since] half a million children in Africa die every year simply from debt service ... . It's estimated that about eleven million children die every year from easily curable diseases, most of which could be overcome by treatments that cost a couple of cents. But the economists tell us that to do this would be interference with the market system (Chomsky, 1997b).

Therefore, basic human rights to food or clean water are discredited as normative considerations by the focus of economic rationality on the market mechanism where money alone provides entitlement to resources.

Growthmania

Economic rationality expresses the political agenda of facilitating and enhancing consumerism through GDP growth. A primary focus on economic growth invariably leads to environmental degradation. Arendt observed that in a capitalist economy 'not destruction but conservation spells ruin, because the very durability of conserved objects is the greatest impediment to the turnover process [of the economy], whose constant gain in speed is the only constancy left wherever it has taken hold' (quoted in Achterhuis, 1994). According to this analysis, continued economic growth is necessary for the very survival of capitalism. This observation pertains to the continual need to expand markets in capitalism. The desire for market expansion extends to the very formula used to calculate GDP, aspects of which must appear unfathomable to non-economists. For example, calculations of GDP treat the depletion of environmental resources as income, rather than as loss or depreciation (Buffett, 1995; Daly, 1995; Korten, 1995; Gowdy, 1999). Thus, supporting the conclusion of Arendt, the process of consuming rather than conserving non-renewable environmental resources such as oil is measured as a social benefit under the calculations of GDP. Even more bizarre is the calculation by GDP of pollution as a double social benefit, firstly for the economic activity that generated the pollution, and then again for the activity required to clean it up. Environmental catastrophes such as the Exxon Valdez oil tanker disaster as well as personal catastrophes, such as the diagnosis of cancer patients, are all recorded in positive terms in calculations of GDP (Lasne, 1998).

Some advocates of economic rationality claim that growth is compatible with environmental protection, or indeed beneficial in this regard, since more resources will thereby become available for environmental protection (Bhagwati, 1995). The logical fallacy of this approach is forcibly documented by Dryzek who demonstrates the inherent ecological damage incurred by all economic growth and resource consumption whereas only a proportion of that growth can be diverted to environmental protection projects (Dryzek, 1990). Other commentators provide convincing evidence that pollution levels in developed states have been reduced in recent years not because of economic growth, but rather as a consequence of a sectoral shift to service industries and the relocation of polluting industries to Third

World states where environmental controls are lax or non-existent (Bartley and Bergessen, 1997).

Economic rationality assumes a scarcity of resources, that the total of available resources is insufficient to meet the needs of all people. Opschoor contends that capitalism itself constructs this notion of scarcity through the idea of infinite human needs (Opschoor, 1994). Gorz reminds us that the concept of the 'sufficient' is a cultural or existential category rather than an economic category (Gorz, 1998). Giddens notes that in many subsistence economies:

> there is no principle of scarcity in operation ... modern economics has invented scarcity in the context of a system which puts a basic stress upon the expansion of production ... Members of primitive societies are characteristically at least as able to provide for their needs as those in the most economically developed capitalistic systems. Most primitive societies have at their disposal, if they so desire, all the time necessary to increase the production of material goods. They do not so desire, since the expansion of material production is not experienced as a driving impulsion (Giddens, 1981, pp. 83–4).

Overall scarcity is a useful concept to excuse the existence of unprecedented opulence alongside widespread poverty since the impoverishment of one section of the global population is thereby normalized and portrayed as an inevitable condition rather than as constructed by global capitalism (Korten, 1995; Korten 1998; Anti-Consumerist Campaign, 1999; Thomas, 1999). The assumption of overall scarcity furthermore accommodates the use of resources for the consumption of luxuries by the affluent since the vital distinction between essential and luxury goods is obfuscated. The market mechanism instead provides the sole legitimizing criteria for claims to products. This again normalizes the denial of essential resources for the impoverished as the market diverts resources to supplying goods to the affluent.

Discounting

Economic rationality encourages systematic environmental destruction as a consequence of assuming the concept of discounting. The discount rate, expressed as a percentage, reflects the economic perception that people attach more value to utility occurring in the present than in the future, an attribute termed time preference (Opschoor, 1994). Discounting is a calculation to equate the future economic benefits and costs of a proposed investment project to the net present value to ensure that the efficient allocation of resources is obtained in the present (MacNeill, Winsemius and Yakushiji, 1991). For example, at a discount rate of 10 per cent, a scheme that results in the depletion of £10 million in 100 years has a net value in the present of £725. Commercial projects that are estimated to incur vast costs in the distant future are legitimized and rationalized by economists utilizing the concept of discounting to reduce the significance of future events for contemporary society. According to the internal logic of economic rationality, it is therefore completely rational to take decisions that will result in even catastrophic ecological destruction in the future when such decisions can be shown to be allocatively efficient today (MacNeill, Winsemius and Yakushiji, 1991).

Discounting stipulates that an investment must earn a high enough return to compensate the investor for the opportunity cost of making that choice, such as the interest that could otherwise be earned from placing the capital in a bank. Policies that benefit the environment in the long run, such as investing in renewable energy plants or forestry projects are invariably rejected on economic grounds since they require large initial outlays and revenue is only received in future years. It is precisely on this point of discounting that Pigou identified a 'defective telescopic faculty' in the discipline of economics (quoted in Opschoor, 1994). From the perspective of power relations, economic rationality can therefore be seen to articulate the interests of members of contemporary societies, especially of those who choose a lifestyle of consumerism. However, this is in no sense an objective position. Rather, the interests of one small proportion of human society, namely those currently alive with disposable income, are privileged over and above those of humans without disposable income and over the interests of non-human life forms and over the interests of future generations to inherit an environment rich in biodiversity, natural habitats and abundant natural resources. The constituency best served by economic rationality is again the economically empowered.

The Practical Manifestation of Economic Rationality in Determining Environmental Human Rights Violations

The epistemological paradigm of economic rationality is fundamentally problematic for the realization of environmental human rights. Through deconstructing constitutive elements of the paradigm, economic rationality has been argued above to rationalize, accommodate or indeed advocate processes that cause systematic environmental degradation in order to serve consumerist lifestyles. To demonstrate the applicability of this discussion of economic rationality to actual events, the subject of analysis now turns to look at how corporations internalize and express the paradigm of economic rationality to create violations of environmental human rights as part and parcel of the capitalist economy.

Corporations are characteristically hostile to public attempts to prioritize social and environmental concerns over economic rationality. This is exemplified in a 1997 letter from Abraham Katz, then President of the United States Council for International Business, to the then US Deputy Trade Representative Jeffrey Lang which stated that: 'we will oppose any and all measures to create or even imply binding obligations for governments or business related to the environment or labor' (quoted in Economic Working Group, 1998). One prominent group campaigning against the toxic pollution of the environment noted that the major problem the organization faced in achieving this goal was presented by industry that was insisting on economic grounds that there be no bans or phase outs of toxic chemicals (Greenpeace, 1999).

Corporations have been eager to retain the right to continue the toxic pollution of the environment to keep operating costs down. BP spent US $171,000 in a successful campaign to prevent new regulations drafted by the Californian state legislature that would have required safety improvements to be made to oil tankers. These developments followed a 300,000 gallon spill from a BP-chartered oil tanker in February 1991 off Huntingdon beach, California (*McSpotlight*, 1998). Brenton extensively details the history of opposition from the shipping and oil industries to proposals for more comprehensive pollution control equipment to be installed in tankers (Brenton, 1994).

In another demonstration of corporate interest defending the ability to maximize profits at the expense of environmental protection, the Methyl Bromide Working Group (which represents three producers of methyl bromide) is actively lobbying to undermine attempts in the US to phase out the usage of the pesticide (*Corporate Watch*, 1998a). This corporate lobbying has continued in spite of the classification of methyl bromide by the US Environmental Protection Agency (EPA) as a category one acute toxin, the most deadly category of substances, and in spite of a history of adverse health effects of methyl bromide on agricultural workers (Methyl Bromide Alternatives Network, 1998). Similarly promoting commercial interests at the expense of environmental health concerns, Rhone Poulem has been reported as defending its exports to the Third World of pesticides that, because of their toxicity, are banned in the US (Greenpeace, 1998b).

Following an explosion on the 2 December 1984, a toxic cocktail of over 40 tonnes of methyl isocyanate, hydrogen cyanide and other gases leaked from a Union Carbide pesticide manufacturing plant in Bhopal, India causing 300,000 people to be injured or killed (*Corporate Watch*, 1997). Over 50,000 people remain permanently disabled as a result of the disaster with diseases of the respiratory, gastro-intestinal, reproductive, musculoskeletal and neurological systems (International Peoples' Tribunal on Human Rights and the Environment, 1998). The response of Union Carbide following the incident exemplifies how a focus on economic rationality violates environmental human rights. The corporation declined to reveal the exact chemical composition of the toxic gases released (Jaising and Sathyamala, 1995). When specifically asked to disclose this information to enable health workers to design effective treatment, Union Carbide refused, using trade secrecy and patent laws to keep its chemical formulas and production processes' secret from its competitors (Jaising and Sathyamala, 1995). The damage to the health of individuals exposed to the toxic gas was thereby exacerbated since as detailed data never became available as to the exact composition of the released gases, no effective treatment could be developed to treat the exposed victims (Agarwal and Narain, 1992).

With regard to the toxic pollutant ozone produced by industry and car users,[3] an oil industry lobbyist explains that people can protect themselves from the health effects of ozone since 'they can avoid jogging, asthmatic kids need not go out and ride their bicycles' (quoted in *Multinational Monitor*, 1997). In response to a World Health Organization (WHO) report that concluded thousands of Europeans exposed to particulate pollution will suffer disease or die,[4] a representative of the oil industry stated that 'to say that particles are dangerous is emotive and irresponsible' (quoted in Edwards, 1995). When European environment ministers met in November 1995 for discussions to reduce the exposure of the public to particulates, the introduction of more stringent limits on emissions was postponed 'under pressure from the motor industry' (Hamer and MacKenzie, 1995). Only after a lengthy period of procrastination were more comprehensive laws on air pollution introduced in the US in November 1990. 'Economic costs' were cited as being the main reason for the delay (Melamed, 1990). Similarly, 'intense lobbying by most car manufacturers in

Europe' delayed the decision of the European Parliament to match American standards of pollution emissions from vehicle exhausts in April 1989 (Gould, 1989). Fearing a downturn in the car market, Peugeot in 1988 lobbied the French government to block European Union (EU) agreement on more stringent exhaust emission standards for small cars (Brenton, 1994).

Corporations in the United States have recently established or funded front groups to campaign against stricter clean air legislation. By coordinating a number of opposition groups, a variety of tactics can be undertaken to shape public opinion, whilst at the same time ensuring that there are multiple targets to which ecological groups have to respond. Citizens for Sensible Control of Acid Rain has connections to electric utilities and mining companies who oppose the 1986 US Clean Air Act, which sought to reduce air pollution (Clearinghouse on Environmental Advocacy and Research, 1998). The Coalition for Vehicle Choice was reportedly created by corporations in the car industry to combat increased fuel efficiency standards (Clearinghouse on Environmental Advocacy and Research, 1998). The Council for Solid Waste Solutions was established by the plastics industry to promote the use of plastic containers (Clearinghouse on Environmental Advocacy and Research, 1998). The National Association of Manufacturers funds and shares addresses with the Air Quality Standards Coalition. This coalition 'represents the industry viewpoint that current air regulations are adequate, and that more stringent regulations would harm business' (Clearinghouse on Environmental Advocacy and Research, 1998). The American Petroleum Institute, the American Plastics Council and the Chemical Manufacturers Association fund Citizens for a Sound Economy, a group that produces advertisements opposing more restrictions on air pollution (Clearinghouse on Environmental Advocacy and Research, 1998). The Foundation for Clean Air Progress opposes regulations designed to force industry to cut pollution emissions, claiming that pollution can be best reduced by members of the public acting more responsibly. The American Petroleum Industry hired the public relations firm Burson-Marsteller to create the Foundation for Clean Air Progress which is housed in Burson-Marsteller's Washington office (Clearinghouse on Environmental Advocacy and Research, 1998).

Whereas fossil fuel usage is a major source of pollution, a number of petrochemical corporations have been actively campaigning for continued reliance on this energy source to promote economic growth. Mr Raymond, the Chairman of Exxon Corporation, urged developing countries to avoid environmental controls that would hinder economic development and encouraged these states to increase fossil fuel usage (*Downstream*, 1997).

Corporate lobbying at the Kyoto conference on climate change exemplifies the position of industry to retain societal dependency on fossil fuels. A series of advertisements was sponsored by lobbyists for the energy and automotive industries warning US consumers of higher prices if the Clinton Administration agreed to cuts in carbon dioxide emissions at the conference (Dejevsky, 1997). The failure to agree legally binding timetables for reductions in carbon dioxide emissions at Kyoto has been widely attributed to the lobbying success of coalitions of influential industries (Corporate Europe Observatory, 1998; Vidal, 1998; Karacs, Dejevsky and Schoon, 1997; Brown, 1997; Kettle, Brown and Traynor, 1997). The Global Climate Coalition whose members include the American Automobile Manufacturers

Association, the American Petroleum Institute, Amoco, Chevron, Chrysler, Dow Chemical, DuPont, Exxon, Ford and Union Carbide was one important industrial lobby group. In the run up to the 1997 Kyoto conference, the coalition sent a letter to President Clinton asking that all current climate proposals be rejected (Corporate Europe Observatory, 1998). Even Conservative MP and then UK Environment Secretary, John Gummer, reported that in Kyoto:

> I saw some of the nastiest big business arm-twisting one could imagine. A corps of 60 lobbyists from the American coal, oil and car industries, masquerading under the Global Climate Coalition ... cajoling and threatening the US delegates and developing countries alike (quoted in Greenpeace, 1998a, p. 1).

Another group, the Global Climate Information Project, is a coalition of industry groups including the American Petroleum Institute and the National Mining Association. In September 1997 the GCIP initiated a $13 million advertising campaign against reducing fossil fuel usage, which warned of the increasing costs of goods that would result from a climate agreement (Corporate Europe Observatory, 1998). In Europe the Employers' Confederation (UNICE), and the European Roundtable of Industrialists have openly disagreed with the EU's proposal to reduce carbon dioxide emissions (Corporate Europe Observatory, 1998).

The same commercial incentives that cause corporations to oppose environmental protection measures also marginalize human rights concerns. The current Burmese government, known as the State Law and Order Restoration Council (SLORC), is one example of a military junta that demonstrates contempt for the concept of human rights, engaging in political tactics of torture and intimidation to stay in power (Strider, 1995). A number of CEOs of petrochemical MNCs have nonetheless chosen to invest in the state. The chief executive of one such corporation, Premier Oil, denied that such investment has any effect on the political situation and 'insisted Premier was politically neutral' (Cowe, 1998). Of course there are many political implications arising from the decision to operate in Burma as pointed out by Aung San Suu Kyi, the democratically elected President kept out of power by the military regime; 'Companies investing in Burma only serve to prolong the agony of my country by encouraging the present regime to persevere in its atrocities' (quoted in Alonso, 1998; Finch, 1998). The response from Premier Oil is however instructive because of the sole focus on economic criteria that dictates investment decisions regardless of even the most egregious human rights violations. Neither is Premier Oil alone in focusing on economic criterion for making commercial decisions at the expense of human rights considerations. Unocal, Total, ARCO and Texaco have all signed contracts with the SLORC for oil, gas and pipeline construction projects (Alonso, 1998; *Corporate Watch*, 1999a).

These examples are not isolated cases, but rather express the corporate pursuit of self-interest in a capitalist political economy. To remain competitive, firms must prioritize profits over social or environmental concerns. In the case of the environment, the editors of *The Economist* for example point out that:

[s]ince companies are not altruists, most will only be as green as governments compel them to be. They will do what is required of them and what they perceive to be in their self-interest (quoted in Brenton, 1994, pp. 149–50).

Supporting this conclusion, a recent corporate survey into business environmental practices found that:

the threat of fines or prosecution has proved the most powerful incentive for adopting greener policies. Forty-eight per cent of respondents cited legislation as the key driver, followed by regulatory requirements (34 per cent) ... . The perception amongst managers is that green policies put up costs with little scope for future payback (Charlesworth, 1998, pp. 18–19).

The purpose of this section has been to illustrate the actual manifestation of economic rationality in corporate activity to demonstrate how this framework encourages indifference to environmental concerns since the focus on commercial criteria predominates. As Greider observes, in neglecting environmental and social concerns, MNCs 'are merely responding to the real imperatives of the present system, doing what they think is necessary to survive' (Greider, 1997). Korten similarly notes that:

Unless a corporation is working in a particular niche situation, and is privately owned by a terribly socially conscious family or manager, it is virtually impossible to manage a corporation in a socially responsible way. Either it will be driven out of the market by competitors, who are pursuing less responsible policies, or it will be bought by a corporate raider who sees the short-term profit in taking those actions. Or, as fund managers themselves become more active in the management affairs of corporations, the managers are likely to be replaced by shareholder action driven by fund managers (Korten, 1996, p. 212).

Economic rationality made manifest in the capitalist structure as commercial self-interest can be identified as determining the continuing violation of the environmental human rights claimed in chapters 5 and 6.

Conclusions

This chapter has analyzed the contested epistemological bases for evaluating the existence of environmental human rights. The fallacy of assuming a singular and universally applicable form of rationality instead of different conceptualizations of rationality, each with specific values and decision-making criteria, was firstly established. An attempt to investigate the basis of environmental human rights solely on grounds of reasoned inquiry was found to be of limited use since this would inevitably reflect the epistemological assumptions of the author and the values of the paradigm of reasoning employed to conduct the analysis. Instead of adopting such a methodology, this chapter has sought to explain how environmental human rights can be either assumed as axiomatic or discredited as irrelevant by different forms of rationality.

The analysis has sought to elucidate the process by which economic rationality has been elevated over and above ecological rationality in characterizing politics in capitalist states. The dominance and legitimacy of a particular conceptualization of rationality over other possibilities was argued to be primarily a function of social power, of serving the interests of powerful social groups who benefit from the resultant outcomes, rather than the result of any inherent epistemological superiority. Throughout this chapter, social interests have therefore been identified as decisive elements in determining the 'rational' from the 'irrational' position in the process of political decision making. Under conditions of capitalism, this process has produced the dominance of economic rationality that hypothesizes and defines rational behavior in terms of the utility maximizing individual. This view of rational action is predicated upon the desired values of private interest, consumerism and private property ownership over conflicting values of protecting the socially vulnerable, preserving biodiversity and habitats or promoting a conception of justice that interferes with the efficient allocation of resources. As (i) an investigation into the construction of the dominant form of rationality and (ii) a juxtaposition to ecological rationality illustrated, the marginalization of environmental human rights by economic rationality is in no sense a neutral position but rather reflects both the interests and influence of the social group from which the economic epistemology derives its legitimacy, authority and dominance. In terms of understanding the political context of environmental human rights, the conclusions in this chapter draw the focus of attention back to the social forces that benefit from capitalism and the forms of power that this group can employ to further its own interest.

Economic rationality serves the agenda of producers and consumers. It addresses questions of resource allocation to privilege the interests of the present generation over those of future generations and the interests of the rich over the satisfaction of the basic needs of the impoverished. This paradigm therefore defines people as consumers rather than as citizens and accommodates rather than discourages (i) the existence of opulence for some alongside deepening poverty of others and (ii) the ongoing depletion of natural resources. The actualization of economic rationality in capitalist states has undoubtedly been of great benefits for a significant sector of humankind, lifting millions out of poverty and facilitating opulent patterns of consumerism for many individuals. Yet, this state of affairs is in no sense impartial, objective or neutral. Rather it is to organize a political economy to serve the desires of those humans in the present generation with disposable incomes at the expense of those without disposable incomes, of future generations and at the expense of non-human life. This latter constituency, whose interests are at best disregarded and at worst thwarted by the value premises of economic rationality, make up considerably more than 99.99 per cent of all life forms on Earth.

Notes

1   See chapter 6 for a detailed criticism of the market allocation of resources from a perspective of human rights.
2   See chapter 6.
3   See chapter 5 for details of the epidemiological effects of ozone.

4   Particulates are pollutants of less than 10 micrometers in length that can become lodged in the alveoli of the lungs, see chapter 5 for more details.

Chapter 2

Structural Power and Environmental Human Rights

There are a thousand hacking at the branches of evil to one who is striking at the root, and it may be that he who bestows the largest amount of time and money on the needy is doing the most by his mode of life to produce that misery which he strives to relieve.

– Henry Thoreau

Introduction

The purpose of this chapter is to establish the role of environmental human rights in the process of political change, taking into account relevant structural limitations. Methodologically, this analysis begins by introducing the relationship between agency and structure, that is the extent to which individuals and organizations constitute, and can therefore change, social and political structures. The position adopted is that constructivism best explains the agent-structure relationship, which argues that the two are mutually constitutive. From this basis, the analysis examines the nature of structural power to conclude that anti-systemic forces are severely limited in their ability to initiate change within formal capitalist structures. Environmentalism and the human rights discourse are examined in turn as examples of how structural power has co-opted the challenges posed by these anti-systemic movements. Structural power will be argued to have assimilated anti-systemic discourses into complimenting, rather than challenging, capitalist structures of economic organization.

The chapter then applies the discussion on structural power, co-option and agency to the potential role of environmental human rights in the process of historical change. The possibility suggested for anti-systemic movements to effectualize political change is to draw public attention to the environmental harm conducted under the day to day operations of the global economy and to the contradictions inherent to the capitalist system. Anti-systemic movements can also contribute to the process of historical change by fostering the growth of ecological and humanitarian values in society. It is important at the outset to draw a distinction between beneficial campaigning for political change through peaceful means on the one hand and through the use of violence on the other. It is the violence perpetrated by the agents of global capitalism to both people and planet that is opposed by anti-systemic forces seeking a political future based on solidarity and ecological values. Anti-systemic acts of violence betray the goal of an alternative political economy based on respect for all forms of life and must necessarily be rejected as a legitimate tactic. Furthermore, acts of violence provide states eager to defend corporate interests with the ideal excuse to use repressive tactics against anti-globalization and environmental protesters.

Structure, Hegemony and the Mechanism of Co-option

Agency refers to the capability of individuals to design social and political systems free of external constraints. By contrast, structures denote those external constraints that both shape and limit the possibilities for the independent action of individuals. Defending the importance of individual agency, Tully claims that changes in structures are caused by changing the practices in which they are embedded, 'it is our routine acting that holds these seemingly autonomous systems in place' (Tully, 1999). The autonomy assigned to individuals in the shaping of political systems is denied by those theorists who interpret the individual as a product of the cultural structures that condition modes of thinking and of behavior. Exemplifying this approach, Kernohan claims that the majority of beliefs that constitute the consciousness of individuals, as well as the background beliefs on which deliberations depend, have been uncritically assumed from the broader social culture (Kernohan, 1998). Similarly stressing structure over individual agency, Hoare and Smith maintain that each individual is the synthesis not only of existing social and cultural relations, but also of the history of these relations (Hoare and Smith, 1971). According to structuralists, the preferences of individuals are not fixed and autonomous, but are instead a function of the structural context in which the preference is formed, for example of the existing legal rules, of past consumption choices and of the actions and the norms of other individuals in society.

Political and economic structures are either recreated or changed over time (Kernohan, 1998). As such, the everyday perceptions and actions of individuals can influence these structures. The subtlety of this interplay between individual agency and the structural context is captured by Barkun who observes that 'beneath the surface of self-serving motives, every decision looks to the past for guidance and every decision bequeaths something to the future, which either reinforces or undercuts some aspect of received norms' (Barkun, 1968). The approach adopted in this research to explain the nature of the agent-structure relationship is that of constructivism that sees agents and structures as constituting each other. Structural change or recreation occurs because of the willful actions and choices of individuals. Yet these individuals are not autonomous or independent agents since their preferences and values have been produced in a social context as the structuralists maintain. The constructivist approach is supported by Cox who paraphrases Marx to contend that people make history, but not under conditions of their own choosing (Cox, 1987). Cox argues that in order to influence political events, it is necessary for individuals to first understand the conditions not chosen by oneself in which action is possible (Cox, 1987).

Attention now turns to describe the nature of the structural power that constrains the capacity of individual agents to initiate political change. Hindess notes that the exercise of power is often not recognized by those who are subject to its effects (Hindess, 1996). Power, Hindess continues 'affects the thoughts and desires of individuals, but it does so primarily through the action of collective forces and social arrangements' (Hindess, 1996). A similar conclusion is suggested by Galbraith's idea of conditioned power which, in contrast to physical force and inducement,[1] is exercised by changing belief (Galbraith, 1984). Galbraith explains that conditioned power is the product of a continuum from visible persuasion to what the individual in the social context has been brought to believe inherently correct (Galbraith, 1984). An important element of social power resides in the capacity to promote an ideological normalization of specific social structures and unarticulated political assumptions (Rosenberg, 1994). This aspect of power can be best articulated through the Gramscian concept of hegemony.

Hegemony combines a social structure, an economic structure, and a political structure to produce social control that combines physical coercion with intellectual, ethical and cultural persuasion (Ransome, 1992; Cox with Sinclair, 1996). The intellectual and ethical elements are integral to the operation of hegemony since these are utilized by the hegemonic power to consolidate strength and maintain popular support (Hoffman, 1988; Gill, 1990). As Mosca argues, hegemony appeals to the universal need in human nature of governing and being governed not only on the basis of material or intellectual force, but on the basis of an ethical principle (Mosca, 1970). The prominent mechanism used by hegemonic orders to negate systemic challenges is through trasformismo. Trasformismo was a term used by Gramsci to refer to the co-option of anti-systemic forces that disempowers potential centers of opposition and prevents the realization of alternative structures of social organization. In a hegemonic order, the dominant power makes concessions to establish an order that can be articulated as expressing the general interest (Cox with Sinclair, 1996). Trasformismo assimilates potentially dangerous concepts and the associated social movements by adjusting them to support rather than question the policies and interests of the hegemonic bloc and thereby diffuses opposition to existing power relations (Cox with Sinclair, 1996). As the following discussion demonstrates, the human rights and environmental discourses have been co-opted by the structural forces of capitalism to negate the potential of these movements to become established as the focus for an alternative social order. In particular, the structures of capitalism and economic rationality manifest social power to abrogate the challenge posed by social movements and to manipulate radical ideas into supporting, rather than criticizing, the ideological basis of capitalism.

Co-option of the Environmental Movement

The commonalty shared by all environmental pressure groups is the objective of implementing some aspect of environmental protection. With the exception of radical environmental groups who explicitly reject political compromises, other commonalties include the desire to avoid political marginalization, to gain and retain access to politicians and other decision-makers and to demonstrate practical achievements to their membership. These objectives lead organizations towards a process of interaction and compromise with governments in an attempt to mitigate the most ecologically damaging effects of the existing political economy. Such an approach invariably results in co-option. Environmental advocacy forces operating within formal political structures in an attempt to influence decisions typically attain minor concessions whilst the main causes of environmental degradation inherent to capitalism remain unchallenged.

The inclusion of environmental NGOs in formal discussions adds credibility to the hegemonic bloc, since it promotes the veneer of an inclusive, open and impartial political system. Many NGOs are eager to enter a dialogue with politicians because of a belief that they can prompt pro-environmental changes. This section demonstrates how this approach of co-operating within the official political structure has facilitated the assimilation of the mainstream environmental movement into the capitalist bloc.

In the domestic politics of the United States, the desire of environmental NGOs to access official political channels was eagerly accommodated by the political establishment as exemplified in the audacious self-description by George Bush (senior) as the 'environmental president' (Waks, 1996). The tactic of mainstream US environmental groups to co-operate within official political channels rather than campaigning for alternative political systems to capitalism became the norm under the Clinton administrations. The de-mobilization of environmental groups in the public arena has subsequently been identified as a contributory factor in accounting for the ability of corporate polluters to secure widespread public sympathy (*Multinational Monitor*, 1994).

One tactic mobilized by corporate interest groups in securing popular support was to assimilate environmental arguments into promoting the existing corporate agenda. The advice of the public relations firm Burson Marsteller to the European Association for Bio-industries (EUROPABIO), advocates strategies to manage public opinion to the benefit of the biotechnology industry. This advice, subsequently leaked to *Corporate Watch*, explained that in order 'to effect the desired changes in public perceptions and attitudes, the bio-industries must stop trying to be their own advocates' (Burson Marsteller, 1998). Environmental arguments are becoming increasingly prominent as a mechanism to promote the corporate agenda as advocacy of commercial self-interest is increasingly untenable or indeed counter-productive in the face of an increasingly well informed public. Thomas points out that the use of environmental discourse by corporate interests has resulted in 'the presentation of the problem as the solution' (Thomas, 1999). The same corporations responsible for environmental damage promote their commercial interests with environmental arguments. The World Business Council for Sustainable Development (WBCSD) is composed of 125 CEOs and describes itself as 'one of the world's most influential green business networks' (quoted in Corporate Europe Observatory, 1997). Livio De Simone, the chairman of the WBCSD has stated that business is now viewed as contributing to solving environmental problems and securing a sustainable future for the planet rather than being depicted as a source of ecological problems (Corporate Europe Observatory, 1998). Greenpeace has contrasted the environmental rhetoric of the WBCSD with its actual political lobbying record that includes opposing environmental taxes and opposing the reduction of governmental subsidies for ecologically damaging products (Greenpeace, 1999). The WBCSD has successfully promoted self-regulation as a strategy to achieve environmental protection as an alternative to governmental regulation (Corporate Europe Observatory, 1997). This approach has improved the environmental image of TNCs whilst simultaneously identifying the needs of sustainable development with those of economic growth and economic globalization (Corporate Europe Observatory, 1997).

On the specific issue of climate change, there is an inescapable conflict between the environmental need to reduce fossil fuel usage and the commercial needs of petrochemical industries to maintain or increase sales volumes. Petrochemical corporations have been lobbying hard against efforts to significantly reduce dependence upon fossil fuels. A memo from the American Petroleum Institute, leaked to the *New York Times* in 1998 for example revealed a plan undertaken by the institute on behalf of Exxon, Chevron, and a number of industry front groups to hinder political efforts to address climate change (*Corporate Watch*, 1999b). The oil industry plan proposed spending \$5 million over two years to set up a Global Climate Science Data Center, ostensibly as an objective public information source on climate change issues, which would be staffed by scientists, 'whose research in this field supports our position' (quoted in *Corporate Watch*, 1999b). In addition the plan proposed to establish a 'Science Education Task Group' that would promote the oil industries position on climate change to school-children (*Corporate Watch*, 1999b).

The co-option of environmental issues is also displayed in the National Wetlands Coalition, whose logo features a duck flying over a swamp. This coalition is in fact sponsored by US petrochemical companies and real estate developers to campaign for the easing of regulations pertaining to the conversion of wetlands into drilling sites and shopping malls (Korten, 1995).

A prominent tactic in the corporate co-option of the environmental agenda is to present a veneer of interest in environmental protection to splinter and weaken opposition movements. Corporations establishing procedural tribunals to deal with public concerns exemplify how potential protests have been pre-empted by redirecting opposition into controlled forums where the corporation retains ultimate authority and decision-making capability. For example, the petrochemical MNC Shell invited 90 'stakeholders' to participate in a series of workshops held on the subject of its oil and gas exploratory activities in the Peruvian virgin rainforest. The discussions at the workshops revolved not around the substantive question of whether the project should go ahead, but only on procedural points of how the project could be implemented to minimize the environmental impact. This process successfully divided the NGO community. Some NGOs were keen to participate to minimize the ecological damage incurred by the drilling whilst radical groups became marginalized by their opposition to the entire consultation process (Rowell, 1999).

The co-option of NGOs was highlighted in a recent study into the influence of social movements on the policy decisions of Global Economic Institutions (GEIs). In this research, the author concludes that the critical voices of NGOs are 'fragmented and polarized' by the process of engagement and dialogue with GEIs (O'Brien, 1997). In particular, the World Bank and the International Monetary Fund (IMF) were so successful in restricting the criticisms that were leveled at them from the groups who had been bought into dialogue 'that with some flexibility GEIs could cultivate a social movement constituency' (O'Brien, 1997). Indicative of co-option rather than reciprocal compromise, NGOs entering into dialogue with the GEIs were found in the study to be relatively ineffectual in changing the environmental and social impacts of GEIs; 'the generalized principles of conduct are subject to debate, but relatively immune from revision' (O'Brien, 1997). Radical NGOs rejecting the tactic of dialogue with GEIs in favor of uncompromising opposition were simultaneously weakened and marginalized by appearing as an extremist minority (O'Brien, 1997).

Co-option of environmental issues by corporate interests was an evident feature of the United Nations Conference on the Environment and Development (UNCED).[2] The organization of the conference facilitated the unprecedented access of environmental NGO representatives to politicians and to the official conference talks, presenting the appearance of NGO participation in conference decisions. Chatterjee and Finger demonstrate that the primary outcome of this inclusion and engagement of environmental NGOs in UNCED was 'the increased legitimization of governments and spotlight visibility for UNCED' (Chatterjee and Finger, 1994). The dynamic of the process of co-option of anti-systemic forces was summarized as encouraging peoples and NGOs to participate actively in the UNCED process, while not allowing them to influence the outcome (Chatterjee and Finger, 1994). This 'led to an overall legitimization of a process that is ultimately destructive of the very forces that were mobilized', specifically those of the environmental movement (Finger and Chatterjee, 1992; 1994). The environmental agenda advanced by NGOs was ignored by the official discussions at Rio, as reflected in the dismissal of the *Ten Point Plan to Save the Earth Summit* sponsored by environmental NGOs. This plan called for radical changes to the global political economy to prioritize environmental protection over corporate interests. Measures included a call for reductions in Northern resource consumption patterns, strong international regulation of TNCs, a reversal of the flow of resources from the South to the North, an end to deforestation, a phasing-out of nuclear power plants and a transition to renewable energy (Chatterjee and Finger, 1994). The complete omission of these pressing topics from legally binding agreements exemplifies how the formal political agenda at Rio was insulated from genuine environmental concerns (Thomas, 1993; Thomas, 1996; Haq, 1997). The opposition from political authorities to any structural change resulting from Rio was made explicit in a US memo leaked to Greenpeace International who revealed that:

On 30 March 1992 at PrepCom 4, members of the US delegation were told privately by Michael Young, US Dept. of State's Deputy Under Secretary for Economic and Agricultural Affairs, to oppose inclusion of certain matters in the Earth Summit agenda. Referring to them as the Ten Commandments, he listed the topics that should be excluded from the Rio Declaration and Agenda 21:

1. the precautionary principle,
2. sharing the benefits of technology,
3. financial resource formulas,
4. liability/compensation for environmental damage,
5. commitments of any kind,
6. environmental impact assessment requirements not consistent with US law,
7. new dispute resolution requirements,
8. references to the military,
9. new institutions,
10. new UN pledges (Curtis, 1992).

Such reservations exemplify the desire to avoid any meaningful change to the capitalist political economy. Instead, the Rio agenda was designed to accommodate corporate interests. Northern governments took on the role of spokespersons of Northern corporations while Southern governments were advocating more economic growth, thereby playing into the hands of business (Chatterjee and Finger, 1994). TNCs were never even mentioned in the UNCED documents as constituting a potential problem for the environment (Curtis, 1992; Chatterjee and Finger, 1994). Indeed, the only mention of corporations in the formal discussions at Rio was to promote their role in sustainable development (Thomas, 1993). No regulatory controls on corporate activity resulted from Rio. The World Business Council on Sustainable Development epitomized the complete failure of UNCED to address corporate causes of environmental degradation when it stated that Rio texts 'have far more to say to government than business' (quoted in *Corporate Watch*, 1998b). As *Corporate Watch* comments, corporate lobbying groups themselves helped ensure this neglect of scrutiny into business activities 'as they relentlessly lobbied UNCED delegates against any criticism of transnational corporations' (*Corporate Watch*, 1998b).

Analysis of the actual texts that emerged at Rio further testifies to the corporate co-option of the negotiations. The Biodiversity Convention is notable for facilitating the continued exploitation of biological diversity rather than implementing any mechanisms to protect or enhance diversity. Further destruction of habitats rich in biodiversity was accommodated by allowing states 'the sovereign right to exploit their own resources pursuant to their environmental policies' (quoted in Chatterjee and Finger, 1994). Biotechnology industry constitutes the vanguard of corporate efforts to commodify the eco-system. Yet this sector of industry was promoted in the Biodiversity Convention as being 'essential for the conservation and sustainable use of biodiversity' (*The Ecologist*, 1993). In a similar accommodation of commercial interests over the needs of habitat preservation, the Agreement on Forest Principles facilitates ongoing deforestation by defending the sovereign right of states to 'convert forests to other uses' (quoted in *The Ecologist*, 1993). Therefore, an international agreement that could have established international laws to preserve forested habitats rich in biodiversity was inverted to accommodate their continued devastation. It is indeed revealing that deforestation is not even mentioned once in the Agreement on Forest Principles as a problem for forest ecosystems (*The Ecologist*, 1993).

Provisions made at Rio that went some way to addressing the causes of social and environmental problems were invariably legally non-binding and have subsequently been ignored in actual practices (Haq, 1997). For example, principle eight of the Rio Declaration strikes at the heart of the consumer culture by calling for the reduction in unsustainable patterns of production and consumption. This principle has conspicuously failed to have any meaningful impact in practice since the rhetoric did not translate into any structural changes to the global economy (Waks, 1996).

In addition to the control over the formal agenda in international environmental conferences, the co-option of the environmental agenda by corporate interests is evident in the phenomena of green consumerism. Green consumerism is the selling or purchase of a product on the grounds of benefiting the environment. This concept is therefore an oxymoron since a focus on environmental concerns requires a reduction in overall consumption patterns rather than a narrow focus of comparisons and shifts in consumption between various products. The goal of reducing overall consumption contradicts the corporate desire to increase sales, to which end environmental logic has been inverted. For example, car manufacturers are attempting to market particular models on environmental grounds:

> Environmentally who is the fairest of them all? Whichever colour you choose, your New Accord will be green. To make it more environmentally friendly, we've used water-based paint instead of oil-based. We've made 91.9 per cent of the car recyclable (easily surpassing the European Community's demands of 85 per cent by the year 2005). And we've made the carbon dioxide emissions a mere 33.5 per cent of the EC's maximum permitted levels. Furthermore, our manufacturing process is one of the most efficient in the world. So instead of just a pale excuse for green, you get a rich, deep, thoughtful green (Honda, 1998, pp. 86–7).

The editors of *The Corporate Planet* noted the evident trend towards the use of wide open spaces, lush vegetation and fresh air replacing scantily clad and large-breasted women as props for car manufacturers to advertise and promote their next generation of gas guzzlers (*Corporate Watch*, 1998c).

In 1999, the word greenwash entered the *Oxford English Dictionary*, defined as 'disinformation disseminated by an organization so as to present an environmentally responsible public image' (quoted in Rowell, 1999). The presentation of environmental responsibility as a means to increase sales epitomizes co-option of the environmental discourse by corporate values since environmental concerns are conceptualized in a framework of marketing, sales figures, commercial arguments and profit margins. Eden provides evidence in support of this trend through a survey of corporations that found 40 per cent of respondents believed that a green image made commercial sense (Eden, 1993). The creation of a green image therefore becomes a useful mechanism to increase sales, a marketing instrument used by companies operating even in the most polluting sectors of the economy. The petrochemical giant Chevron for example began its 'People Do' advertising program in 1985 which, at an estimated cost of $5 to $10 million per year, advertised a series of environmental projects that it had funded (*Corporate Watch*, 1998d). *Corporate Watch* notes that Chevron can spend more on advertising the projects in television and print media than on managing the projects themselves (*Corporate Watch*, 1998d). One example relates to the El Segundo butterfly sanctuary established and maintained by Chevron at a cost of $5,000 per year. This project was the content of a 30 second advertisement that cost as much as $200,000 to produce (*Corporate Watch*, 1998d).[3]

Green consumerism is ultimately an expression of economic rationality since it appeals to people as consumers, rather than as citizens, seeking answers to ecological problems through the market mechanism rather than through broader social or political change. Consumption preferences expressed through the market mechanism are suggested by the notion of green consumerism to be the appropriate method of addressing ecological concerns (Barry, 1993). Green consumerism restricts the focus of attention to individual products and deflects attention away from the structural aspects of capitalism that cause environmental degradation.[4] Most importantly, green consumerism promotes a continuation of corporate freedom since the market is assumed to ensure the production of the hypothesized environmentally friendly products without additional regulations. The concept of green consumerism ultimately supports corporate interests since any form of environmental regulatory controls over commercial activity are deemed unnecessary and the dominance of the market remains unchallenged.

The final aspect of the co-option of the environmental movement by structural forces described in this section is articulated through the polluter pays principle. This principle states that the originators of pollution must pay a specified price for the toxins emitted into the environment so that the costs of pollution are paid for by the originator of that pollution, rather than passed on to the rest of society (Pearce and Turner, 1990). The polluter pays principle is now a widely recognized principle of international environmental law (Morita-Lou, 1999). The purpose of the principle is to discourage excessive pollution through a market based approach. One economist states that such a mechanism is required to reduce pollution since, 'if the firm can pollute the lake without cost, its self-interest will lead it to pollute' (Begg *et al.*, 1987). The polluter pays principle may be institutionalized through a variety of mechanisms, for example, through a pollution tax (Begg *et al.*, 1987). Another prominent example is a system of tradable pollution permits whereby a polluter requires a permit to legally emit a unit of a specified pollutant (Peace and Turner, 1990). These permits are bought from a total number reflecting the optimum level of pollution and at a price decided by market forces (Peace and Turner, 1990). Whichever form the polluter pays principle eventually takes, the commodification of pollution units is a necessary prerequisite for either a tax based system or for the market to determine the efficient allocation and cost of pollution permits. Commodification refers to the economic process by which elements previously external to market considerations become perceived and traded through market transactions to ensure the efficient allocation of resources. In this instance, pollution is perceived as an exchangeable commodity. The polluter pays principle has been championed by both NGOs and environmental theorists as a method of environmental protection (Friends of the Earth, 1998a). Glazewski goes so far as to claim that the basis of environmental human rights resides in the acceptance of the norms of sustainable development and of the polluter pays principle (Glazewski, 1996).

Yet, expressed through the polluter pays principle, the market facilitates the continued pollution of the environment since the right is ascribed to the polluter as opposed to the right of people and ecosystems in general not to be exposed to pollution. The polluter pays principle institutionalizes the continued pollution of the environment with the only requirement that polluters pay a specified sum for engaging in the process, effectively expanding the remit of the market by commodifying units of pollution. As such, the allocation of pollution rights under the polluter pays principle ensures the continued systematic violation of the claimed human right to an environment free from toxic pollution with the only condition being that polluters pay a price for the environmental harm that they incur. Through promoting the polluter pays principle, environmental NGOs are legitimizing and underpinning the epistemological paradigm of economic rationality, which is the main cause of environmental degradation, and thereby help normalize and endorse the continued toxic contamination of the environment.[5]

To accept that the right to pollute can be purchased, and thereafter overrides the claimed right to an environment free of toxic pollution is to adopt the logic of capitalist rationality for which allocative efficiency and the market mechanism, rather than human rights, is central. In contrast, the focus of ecological rationality on the well being of the whole eco-system would necessarily regard the purchasing of a permit to pollute as an illegitimate claim to damage the biosphere. To accept the application of the market in determining the extent the of toxic pollution of the environment is to accept (i) economic efficiency as the principal criterion employed in the decision-making process, to which considerations of the biosphere are to be subordinated, (ii) the ability to place a monetary price on the destruction of life exposed to toxic pollution and (iii) the legitimacy of the damage subsequently incurred by the application of this formula. As Sagoff reminds us, there is nothing impartial about this endorsement of market values since efficiency is one particular value rather than a neutral arbiter between incommensurate values (Sagoff, 1984).

Co-option of the Human Rights Discourse

The following section examines evidence of co-option of the human rights discourse to serve the needs of the capitalist political economy. Contrary to the assertion of some analysts, violations of human rights occur not because current rights legislation is too extensive, and consequently requires an unattainable level of resources to be implemented in practice but rather because stipulations fail to go far enough in requiring structural changes. Cranston dismisses needs based rights by claiming that it would be impossible to translate social and economic rights into positive rights through the same political and legal actions that can realize civil and political rights (Cranston, 1967). In fact, like their social and economic counterparts, civil and political rights require a plethora of resources in order to be enforced in practice. Specifically, they require a police force, a judiciary and prisons and a host of auxiliary resources which undermines a rejection of social and economic human rights based upon the claim that such rights alone require resources to be implemented. This conclusion is also supported by the observation made by Donnelly that most critics of economic and social rights effectively destroy their own arguments by defending a right to private property, clearly an economic right (Donnelly, 1993). The argument that social and economic human rights are not 'real' human rights is an instructive example of how the human rights discourse can be used to defend the interests of power and privilege by asserting an ideology of possessive individualism. Theorists have expanded on this argument to describe how the discourse of civil and political rights articulates capitalist definitions of freedom and thereby ideologically underpins and vindicates the capitalist economy (Rupert, 1995; Evans, 2000). Less prominent in the existing literature is the service that social and economic rights perform in support of existing structures of economic power. Indeed, economic and social rights have been assumed to constitute a radical challenge to capitalism. The following discussions balance this contention by demonstrating how social and economic rights can support the capitalist political economy.

The right to self-determination was used as a mechanism to accommodate the expansionary needs of US capital following the Second World War.[6] Planning documents produced by the US Council on Foreign Relations advanced the concepts of human rights and internationalism to promote American trade interests abroad by reducing foreign barriers to trade (Gill, 1990). In particular, the right to national self-determination could be used to dismantle colonial spheres-of-influence that were a significant hindrance to US investors trying to access Third World markets (Gill, 1990). Rosenberg similarly produces evidence testifying to the use by US economic planners of the rhetoric of freedom and self-determination to seek unrestricted access for American corporations abroad (Rosenberg, 1994). Therefore, the human right to self-determination was promoted by the hegemonic power not as an end in itself, but rather as a means to secure another goal, specifically that of ensuring global market access for US businesses (Evans, 1996). Arguments relating to human rights and self-determination are tactical devices for the US to claim ethical legitimacy for the globalization of its capital, which was required because of the success of nationalist forces fighting colonialism (Rosenberg, 1994; Evans, 1996). Attacking the ethical basis of colonialism was useful for the promotion of US capital interests since corporations could thereby access markets that had previously been monopolized by a colonial power.

The co-option of human rights to accommodate the expansionary need of capital is evident through the promotion of economic and social rights that impact negatively upon the cultural traditions of marginalized groups. One such instance of cultural imperialism is evident in the implementation of the right to social security for First Nation people in Canada. The ICESCR states that 'the States Parties to the present Covenant recognize the right of everyone to social security, including social insurance'.[7] This economic right has been used to assimilate indigenous cultures into both state and global economic structures. Economic rights negate, through creating dependency on welfare payments, the social challenge that could otherwise be mobilized by diverse indigenous communities, who in Canada represent significant constituencies with distinct non-capitalist cultures.[8] The criticism that universal human rights violate cultural diversity is not particularly new, nor necessarily accurate, nor is it the argument presented here. It is rather the contention that the specific manifestation of rights stipulated in the ICESCR facilitates the expansionary needs of global capital through incorporating non-capitalist cultures into the global economy by engendering a culture of dependency. These rights are implemented to compliment, rather than challenge the interests of capital. By way of a comparison, this contrasts with the proposed environmental right to natural resources,[9] that could empower local communities to construct their own cultures, liberating them from dependency upon economic structures external to their own cultural traditions.[10]

Economic rights can create the very dependency that they purport to alleviate. The dignity of humanity is undermined by the culture of dependency on handouts that characterize existing economic rights. The implementation of economic rights in capitalist systems has degraded the vision of an equal and just society into under-funded and stigmatized social welfare programs (Waks, 1996). Economic rights do not address the human rights violations that are caused by the operations of the capitalist economy. Rather, these rights seek only to mitigate the subsequent desperate plight of the marginalized. The focus of economic rights is in this sense analogous to shutting the stable door after the horse has bolted.

The ICESCR stipulates a 'right to work'.[11] For the marginalized in the global capitalism, this freedom manifests itself as, in effect, paid slavery.[12] Under a banner of freedom, the right to work locks people into a capitalist economy whose reality for those in the periphery is a life of continued poverty and dependency. Although the ICESCR stipulates a right of workers to fair wages,[13] no further details are given. Such ambiguity allows employers currently paying below poverty line wages to argue that these wages are fair since they, for example, reflect market conditions of supply and demand.

The commodification of labor is the attaching of a market specified monetary price to human work and is itself problematic from a position focusing on human dignity, since it reifies the separation of workers from the means of production and thereby ensures the continued dependency of workers on the capitalist exchange economy. As Marx argued in his theory of alienation, labor is treated like a commodity in the capitalist economy, resulting in the domination of people by the market, instead of society controlling productive activities (Collins, 1982). Although the commodification of labor has been normalized in Western society to the extent that it has now acquired the status of an unquestionable fact, Rosenberg observes the exceptional nature of the concept. Rosenberg points out that the commodification of labor distinguishes modern society from previous systems of social organization that were typically based around personal relations of mutual dependence that authorized commands over labor (Rosenberg, 1994). Chomsky reminds us that wage labor was considered hardly better than slavery in American political culture through much of the 19th century, not only by the labor movement but also by Abraham Lincoln, the Republican Party and the mainstream media (Chomsky, 1997a). Through endorsing wage labor, existing economic rights normalize and legitimize a central and dehumanizing feature of capitalism, obfuscating this cause of oppression and exploitation.

By way of a comparison, the right to environmental resources could be expected to help ensure greater autonomy from the tyranny of the market.[14] Without wanting to romanticize the desperate plight of the medieval peasant, Rosenberg comments that 'unemployment held no terrors for the peasantry of medieval Europe, for they were in possession of the means of subsistence, "free" labor is dependent in ways that tied labor never was' (Rosenberg, 1994). Unlike existing economic rights, the claimed human right to environmental resources is not based around a concept of handouts where the recipients are inactive and disempowered receivers. Neither does it state a right to work, which in practice operates to lock people into an economic order that recreates the conditions of their continuing poverty. To escape patterns of dependency and environmental degradation created under capitalism, individuals and communities require the land and environmental resources to create and work within alternative economic structures based upon principles of subsistence, respect for the local environment, independence and self-reliance.

A further way in which stipulated social and economic rights support the capitalist system is by acting as a means to defuse destabilizing popular unrest and opposition. A welfare state ameliorates the poverty of some of those who have been excluded from the material benefits of capitalism, preventing organized opposition through the offer of token handouts (Dryzek, 1992). Stammers convincingly demonstrates that the welfare state exists to manage the social order to protect and legitimize power inequalities rather than to aid the deprived (Stammers, 1995). The absence of any redistribution in a capitalist economy would most likely create social upheaval resulting in either (i) authoritarian repression of the general population on behalf of the beneficiaries of the capitalist system or (ii) structural changes to address the dynamics that create inequality. Both of these eventualities would challenge the fundamentals of the present system. Authoritarian repression in defense of global capital interests would jettison the moral component of hegemony and openly demonstrate contempt for justice that could only further fuel social unrest and popular opposition. This is best exemplified in the spiraling levels of instability in the South following the imposition of Structural Adjustment Policies (SAPs) and other attacks on state support for the impoverished (Walton and Seddon, 1994). The second option, structural changes to prioritize human needs over the ability of capital to accumulate, would, by definition, be the end of capitalism. Economic rights can therefore be identified to support capitalism by acting as a pressure valve to negate popular opposition and obfuscate the inequalities caused by capitalism. Gorz explains that:

> the condemnation of the welfare state in the name of economic liberalism is thus a piece of mindless ideology. State provision does not stifle society and limit the spontaneous deployment of economic rationality; it is born of this very deployment... and as a necessary framework preventing the market economy finishing up in a collective disaster (Gorz, 1988, p. 132).

Russell similarly comments on the tactic of limited redistribution as an instrument of co-option used by capitalist forces:

> Will capitalists, in fact, exploit their control to the uttermost? Where they are prudent, they would not do so, for fear of just the consequences as Marx foresaw. If they allow the workers some share in prosperity they may prevent them from becoming revolutionary; of this the most notable example is in the United States, where the skilled workers are on the whole Conservative (Russell, 1948, p. 136).

The actual implementation of economic rights is more a function of the structural conditions of the capitalist system than it is a realization of the protection of human dignity. Several theorists have demonstrated the use of economic rights as a Keynesian mechanism to manage aggregate demand and other macro economic variables upon which future economic growth depends (Wallerstein, 1991; Dryzek, 1992). The concept of progressive realization allows states a large degree of flexibility in the extent to which they implement social and economic rights, taking into account economic conditions. As Bauer observes, governments have interpreted their obligation under the ICESCR as implying that a certain level of economic growth must be attained before economic rights become effective (Bauer, 1998). The economic rights of individuals and groups can be thereby subordinated to the development goals selected by states (Bauer, 1998). Thus interpreted, the ICESCR paradoxically facilitates violations of its own provisions since the notion of progressive realization subordinates human needs to the focus on macroeconomic variables. The increase of opulence in the world economy exposes the inadequacy of the claim that economic rights remain unfulfilled because of a lack of aggregate resources. The skewed distribution of these resources under capitalism ensures the deepening of absolute poverty alongside the increasing opulence that is similarly produced by the operations of the market.[15]

Economic rights perform a further function in legitimating the capitalist economic structure in that they are presented as a radical extreme, a wish list of a rise in living standards for the general population. This is typified through Cranston's claim that the realization of economic rights is impossible (Cranston, 1967). Yet, in being presented as an extreme, economic rights perform an important function to negate the challenge posed to capitalist structures by the social values inherent in the project of universal human rights. The presentation of the human rights agenda as ranging from civil and political rights on the one hand to social and economic rights on the other serves to control the challenge posed since more radical demands, such as the environmental human rights claimed in chapters 5 and 6 of this research, are excluded from the mainstream human rights discourse. The presentation of economic rights as an alternative to capitalism co-opts opposition by creating support amongst anti-systemic forces for a set of rights that, in contrast to the way that they are portrayed, do much to support, rather than challenge, hegemonic economic structures. The effectiveness of the set agenda to limit creative discourse and establish conceptual prisons is best exemplified not in the general lack of existing criticisms of economic rights from a social perspective, but rather through the unquestioning endorsement of existing economic human rights by many critics of global capitalism.

Environmental Human Rights as Praxis

None of the foregoing discussion is to deny that environmental and human rights groups can mitigate instances of environment degradation and human rights violations produced by the capitalist system. However, the potential for social movements to extract concessions in the formal political forum is circumscribed by the politics of power that ensures an ongoing prioritization of commercial interests. There is also a price to pay for anti-systemic forces operating within official political channels. Social movements accommodate, condone and legitimize existing political structures and thereby play a part in the reproduction of the capitalist world order. Time and effort spent debating with and lobbying politicians is committed at the expense of campaigning for broader value changes in society.

To address the fundamental causes of violations of the claimed environmental human rights, there is a need to challenge existing political structures, both through academic challenge and campaigning in society. This approach is championed by Wallerstein:

> we do not live in a modernizing world but in a capitalist world. What makes this world tick is not the need for achievement but the need for profit. The problem for oppressed strata is not how to communicate within this world but how to overthrow it (Wallerstein, 1979, p. 133).

Radical change cannot be initiated by dialogue within formal political forums since these exclude NGOs with alternative, radical agendas from engaging in negotiations (Taylor, 1998).

The remaining possibilities for systemic change in the historical context then becomes the most pressing subject of analysis. A central constraint on the possibilities for political change has been identified in this chapter as the hegemonic mechanism of co-option. As Cox and Sinclair remind us:

> hegemony is like a pillow: it absorbs blows and sooner or later the would-be assailant will find it comfortable to rest upon. Only where representation in international institutions is firmly based upon an articulate social and political challenge to hegemony – upon a nascent historic bloc and counter hegemony – could participation pose a real threat (Cox with Sinclair, 1996, p. 139).

For a counter hegemony to emerge, the environmental movement must (i) present a popular challenge to capitalism, (ii) possess the resources to affect alternatives and (iii) gain more power in affecting changes in international institutions (Taylor, 1998). Although anti-systemic forces have thus far failed to secure any of these requirements, challenges to the existing world order continue (Elliott, 1998a; Reynolds, 1999), and now find expression in the most unlikely sources. George Soros, manager of the Quantum investment fund, for example refers to the global financial markets as a 'wrecking ball' and a 'bubonic plague' (quoted in Coyle, 1998). Predictions from more radical analysts of the demise of capitalism have been circulating since Marx first noted the inherent contradiction between capital and labor in an exchange-based economy (McLellan, 1990). More recently, O'Connor has coherently argued that environmental degradation produced through capitalist production constitutes a second contradiction of capitalism (O'Connor, 1997). As capital degrades the environment, it increases future costs of expansion and hence leads to its own eventual demise (Bartley and Bergessen, 1997; O'Connor, 1997). Benton has similarly argued that capitalism is predisposed to undermining its own ecological conditions of existence (Benton, 1997). Claims to the demise of capitalism are inevitably open to the charge of conjecture since they are concerned with speculating about a future event. The current dominance of capital interests in determining political structures furthermore suggests that the systemic demise of capitalism is neither inevitable nor imminent. Yet, possibilities for systemic change nonetheless exist, dependent upon anti-systemic values achieving more popular support. This could either happen through a rise in the political saliency of environmental values or the failing of capitalism on its own terms, that is the inability of capitalism to continue providing aggregate economic growth because of, for example, the reasons suggested by Marx, O'Connor and Benton.

Seemingly remote structures only exist because of implicit consent or explicit approval by which they are normalized and internalized by individuals. As such, the possibility for structural change exists through the actions of individuals, as an expression of praxis. Praxis relates to human actions performed by knowledgeable agents who construct the social world and are simultaneously conditioned by the external world (Giddens, 1981). Praxis is the identification of theory and practice as an instrument for the construction, reproduction or change of political structures.

Praxis is the method of constructing a counter hegemonic bloc through the development of an alternative ideology (Gill, 1990). Environmental human rights constitute an instrument of praxis for structural challenge for the reason suggested by Brazier; 'if there is to be a way forward for the world it will lie in a new union of ideas previously labeled separately as Red and Green' (Brazier, 1998). Environmental human rights can articulate the union of human security and environmental concerns that provides a broad basis for a counter hegemonic bloc. The environmental human rights claimed in chapters five and six are less susceptible to systemic co-option since they have been devised to constitute an uncompromising defense of social and environmental over capitalist values. Furthermore, the two claimed rights benefit from being derived from existing legally recognized human rights. Rather than being restricted to philosophical expressions of deep or social ecology that can be readily dismissed or ignored by the legal system, the two claimed environmental rights are necessary for the realization of the most fundamental of existing human rights. Campaigning for environmental human rights is simultaneously a practical method of raising the prominence of environmental values in society. Such a change in values is the necessary requirement for the emergence of a political culture based on ecological, rather than economic, rationality.

The existing political economy cannot be reformed by existing political institutions to subordinate the interests of capital accumulation to those of biodiversity preservation. Suggestions to the contrary simplistically envision gradual reforms to create some hypothesized ecologically friendly form of capitalism. Such a project is a fundamental contradiction in terms and an idealistic pipe dream for it disregards the operational dynamics of the politics of power. Power relations have been highlighted in this research as facilitating, rather than restricting the continued ecological degradation and exploitation of environmental resources to serve the capitalist political economy. In order to effect meaningful environmental protection, it is first essential to change the power relations that determine political outcomes. As already stated, such a change in power relations cannot be achieved through violent struggle. Violence conducted by anti-systemic forces is likely to be counterproductive as well as contravening the principle of respecting all forms of life that lies at the heart of ecological ethics. A critique of capitalism based on the principle that the system is inherently violent towards people and the planet is non-sensical if articulated by a movement that itself utilizes violent tactics. Violent struggle will in any event legitimize repressive force by states keen act in the defense of corporate interests.

A more productive avenue to achieving social change is through epistemological discourse and campaigning for value change in society. Thinking outside of mainstream terms of reference that have been created by, and defend, existing power relations can help critique those relations. In particular, evident contradictions in the capitalist system can be highlighted and used as campaigning tools to demonstrate the partiality and therefore also the injustice of the system. This theme is developed in the remaining chapters of this book. Chapter 4 looks at the rule of law in capitalist states not as an impartial rules based instrument but rather as a reflection of existing power relations. Chapter 5 examines how legal systems accommodate widespread harm when this results in the efficient allocation of resources.

Increasing the importance of ecological values relative to economic values in society will draw attention to the contradictions of capitalism that are obfuscated by the present self legitimizing structural focus on economic values. Environmental human rights can play a part in this process to increase the saliency of ecological values relative to materialistic concerns in human societies. As chapter 3 explains, a number of NGOs are already playing a positive role in this process. To the extent that NGOs achieve environmental awareness and increased saliency for ecological values through their campaigning activities they act as anti-systemic forces and positive engines for social change. Evaluating the extent to which NGOs have succeeded in this task lies outside the remit of this research and is in any event extremely problematic to quantify since NGOs form just another influence on the consciousness of the general population.

A discourse of environmental human rights could also act as an instrument of praxis by protecting the interests of future generations. Reducing (i) toxic pollution and (ii) the overuse of natural resources in the present will directly benefit future generations. Future generational rights have not been stipulated in legally binding human rights texts and consequently lie outside the remit of this research. A brief discussion of future generational rights is nonetheless appropriate at this stage to illustrate how the interests of this group have been neglected under the existing human rights regime. Goodin highlights the poverty of existing research into the subject of intergenerational rights by noting that the debate remains on the level of whether we owe future generations anything at all, constructing an agenda favoring the opponents of intergenerational justice (Goodin, 1985). One such opponent is Hillel Steiner who contends that future generations cannot have rights since, it is argued, moral principles cover only people who can reciprocate and future generations cannot demand the present recognition of their rights (Steiner, 1994). In contrast to this assertion, ethical principles can be based around a notion of justice conceptualized as (i) altruism, (ii) an ethic of respect for others or (iii) protection of the vulnerable, rather than being restricted to a more circumscribed notion of reciprocity (Goodin, 1985). By way of an analogy, the severely mentally disabled are incapable of reciprocal relationships, and indeed, lack the reasoning faculties to demand the recognition of their rights, yet this in no way deprives them of those rights. Rights are indeed required most urgently in relationships based not around reciprocity, which implies a parity of power between parties, but rather in conditions of structural exploitation and dependency, where power resides with one party and is used at the expense of the other. This abuse of power is sanctioned by a strict delineation of the subjects of human rights to exclude future generations. Goodin demonstrates that future generations are completely dependent on the present generation regarding environmental factors such as toxic pollution, climate change and resource depletion (Goodin, 1985). Goodin furthermore makes a compelling case in arguing that the responsibility accompanying this vulnerability can be expressed through extending human rights to future generations (Goodin, 1985). Using an alternative approach, du Bois derives the human rights of future generations from an application of the right to equality of opportunity on an intergenerational scale (du Bois, 1996). There are therefore a variety of methods for deriving future generational human rights from divergent approaches in political philosophy.

The main obstacle in realizing future generational rights resides in the self-interested politics conducted by the present generation. A policy of protecting the environment and conserving resources for future generations would require the present generation to decide to allocate resources in a way that does not maximize its own consumption levels. Since the beneficiaries of future generational rights have no voice in the present (and therefore no effective power), their interests have hitherto been ignored in capitalist states in favor of focusing on the efficient allocation of resources for the existing generation.[16] The economic structures of capitalism effectively dismiss environmental responsibilities to future generations through a focus on consumption in the present.[17] Under capitalism, ethical imperatives and broader considerations of justice tend to be marginalized by the structural focus on individual materialistic concerns.[18] The absence of any future generational rights in existing human rights covenants facilitates the needs of capital by refusing to acknowledge a constraint that would limit the scope of the market and in particular would restrict the access of corporations to environmental resources. The conclusion of this brief examination of future generational rights is to draw the use of the claimed environmental human rights back into focus as an instrument of praxis to protect the interests of future generations by countering the tendency of the market to destroy Earth's organic heritage.[19]

Conclusion

This chapter has examined the possibilities for structural change in world politics and has suggested a role for environmental human rights in this process. The relative influence of agent and structure was firstly introduced in order to establish the meaning and extent of the limitations on the ability of individuals to reform political structures. The conclusion of this analysis suggested a capacity of structures to condition the actions of individuals. In particular it identified the hegemonic function of co-option, which was found to act as a structural mechanism to negate systemic challenges by assimilating aspects of these challenges without altering fundamental traits of the hegemonic bloc. This framework was applied to an analysis of the environmental and human rights movements where co-option was identified in a multiformity of aspects. The conclusion of this examination suggested an ineffectuality for NGOs of adopting the tactic of co-operating with official political structures in an effort to modify the capitalist hegemonic bloc to prioritize environmental and social values.

The potential role for environmental human rights as an instrument for initiating political change was then analyzed. The environmental human rights detailed in chapters five and six reject compromising environmental values and instead institutionalize a concern for ecological and human security needs over considerations of economic efficiency. A challenge to capitalism based around a radical conception of environmental human rights is therefore less susceptible to co-option than an approach based on more mainstream claims to human rights and environmental law. A role for environmental rights was furthermore suggested both as a goal that could institutionalize the political prioritization of social and environmental values and as a campaigning instrument with which to realize structural change.

Notes

1 Termed condign power and compensatory power respectively.
2 June 1992; also known as the Rio Conference.
3 A figure that excludes the cost of magazine space and television time.
4 See chapter 1.
5 See chapter 1.
6 Article 1, International Covenant on Economic, Social and Cultural Rights, 16 December 1966 and article 1, International Covenant on Civil and Political Rights, 16 December 1966.
7 Article 9.
8 Interview conducted at Southampton University with Dr Taiaiake Alfred, director of indigenous governance programs, University of Victoria, 29 April 1999.
9 See chapter 6 for details.
10 See chapter 6 for details.
11 ICESCR part III, article 6 stipulates 'the States Parties to the present Covenant recognise the right to work, which includes the right of everyone to the opportunity to gain his living by work which he freely chooses or accepts, and will take appropriate steps to safeguard this right'. Article 23 of the *Universal Declaration of Human Rights* (1948) stipulates that 'everyone has the right to work, to free choice of employment, to just and favourable conditions of work and to protection against unemployment'.
12 See chapter 4.
13 Part III, article 7(a).
14 See chapter 6.
15 See chapter 6.
16 The notable exception being a declaration of the United Nations Economic, Social, and Cultural Organisation (UNESCO) in 1995 which included as one of its nine 'main targets' for social development 'the preservation of the environmental rights of future generations'; see 'Fact File', *United Nations Economic, Social and Cultural Organisation Courier*, March 1995, p. 30.
17 See chapter 1.
18 See chapter 1.
19 See chapters 5 and 6.

Chapter 3

Social Demands for Environmental Human Rights

The environment is man's first right.

– Ken Saro-Wiwa

Introduction

The purpose of this chapter is to detail the nature and extent of claims to universal environmental human rights made by NGOs in the environmental and human rights movements. A questionnaire was devised and circulated to a total of 196 NGOs to elicit information on the extent to which these organizations recognized, advocated and campaigned in terms of environmental human rights. Three other questionnaires were circulated to a selection of (i) states, (ii) MNCs and (iii) global institutions in order to establish the attitudes to environmental human rights held by institutions of political and economic power. The response rate from NGOs was significantly higher than for the other three questionnaires and constitutes the majority of the data analyzed in this chapter. The questionnaire circulated to states concerns the formal political responses to claims of environmental human rights and the small number of replies are discussed in chapter 4.

The questionnaire to NGOs did not explicitly inquire how each organization related to formal political institutions of power. It rather focused on the central theme of recognition of specific environmental human rights. To keep this focus, the human rights and environmental movements will be evaluated as a whole in this chapter. The context of structural power is nonetheless addressed by discussing how NGOs perceive or have indeed used environmental human rights claims to promote an alternative vision to the capitalist political economy. Reference will also be made to NGOs working within formal political channels to realize environmental human rights but this topic is not discussed in depth since the formal response to environmental rights claims forms the subject of analysis in chapter 4.

The questionnaire to NGOs was designed to elicit information on (i) which environmental human rights were recognized, (ii) on what grounds these rights were recognized and to (iii) identify campaigns that had been run on the basis of the environmental human rights demanded. The questions were therefore formulated to elicit qualitative rather than quantitative data. Consequently, no statistical analysis is included in the methodological interpretation of the data in this research. Instead, the data is analyzed through thematic method. Firstly, the conceptual results of the research that relate to the justification of environmental human rights will be examined. This section also addresses the potential for the use of environmental human rights as an anti-systemic instrument. Secondly, the level of recognition by NGOs of specific environmental human rights will be evaluated. Thirdly, the analysis proceeds to the practical agenda of how environmental human rights claims have been used by NGOs as a tactical instrument of praxis to initiate and promote political change to benefit human rights and environmental protection. Fourthly, the data evaluation details the nature and extent of political campaigns for environmental human rights. These campaigns will be differentiated into two categories. The first category details efforts aimed at the recognition of environmental human rights conducted on the level of global politics (hereafter termed the structural level). The second section examines campaigns for environmental human rights based at the local level, focusing on two brief case studies of protest movements in Nigeria and Irian Jaya.

Environmental Human Rights as a Conceptual Component of Social and Environmental Campaigns

The questionnaire results testify to a widespread conceptual advocacy of environmental human rights amongst social movements. In response to the question of whether NGOs recognize environmental human rights, 54 organizations answered affirmatively, 36 declined to state a position and only three; Amnesty International, Earth Share and Ozone Action, stated that they did not recognize environmental human rights. Of the three dissenting groups who rejected environmental human rights, Earth Share gave no grounds for its decision.[1] The reason given by both Amnesty International and Ozone Action for rejecting environmental human rights was that the focus of campaigns would be lost through linking environmental protection to human rights claims.[2]

Before examining the details of the positive responses, a brief explanation of the conceptual framework within which affirmations of environmental human rights were contextualized may be informative. In particular, the existence of environmental human rights was presupposed as natural and as universal because of the holistic philosophical paradigm that characterized the politics of a number of NGOs. This paradigm identified human society as a part of the wider environment and rejected a strict ontological distinction between the two categories. This perception is significant for the study of environmental human rights since the fundamental distinction made by proponents of economic rationality between human societies on the one hand and the environment on the other is thereby rejected. The normalization of human societies exploiting the environment for the benefit of material accumulation is denied by an ecological perspective which refutes the separation humans from the environment. From the ecological perspective, human rights are seen as a mechanism to protect holistic environmental concerns incorporating human and environmental needs alike, rather than as an argument used in support of supplying human wants at the expense of environmental considerations. The Tibet Foundation for example defends their support of environmental human rights because 'we are human and as such we are part of the environment, and also this ties in with the Buddhist philosophy of interdependence'.[3] Another respondent similarly comments that:

we share the Earth and thus must share the responsibility which comes with it ... Connecting human rights to the environment helps people to see that they are not separate from the Earth.[4]

Earth Sangha states that 'we hold the Buddhist belief that all life is inextricably bound together'.[5] This holistic theme continued in the response from Borderlinks who explain that:

we believe that social justice is inextricably intertwined with human rights. All living creatures are bonded and dependent to or on the environment. Therefore, when the environment is violated, human rights are dually violated. [6]

Grossman explains that the Midwest Treaty Network recognizes an intrinsic environmental component of human rights because 'the overall Native America philosophy does not see human beings as separate from nature, unlike development advocates that prioritize humans, or wilderness advocates who prioritize non-human nature'.[7] The perception of unity between all elements of the biosphere was similarly asserted by Geist who responded that 'when we begin to acknowledge that the land has its own right to exist, we see ourselves as part of this community, part of the land, and that the only thing that separates us is the divisibility of the words themselves'.[8]

This ecological paradigm produces a more complex, interconnected and comprehensive conceptualization of human rights when juxtaposed to the capitalist perception of human rights which assigns (principally property) rights to autonomous individuals. The conceptual basis of environmental human rights given by the NGOs quoted above includes general environmental protection as an axiomatic human right since the unification of all elements of the biosphere means that harm incurred on one part of nature is perceived to necessarily also harm all other parts. Reasoning within this paradigm results in the inescapable conclusion that harming the land will necessary harm the people connected to that land. This perception is exemplified in the Guarani nation in South America who use the same word to refer to their tribe as they do to relate to the land that they inhabit.[9] Thus, the complete identification of the tribe with the land prevents any differentiation between the two entities within both the language and culture of the tribe. Opposing forced relocation by the authorities of the Brazilian state, a member of the tribe stated that 'we're part of the land and the land is a part of us ... that's the reason why we cannot live without our land'.[10] This holistic paradigm challenges capitalism since social and environmental values are assimilated into a unified whole and assume a much higher importance in the relative position of competing values than that evident in the neo-classical economic paradigm. Although this holistic paradigm was only expressed in a minority of NGO responses, the trend is notable because no mention of the holistic paradigm was made on any of the questions. This meant that all the respondents referring to the concept as a justification of environmental human rights asserted the idea themselves.

The trend towards recognition of unity between human societies and the rest of the biosphere described above suggests a role for environmental human rights claims as an anti-systemic instrument of praxis for social forces to campaign for the institutionalization of social and environmental values over the focus on economic competitiveness characteristic of the capitalist paradigm. The interpretation of environmental human rights as an anti-systemic instrument is endorsed by the overwhelming rejection of the concept by corporate responses to the research questionnaire. The only exception to this trend was provided by Xerox which replied that:

> all of our stakeholders (employees, customers and neighbors) are entitled to a clean, safe and healthy environment in which to work and live ... we promote the right of all stakeholders to a safe and healthy workplace and/or community environment.[11]

The health and safety policy of Xerox further states that 'protection of the environment and the health and safety of our employees, customers, and neighbors from unacceptable risks takes priority over economic considerations and will not be compromised'.[12]

Denying that environmental degradation is necessarily linked to human rights violations, a spokesperson for the European Roundtable of Industrialists (ERT), argued that 'while a company or government may be accused of both damaging the environment and infringing generally accepted human rights, there is no direct logical link between the two'.[13] Although the ERT has an environment group, its agenda is 'restricted to certain cross-sectoral issues related to climate change and environmental liability ... . Questions of human rights do not appear on the agenda'.[14] The questionnaire response from the ERT stated that the organization has not referred to the environment in terms of human rights protection since 'we are not an NGO for social issues'.[15] The ERT does however advocate 'rights to life, liberty and freedom of movement'.[16] In a follow-up correspondence to clarify the meaning of the advocated freedom of movement, the focus on capital was made explicit, 'reductions in immigration controls' were not intended, rather the pro-corporate lobbying organization advocates 'freedoms of individuals to do business in other states'.[17] This response is instructive for understanding the position of business on the subject of environmental human rights since the organization promotes the interests of its member corporations and the ERT therefore articulates a cross section of business opinion. Furthermore, the lobbying efforts of the ERT have been consistently influential in European political decision making circles (Corporate Europe Observatory, 1999).

Global economic institutions responding to the questionnaire demonstrated a general disregard for the concept of environmental human rights. A spokesperson for the World Trade Organization stated only that 'we do not deal specifically with that matter'.[18] A response from the International Monetary Fund declined to answer any of the questions posed in the questionnaire, opting instead to direct any research to the IMF web site.[19] The Organization for Economic Co-operation and Development, replied 'the OECD does not have any information on the human rights side of the environment as we are an economic institution'.[20] All these responses exemplify the trend for systemic forces to discount the importance of environmental human rights in favor of a focus on economics, again suggesting the anti-systemic nature of these rights.

The conclusion of this conceptual analysis is to draw attention to the way in which recognition of environmental human rights tends to be a function of the theoretical paradigms within which different organizations operate and which attribute differing degrees of importance to competing values. The general conceptual endorsement of environmental human rights evident in the NGOs' responses to the questionnaire reflects the tendency for these social forces to prioritize social and environmental values over the concern of capital accumulation which characterizes the capitalist paradigm. The conceptual endorsement also suggests a potential role for environmental human rights as an anti-systemic instrument of praxis to strengthen social and environmental claims vis a vis competing demands of economic competitiveness. Attention now moves to examine which specific environmental human rights are recognized by NGOs.

Recognition of Environmental Human Rights by Social Movements

To avoid presenting potentially leading questions, the NGO questionnaire did not mention any particular rights. Instead, the relevant question asked 'Do you recognize environmental human rights? Which Ones? and Why?'. Thirty-three NGOs replied that they recognized some formulation of a human right to an 'unpolluted', 'clean' or 'healthy' environment.[21] Eleven NGOs replied that they recognized the environmental human right to resources.[22] Five NGOs identified a right to environmental justice.[23] Environmental justice is a concept coined (and is still largely restricted to) within US domestic politics. The environmental justice movement opposes the location of pollution creating industries in areas inhabited by minority and impoverished groups.[24] Two other environmental rights were suggested by NGOs; Action in Solidarity with Indonesia and East Timor advocates 'a right to sustainability' and the Austin, Texas Sierra Club defends a right to 'family planning'.[25]

The following five respondents affirmed their support for the concept of environmental human rights but declined to define any specific rights. The indigenous peoples protection group Midwest Treaty Network recognizes environmental human rights because 'the impact of environmental decisions falls on human beings as well as non-human nature'.[26] Another respondent recognizes a link between the environment and human rights since 'the destruction of the environment is an abuse of the rights of all people who need that environment'.[27] The Sustainable Development Institute 'applaud wholeheartedly' the concept of linking the environment and human rights'.[28] Asked whether the organization recognizes environmental human rights, the Peoples Decade of Human Rights Education responded 'of course we do and it is part of our fully comprehensive program for the learning of human rights'.[29] Another organization recognized environmental human rights since this 'builds on the understanding of human rights as a universal concept and helps to broaden understanding about what constitutes these rights'.[30] The 'primary vision' of Cold Mountain, Cold Rivers was:

> to communicate people's environmental and human rights struggles to the world. As such we have found that though the words are divisible the spirit of them is not.[31]

Two organizations recognized environmental rights according to the criteria of existing human rights international law. Legitimate environmental human rights were perceived by these two groups as those which are required to fully implement existing universal human rights stipulations. The Institute for Agriculture and Trade Policy recognizes environmental human rights that are 'fundamental to the Universal Declaration of Human Rights' and 'to the right to life'.[32] Rights International advocates recognition of 'the right of human beings to the protection of an environment that is necessary for the protection of civil and political rights as well as economic, social and cultural rights of human beings'.[33] Both groups however failed to suggest any particular rights that would be justified under this criterion.

Endorsing the environmental human rights claimed in this research project, the two specific rights recognized by a significant number of NGOs responding to the questionnaire were those to an environment free from toxic pollution and to environmental resources. Exemplifying claims to the former, the Legal Environmental Assistance Foundation contends that 'all people have the right to a clean and healthy environment'.[34] Another group similarly claims that 'all humans on the earth have the right to live in a world where they have clean air, clean water [and] enough nutritious food to eat'.[35]

Another respondent explained that:

> Cold Mountain, Cold Rivers helped found Montana CHEER (Coalition for Health, Environmental and Economic Rights) back in 1995. As the name indicates we acknowledge that human beings have a right to a healthy environment, a right to breathe clean air, to drink clean water, to bargain collectively for living wages, a safe workplace and so on. We acknowledge these rights, and of the land (as expressed as a whole of the biotic community) itself, because they are central to who we are, and [to] our continuing existence.[36]

This response is instructive because of the linkage made between environmental and economic rights claims. This linkage demonstrates a practical instance of how environmental and economic rights claims have been recognized to be mutually reinforcing as an instrument to subordinate the systemic power of capital to ecological and human needs.

Continuing the trend of anti-systemic social movements recognizing rights to an unpolluted environment, another questionnaire respondent states that:

> the right to a sustainable, liveable, healthy environment should be the right of all people. These are very basic demands – that the environment which we require to live, should not be destroyed – rather it should be maintained for the needs of all people.[37]

The Campaign for Peace and Democracy claim that 'a liveable environment is as much a right as freedom of press, right to a job'.[38] A spokesperson for the Center for Environmental Citizenship affirms that 'the rights of humans to clean water, air, etc. are equally important as other environmental concerns'.[39] Tenuto states that 'each person or community has the right to a healthful environment'.[40] Porter asserts that 'clean air, water and safety seems to be a basic need and right'.[41] The Center for Economic and Social Rights contends that:

the human right to health includes the right to a healthy environment, including clean air and water ... . The health of the environment is directly linked to the health of human beings and health is a human right. Therefore, we feel that we cannot talk about the right to health without talking about the right to a healthy environment.[42]

All of above these questionnaire responses represent the positive recognition of the right to an 'unpolluted', 'clean' or 'healthy' environment by politically active social forces.

The right to environmental resources was the second environmental human right asserted by a number of NGOs in questionnaire responses. Recognition of the human right to environmental resources is not as widespread as that to an unpolluted environment. Only 11 NGOs suggested some variant of a right to environmental resources compared to 33 who identified a right to an unpolluted environment. All the organizations recognizing the right to environmental resources did so in addition to identifying the right to an unpolluted environment. The Pacific Institute for example advocates 'policy principles such as the basic right to have access to clean water [and] the right of communities to be involved in decision making processes related to natural resources'.[43] Another NGO recognized variants of the rights to an unpolluted environment and to environmental resources by advocating 'rights to live in a healthy environment, to have a right to life, habitat and to safe food'.[44] A right to habitat is, however, a rather ambiguous claim that could be interpreted to mean anything from a right to access natural areas to a right to control or to ownership over land.

Unifying human rights to an unpolluted environment and to environmental resources, El-Roy contends that 'environmental conditions [are] at the base of any living creatures existence. Pollution and shortage of resources threatens not only the health and life of people but also their livelihood and quality of life'.[45] Earth Rights International states that:

> it is a fundamental human right of all people to have a secure and healthy environment in which to live. Natural resource exploitation and other environmental degradation not only negatively affects the health and security of local communities and indigenous peoples, but also often goes hand-in-hand with fundamental human rights abuses, such as suppression of civil and political rights, summary executions, torture, rape and forced labor.[46]

This response is notable for the linkage made by the respondent to current processes of resource exploitation that cause both human rights violations and environmental degradation. Another respondent recognized such an important link between the protection of human rights and of the environment that any differentiation between the two concepts was rejected:

> In many situations human rights abuses and environmental abuses go hand-in-hand. Local people who are engaged in the struggles to protect their communities do not distinguish between human rights abuses and environmental abuses – they experience it all together ... . It is important to work with communities based on their experience of injustice, independent of such categories as human rights and environmental destruction.[47]

In summary, the questionnaire results therefore demonstrate considerable NGOs' support for two environmental human rights. Support for a variation of the human right to an environment free from toxic pollution was considerably more widespread than support for the right to environmental resources.

Environmental Human Rights as a Tactical Device for Social and Environmental Campaigns

The recognition of environmental human rights by NGOs demonstrated above is of limited significance by itself. However, when these rights are demanded to be universally implemented or are operationalized in specific campaigns, they become a potential instrument to enact political change.

There is an evident recognition amongst NGOs responding to the research questionnaire that the linking of environmental to human rights demands strengthens the nature of both of the claims made. Environmental human rights claims are perceived as a useful means to achieve the social and environmental goals that the organizations seek. In response to the question 'do you think that the linking of human rights to environmental concerns leads to the promotion, or helps to strengthen the case of either of the issues?'. Forty-five NGOs responded affirmatively, 45 left the question unanswered or replied that they did not know, and only three groups answered the question negatively. As for the responses given in the negative, Californians Against Waste replied 'not necessarily'; a spokesperson for Citizen Alert stated 'not as far as I can tell' and Grassroots World Government claimed that 'both are a threat to certain regimes and economies and it is unlikely [that] the linking would give any benefit to either one. It is likely that it would expand the front against each one as it adds to the enemies of the other'.[48]

The remaining 45 NGOs who expressed an opinion stated that linking environmental to human rights concerns would strengthen both campaigns and constitutes a useful tactical approach for achieving political change. Twelve organizations that gave specific reasons in support of this recognition stated that linkage of the environmental to the human rights agenda was tactically beneficial since the social base and appeal of a campaign could be broadened and strengthened. Earth First! stated that 'any time you join forces with other oppressed individuals you strengthen your cause and widen your base of support'.[49] Similarly, other organizations claimed that 'by having different angles, you can appeal to a broader group of people',[50] 'collectively we are strongest',[51] and 'unity is strength'.[52] Earth Rights International make the same point whilst also drawing attention to the more efficient use of resources achieved by operating campaigns which link environmental to human rights issues:

> there is a lot of duplicate work being done by environmental and human rights organizations. By linking the two issues, such groups can launch joint campaigns, maximize resources, personnel and expertise and benefit from an expanded constituency for their concerns.[53]

The Center for Economic and Social Rights claimed that 'linking environmental rights to human rights allows communities and people to work across borders and disciplines'.[54] An organization campaigning for the rights of First Nation peoples stated 'there is a strong link between treaty rights of Native peoples and environmental concerns... The link between the two can often lend to the efficacy of a campaign, because truly these concerns are very linked and can increase public involvement in a campaign'.[55] Claiming a mutually strengthening nature of environmental and rights claims, another activist asserts that 'this linking [of the environment to human rights] strengthens the case for both'.[56] Landy likewise identified a 'mutual reinforcement' by linking environmental concerns to human rights.[57] Similarly, Martin states that environmental human rights 'brings two communities of activists together resulting in greater political leverage'.[58] Another organization advocates the linkage of the human rights and environmental campaigns on the grounds that:

> both movements can benefit by expanding their constituent base and areas of interest. The environmental movement has been hurt by its inability to reach out to a broader cross section of society. Linking environmental issues with human concerns will bring more communities and people into the movement.[59]

The tactical importance of human rights for environmental protection was stressed in the response of the Alliance for the Wild Rockies who reported that 'without supporting human rights our wilderness protection efforts would not succeed'.[60] The second tactical reason given by a number of NGOs advocating the use of environmental human rights claims in campaigns argued that a discourse of human rights makes more tangible the otherwise abstract concept of environmental protection. Training for Change advocate using environmental human rights in campaigns since 'all too often people just can't relate to the natural environment unless it directly affects people'.[61] The Midwest Treaty Network advocates linkage on the grounds that 'we have found that the argument that corporations limit local economic control and local political democracy attracts rural and working class people who otherwise would not be concerned with defending endangered species or nature for its own sake'.[62] Croft advocates linkage since 'environmental issues are best put in human terms ... because I think it is easier philosophically to treat values within a humanistic model'.[63] An example of the claim that environmental protection can be achieved through utilizing the human rights discourse is provided in a questionnaire response from another organization that contends 'there is greater public support for public health versus environmental protection'.[64] A spokesperson for Charter 88 points out that 'anti-environmentalism arguments ... usually begin with "but what about people, aren't they more important?"'.[65] The argument forwarded by the respondent is that this criticism is refuted by the formal anthropocentrism of environmental human rights. These questionnaire results support the findings of Eckstein and Gitlin that where human rights and environmental groups have converged, they have used the discourse and discipline of the other to secure their own goals (Eckstein and Gitlin, 1998).

In summation, the questionnaire results demonstrate that a significant number of NGOs advancing human rights and environmental causes have recognized linkage of the two issues as a useful tactic for initiating political change. The following section demonstrates how NGOs have campaigned for the formal recognition and implementation of environmental human rights. This will be referred to as a structural focus since it relates to the demands that have been made by social movements for the general recognition of environmental human rights in formal legal regimes. The analysis then progresses to examine how anti-systemic social forces have used claims to environmental human rights in specific campaigns, including two brief case studies relating to the protest movements mobilized against Shell in Nigeria and against Freeport McMoran in Irian Jaya.

Campaigns for the Structural Recognition of the Right to an Unpolluted Environment

Campaigns focusing on the structural recognition of environmental human rights may appear more abstract and less productive than campaigns focusing on specific instances of violations of environmental human rights. However, campaigns aimed at the structural level seek to address the long-term systemic causes of environmental human rights violations. The success of the demands for environmental human rights made by NGOs in the formal political arena is discussed in chapter 4. The purpose of the analysis in this chapter is limited to establishing that NGOs are actively lobbying governments to realize environmental human rights.

A number of NGOs are campaigning for the structural implementation of a universal human right to an unpolluted environment. Friends of the Earth assert that:

> the natural heritage that is everyone's shared birthright – an inheritance independent of status or worth – is becoming a poisoned, corrupted legacy for present and future generations. Environmental rights should equally define the guarantees that the State offers to the people it serves (Secrett, 1993, p. 1).

The organization claims that:

> much of the water we drink is polluted, as is some of the land on which we grow our food and build our homes. The polluters – including chemical companies and waste disposal firms – are denying us our right to a healthy environment. And the Government is opposed to strengthening the legal framework which should protect our rights. Much of Friends of the Earth's work is about defending these basic rights (Friends of the Earth, 1993, p. 13).

World Information Transfer has advocated 'that each person has a right to a healthy environment', and the organization 'work[s] to educate [their] audience about them'.[66] The World Institute for a Sustainable Humanity declared in its response to the questionnaire that 'it is our job to demonstrate the interconnectedness of environmental issues to human rights' to governments around the world.[67] The Center for Economic and Social Rights defends its advocacy of environmental human rights on the basis that, 'the health of a community depends upon the health of its environment' (Center for Economic and Social Rights, 1997). Similarly, Altai promotes environmental human rights 'because they are directly connected with the main human right – right for living'.[68]

A number of environmental NGOs have been actively campaigning in the United States for the constitutional recognition of a domestic right to an environment free from toxic pollution. Since 1995 the Sierra Club, the Public Interest Research Group and the Natural Resources Defense Council have been petitioning the United States government to adopt an Environmental Bill of Rights affirming the right to a 'safe, secure and sustainable natural environment' (Bergman, 1995). Another organization has lobbied the US government to implement 'rights to clean air, soil and water and the right to defend these vital resources' stating 'what could be more fundamental?'.[69] Earth First! has demanded environmental human rights in the course of conducting ecological campaigns for improved air and water quality and forestry protection in the US.[70] The South West Organizing Project,[71] produced their own Community Environmental Bill of Rights which demanded the implementation of a number of environmental rights:

> we have the right to say 'no' to industries that we feel will be polluters and disrupt our lifestyles and traditions ... . We have the right to be safe from harmful exposures imposed on us against our will that would affect our health or disrupt our lifestyles. It is our right to have a comfortable lifestyle, safe from toxic chemicals, other hazardous waste and nuisance. This means having safe water, clean air, and being free of excessive and constant noise from industry (South West Organizing Project, 1998).

Other demands included rights to:

> participate in the formulation of public policy that prevents toxic pollution from entering our communities ... the right to know what toxic chemicals industry, corporate polluters, and government have brought or intend to bring into our communities... the right to participate in the formulation of strong laws controlling toxic wastes and vigorous enforcement of those rights... [and a] right to clean up: The polluters shall bear the financial burden of clean-up (South West Organizing Project, 1998).

Individual state officials have also articulated demands for the recognition of environmental rights. The secretary of the Florida Department of Environmental Protection testified to the state constitution revision commission that 'we have a right to live in an environment that is free from the toxic pollution of man-made chemicals' (Langer, 1997). The judgment of the Permanent Peoples' Tribunal on Human Rights and Industrial Hazards, declared in Bhopal, India in October 1992, provides an example of a social demand for the implementation of universal environmental human rights (Permanent Peoples' Tribunal, 1993). This judgment has no legal force, but is a product of the work of legal, social and political academics and activists; that is to say of members of civil society working outside the formal political institutions of government (Permanent Peoples' Tribunal, 1993). The document calls for the implementation of a number of universal environmental human rights claims including the right of communities to refuse the introduction of hazardous activities to their environment;[72] permanent sovereignty over natural resources;[73] a right to a living environment free from hazards;[74] a right to environmental information;[75] a right to environmental monitoring;[76] a section devoted to the rights of workers focusing on health and safety rights and a section on rights to relief, focusing in particular on compensation rights.[77]

All these examples demonstrate that a number of environmental advocacy groups are actively campaigning for the structural implementation of a universal human right to an environment free from toxic pollution.

Campaigns for the Structural Recognition of the Right to Environmental Resources

Indigenous groups are prominent in demanding governmental recognition of the communal right to land. The 1977 Conference on Indigenous Peoples and the Land culminated in a statement demanding that:

> the right should be recognized of all indigenous nations or peoples to the return and control, as a minimum, of sufficient and suitable land to enable them to live an economically viable existence in accordance with their own customs and traditions, and to make possible their full development at their own pace ... that the ownership of land by indigenous peoples should be unrestricted, and should include the ownership and control of all natural resources. The lands, land rights and natural resources of indigenous peoples should not be taken, and their land rights should not be terminated (Nettheim, 1992, p. 115).

Claims to land rights from indigenous peoples were affirmed at the 1981 Legal Commission of the International NGO Conference on Indigenous Peoples and the Land held in Geneva. The declaration produced at this venue stressed the 'inseparable connection between land rights of Indigenous Peoples and the right of self-determination' (Nettheim, 1992). The 1986 Quito Declaration by the indigenous people of Latin America further demanded 'an end to assimilationist policies, juridical recognition of territorial rights based on prior ownership including rights to the resources of the sub-soil and recognition of systems of self-government' (Smith, 1992).

These rights claims are furthermore supported by specific campaign initiatives. The mission of the South and Meso American Indian Rights Center is 'to promote and work for the self-determination of Indigenous people in Meso and South America'.[78] The organization declares that it is 'always campaigning for environmental human rights' for indigenous peoples.[79] The centrality of structural resource rights claims to the campaigning work of this NGO is revealed in the response from the Center that:

> Environmental human rights is a central component of the advocacy work that we do ... . We recognize Indigenous territorial rights. We believe that Indigenous nations ... [are] the only ones that can properly determine the use of the resources available on the land ... . In most of our work, human rights and environmental concerns are inseparable. The rights of Indigenous people involves the protection of their territories, the natural resources and the knowledge and cultural connection that they have with the land.[80]

Although these claims to land rights are not universal human rights demands since they are specifically claimed for indigenous peoples, they are significant to this research firstly because they represent claims to environmental resources based around a discourse of rights and secondly because they constitute a possible framework for the universal implementation of the right to environmental resources.[81]

Anti-systemic social forces are therefore actively campaigning at the structural level for the recognition of human rights to an environment free from toxic pollution and to environmental resources. Social movements have also actively used claims to universal environmental rights in specific campaigns as a vehicle to enact political change at a local level.

Campaigns on the Specific Implementation of Universal Environmental Human Rights

The questionnaire results suggest that specific campaigns demanding environmental human rights can be differentiated into the two general categories of (i) protests against toxic pollution and (ii) campaigns for the ownership of environmental resources.

Exemplifying human rights campaigns directed against toxic pollution, Wisconsin's Environmental Decade has run campaigns demanding environmental protection as a human right on the issues of children's safety, reducing pesticide usage, breast cancer and mercury contamination of the environment.[82] The environmental protection and peace advocacy group 20/20 Vision 'have done action alerts on a variety of environmental human rights issues' related to toxic pollution and provided examples of organizing campaigns against the exposure of strawberry and banana workers to pesticides and against the construction of plastic manufacturing plants.[83] Borderlinks is currently campaigning against an international toxic waste dump located in Hermosillo, Mexico, through a claim that the pollution escaping from the dump constitutes a violation of the human right to health of local residents.[84]

The Asia Pacific Center for Justice and Peace has 'campaigned for environmental protection in terms of human rights ... around the issue of toxic contamination on and near US military bases in the Pacific'.[85] Linking pollutants to the human right to health the Center comments that 'as the US military refuses to reveal the extent of toxic waste on its sites, communities are at high risk without full awareness and knowledge, while they suffer high rates of cancer, birth defects, etc. – a clear human rights violation'.[86] When asked whether the organization had campaigned for environmental protection in terms of human rights, Altai responded affirmatively giving the example of an ongoing campaign against the toxic pollution resulting from the testing of space shuttles and satellites in Russia.[87] The South and Meso American Indian Rights Center has operationalized claims to environmental human rights in a campaign that publicized the hazards of agricultural pesticides on the health of the Huichole in Mexico.[88] Another campaign by the same organization used claims to environmental human rights to protest against the detrimental health effects to local communities resulting from mining and deforestation activities in South America.[89]

Demonstrating that claims of human rights to environmental resources have likewise been used in specific campaigns, the Alaska Rainforest Campaign reports that 'subsistence rights have helped our campaign ... . Lawsuits, media, lobbying have focused on the rights of Alaskans both native and non-native to live off the land'.[90] The indigenous Huaraoni and Quichua peoples of Ecuador responded to repeated oil spills produced by petrochemical companies by demanding rights to control their environmental resources, which they expressed by occupying oil drilling sites. This tactic has resulted in the official recognition of land rights and the successful expulsion of a number of oil companies from indigenous peoples land (Grossman, 1995).

The Midwest Treaty Network stated that it has united indigenous people throughout the Third World to support the efforts of native tribes to protect traditional lands from mining and to protect the rights of indigenous peoples to the natural resources of their lands.[91] The environmental organization Earth Sangha has used claims to resource rights to support the efforts of forest monks in Thailand to maintain dwindling forests and 'to stem the development that is hurting the indigenous people of that region'.[92] The Brazilian Movement for Landless People (MST) advocates land redistribution in terms of rights through calling for policies to expropriate the areas of land which multinationals own, to expropriate ranches which are not currently used for agricultural purposes, and a specified maximum size for each rural property (*Brazil Network Newsletter*, 1996b). Since the inception of the MST in 1984, 140,000 families organized around productive co-operatives have received land titles (*Brazil Network Newsletter*, 1996b).

The right to food is campaigned for as an environmental human right by two organizations responding to the questionnaire. The Artist Hunger Network campaigns for the right to those environmental resources required to ensure food self-sufficiency since 'all humans have a basic right of accessing food that grows from the earth. Denial of this right is a violation of human rights'.[93] The 1990 'renewing the earth' action organized by CAFOD unified claims to an unpolluted environment and to environmental resources by campaigning for access of the rural poor in the Third World to productive land free from toxic pollutants in terms of environmental human rights.[94] The Food and Agriculture Organization (FAO) similarly replied that they focus on implementing 'the right to food, which lies at the heart of its mandate. Inherent in the right to food is the notion of sustainability, both social and environmental'.[95]

Space limitations prevents the detailed analysis of the specific campaigns mentioned above. However, to illustrate and contextualize particular campaigns, the focus now turns to two brief case studies of campaigns conducted for the recognition of environmental human rights. The first campaign relates to the struggle of the indigenous peoples of Ogoniland whose homeland has suffered environmental degradation as a result of oil exploitation and the second of which concerns the struggle against the mining operations of the Freeport McMoran corporation in Irian Jaya. These examples have been chosen firstly because the two campaigns unify the demand of a right to an environment free from toxic pollution with the right to environmental resources. Secondly these examples have been chosen because of the interplay between economic forces, pollution, resource depletion and political repression that are expressed in similar patterns in both cases.

Johnston observes that 'human rights violations often occur as a result of efforts to gain control of land, labor and resources of politically and/or geographically peripheral peoples' (Johnston, 1994). The validity of this claim is exemplified in the case of oil exploitation in the Ogoniland area of Nigeria where systematic pollution combined with political repression has characterized much of its recent political history. This case study contextualizes claims of resource rights in the wider political economy and demonstrates that human rights claims to resources conflict with the private economic interests that benefit from capitalist ownership rights as well as with the right to pollute. The case study reveals that the interests of global capital have been consistently protected by the Nigerian state above the environmental human rights claimed by the indigenous population.

The role of the Shell Petroleum Development Company (SPDC) has been central to both oil exploitation and environmental human rights violations in Ogoniland. The company has made approximately 30 billion US dollars in revenue from Niger delta oil since it started operations in the region in 1958 (Frynas, 1998). As of 1993, the SPDC had only invested an estimated 0.000007 per cent of its oil revenue from Ogoniland in social or environmental projects in the area itself (Frynas, 1998). Neglect of the local area has resulted in the systematic pollution of the environment. One report informs us that the:

> flaring of gas, poor pipeline placement, chronic oil spills, and unlined toxic waste pits plague the Nigerian Delta region ... . The antiquated pipeline routinely spills oil. According to an independent record of Shell's spills, Shell spilled 1.6 million gallons from its Nigerian operations in 27 separate incidents from 1982 to 1992 (*Multinational Monitor*, 1995a).

At Bonny terminal, where Shell separates water from crude oil, the concentration of oil in river sediments has been described as 'lethal' at 12,000 parts per million (Rowell, 1996). Unlined toxic waste pits in Ogoniland allow oil pollution to seep into drinking water; open gas flares have destroyed plant life, caused acid rain, and have deposited soot on nearby Ogoni homes and corroded pipelines have rendered formerly fertile agricultural land unproductive (Sachs, 1996a; *Corporate Watch*, 1998e; Greenpeace, 1998c).

Severe environmental degradation in Ogoniland led to the formulation of a protest campaign against the SPDC and other oil companies by the indigenous population articulating a claim for environmental human rights. A central figure in that campaign was the author Ken Saro-Wiwa who proclaimed that 'the environment is man's first right' (quoted in Sachs, 1995). Ken Saro-Wiwa unified claims to environmental protection and human rights in the campaign against foreign MNCs operating in Nigeria, stating on one occasion that:

> what Shell and Chevron have done to Ogoni people, land, streams, creeks and the atmosphere amounts to genocide. The soul of the Ogoni people is dying and I am witness to the fact (quoted in *Corporate Watch*, 1998f).

The Ogoni people organized a series of protest marches to demand a cessation of further degradation and compensation for the ecological damage incurred by oil operations in Nigeria. At one rally held in January 1993, an Ogoni leader stated that:

> our atmosphere has been totally polluted, our lands degraded, our waters contaminated, our trees poisoned, so much so that our flora and fauna have virtually disappeared ... we are asking for the basic necessities of life – water, electricity, roads, education; we are asking above all for the right to self-determination so that we can be responsible for our resources and our environment (quoted in Rowell, 1996, p. 297).

This demand is notable for the way in which the communal ownership of the environment and natural resources is claimed to be derived from the right to self-determination, a theme developed in chapter six of this research. The Iko people who live alongside the Ogoni have likewise been campaigning in terms of environmental human rights, in 1980 demanding from Shell 'compensation and restitution of our rights to clean air, water and a viable environment where we can source for our means of livelihood' (quoted in Rowell, 1996).

The two most notable features of the response from political authorities to the campaign for environmental human rights in Ogoniland were (i) the level of repression employed and (ii) in defense of (and partly funded by) global corporate interests. The response of the Nigerian state to the campaign for environmental human rights was to send the Internal Security Task Force into Ogoniland. The Task Force has subsequently been accused of conducting a terror campaign consisting of beatings, rape and extra judicial killings (Wiwa, 1995; Rowell, 1996).

The revealing insight provided by an examination of the repressive response to the environmental human rights campaign in Ogoniland is the way in which this served global capital interests. Recognition of environmental human rights allowing local communities to control natural resources and address endemic pollution would, at the least, have forced up the costs to oil companies operating in Ogoniland and could have precipitated the expulsion of foreign companies. Subsequently, the petrochemical MNCs operating in Nigeria were eager to see the environmental human rights campaign fail and the economic power wielded by these organizations ensured the compliance of the state authorities in achieving that result. The active role played by the SPDC in the repression of the Ogoni environmental human rights movement is exemplified in the execution of Ken Saro-Wiwa in 1995 on falsified charges of murder following a riot on 21 May 1994. Two of the prosecution witnesses in the case have since signed sworn affidavits that they and others had been bribed by Shell to lie about who started the riots in order to falsely incriminate Ken Saro-Wiwa (Rowell, 1996; Sachs, 1996a). In an interview the brother of Ken Saro-Wiwa, Owens Wiwa, revealed that he pleaded with the head of Shell in Nigeria for the company to intervene to save the life of his brother (Owens Wiwa, 1996). The condition reportedly set by the head of Shell was that Owens Wiwa should write a press release saying there was no environmental devastation in Ogoniland and to call off the international campaign against the Nigerian military regime and Shell (Owens Wiwa, 1996). Owens Wiwa forwarded the request to his brother who wrote back to him, rejecting the conditions made by Shell and saying that the campaign should only be stopped once Shell responds to the environmental concerns of the

Ogonis (Owens Wiwa, 1996). After the subsequent hanging of Ken Saro-Wiwa a prominent spokesperson for Greenpeace commented that:

> Shell has blood on its hands. Ken Saro-Wiwa was hanged for speaking out against Shell. He was trying to secure the most basic of human rights, the right to clean air, land and water (Black, Bowcott and Vidal, 1995).

Supporting this conclusion, two days after Ken Saro-Wiwa's execution, Shell Oil signed a $2.5 billion gas contract with the Nigerian government (Johnston, 1997).

The role of Shell in the repression of the campaign for the recognition of environmental human rights in Ogoniland extended beyond the case of Ken Saro-Wiwa. In 1987 Shell provided speedboats for the notorious Mobile Police Force to break up peaceful demonstrations protesting against the operations of Shell (Rowell, 1996). In response to one such protest against Shell on 29 October 1990 by the Etche people at Umuechem, Shell requested security protection which was subsequently provided by the Mobile Police Force. An ensuing massacre conducted by the police resulted in 80 deaths and the destruction of 495 homes (Rowell, 1996; Steele, 1997). Human Rights Watch report that:

> Shell cannot absolve itself of responsibility for the acts of the military ... . The Nigerian military's defence of Shell's installations has become so intertwined with its repression of minorities in the oil-producing areas that Shell cannot reasonably sever the two (Rowell, 1996, p. 315).

Project Underground supported this conclusion when in 1997 the NGO revealed that Shell provided logistical and financial assistance to the Nigerian military (Project Underground, 1997a). A report from the International Peoples' Tribunal on Human Rights and the Environment likewise concluded that 'Shell equips and maintains a police force to protect its operations in Ogoni' (International Peoples' Tribunal on Human Rights and the Environment, 1998). The Tribunal quotes a letter from SPDC Managing Director PB Watts in which the company pledged:

> to provide complete logistics accruement and welfare support to the Opapco Police Force which will be assigned to protect SPDC's Operations ... SPDC will fully support the cost of setting up and maintaining the contingents (International Peoples' Tribunal on Human Rights and the Environment, 1998).

Shell spokesman Eric Nickson admitted that the company had also imported guns for military units sent into Ogoniland, underwritten the costs of troop transportation and paid salary bonuses to soldiers (Sachs, 1996a; Steele, 1997; *Corporate Watch*, 1998e). Owens Wiwa states that the SPDC:

> bought and supplied arms to the military, the same arms which the military used to devastate Ogoni villages and kill 2,000 people, just to stop our legitimate protests for our rights – for our environmental rights, for the right to our land and for the right to our rivers' (Wiwa, 1996).

The concept of human rights is nonetheless a useful marketing instrument for Shell whose advertisements re-write history to explain that:

> At Shell, we are committed to support fundamental human rights .... We've also spoken out on the rights of individuals – even if the situation has been beyond our control. It's part of our commitment to sustainable development, balancing economic progress with environmental care and social responsibility (Royal Dutch Shell Group, 1999).

A similar pattern of events is discernible in the case of the copper and gold mine owned and operated by Freeport McMoran in Irian Jaya. The company has mined the Puncuk Jaya mountain since 1972. As a waste product from this operation, up to 110,000 tonnes of tailings (waste sediments) have been dumped daily into the local Aghawagon river (Chatterjee, 1996). These tailings have had a considerable environmental impact on the local river system, rainforest and agricultural land (Knight, 1998). The environmental damage incurred by this operation became so severe that on the 31 October 1995 the United States Overseas Private Investment Corporation[96] revoked the political risk insurance of Freeport McMoran since:

> massive deposition of tailings from Freeport's operation has degraded a large area of lowland rainforest posing unreasonable or major environmental, health or safety hazards with respect to the rivers that are being impacted ... the surrounding terrestrial ecosystem, and the local inhabitants (Eyal Press, 1998).

As in Nigeria, the local people responded to the environmental degradation by organizing a protest campaign directed against the mining MNC based on a claim to environmental human rights. Statements issued by the local Dani, Amungme and Komoro tribes state that 'we fight against [Freeport CEO] Jim Bob Moffett, Freeport and the government ... because our rights are not recognized, our resources are extracted and destroyed while our lives are taken' (quoted in Chatterjee, 1996). 'For us' reads another statement from the Amungme, 'the root cause of the human rights violations is Freeport .... Our sacred lands have been defiled and destroyed, our lands seized and taken over' (quoted in Eyal Press, 1998). In these statements the process of human rights violations is articulated as being synonymous with the resource appropriation and environmental degradation caused by the mining operations.

As in Nigeria, the campaign for environmental human rights was met with repression from a mutually supportive combination of state violence and corporate self-interest. One report reveals that Freeport McMoran provides the Indonesian military forces that protect its mine with food, shelter and transportation (*Corporate Watch* and Project Underground, 1998). The close ties between the Indonesian military and Freeport are further illustrated in that the company is helping to build a naval base for the Indonesian military near their portside at Amamapare (*Corporate Watch* and Project Underground, 1998). Freeport security personnel have themselves been accused of violence against indigenous rights campaigners. In April 1995, the Australian Council for Overseas Aid reported that 37 Irianese civilians had been killed by Indonesian military personnel operating in the area of the mine, and that Freeport security personnel 'engaged in acts of intimidation, extracted forced confessions, shot three civilians, disappeared five Dani villagers and tortured 13 people' (quoted in *Corporate Watch* and Project Underground, 1998).

These two brief case studies exemplify campaigns based on claims to environmental human rights conducted by indigenous communities opposing environmental destruction and resource exploitation. The conclusions of these studies relate to the conflictual and competing nature of rights claims to natural resource. Whereas the forces campaigning on the basis of environmental human rights derive rights from social and cultural criteria, the corporate claim interprets resource rights in terms of private property ownership. The dominant influence of corporate interests in the politics of both of the cases examined is exemplified through the use of the state apparatus to repress the campaign of environmental human rights to facilitate the continued resource extraction by the MNCs.

Conclusion

The purpose of this chapter has been to detail and evaluate the nature of claims to environmental human rights made by social organizations dedicated to political change. The conceptual grounds provided by NGOs for advocating environmental human rights was examined and a trend was noted that evidenced a philosophical assumption of interconnectedness between all elements of the environment, including human societies. This ecological interpretation of human rights promoted rights as a mechanism to protect holistic environmental concerns, rather than as an argument used in support of economic growth at the expense of environmental considerations.

With only three exceptions, all the NGOs responding to the questionnaire who stated a preference replied that they recognized environmental human rights. Differentiating between the specific environmental rights subsequently advocated by responding NGOs, the results of the questionnaire indicated the affirmation of two categories. Most commonly asserted was the right to an 'unpolluted', 'clean' or 'healthy' environment whilst a right to environmental resources was additionally identified by a smaller number of respondents. The conclusion of the conceptual analysis was to suggest the possible use of environmental human rights as an anti-systemic instrument to prioritize social and environmental over economic concerns. This conclusion was supported by the generally dismissive response to the concept of environmental human rights which was noted from the results of the questionnaire sent to selected MNCs and GEIs.

Moving from the conceptual to the practical findings of the questionnaire, evidence demonstrating widespread recognition of environmental human rights as a tactical instrument to prioritize social and environmental values was the key finding. The questionnaire responses further revealed evidence that social movements are campaigning for the implementation of environmental human rights on the structural level as a long term goal. A number of specific local campaigns opposing pollution, environmental degradation and resource exploitation based on ethical claims to environmental human rights were also noted, regardless of the legal status of such rights. These campaigns rely upon an ethical claim to rights, meaning that they are asserted with their validity being legitimized by criteria constitutive of the political ethics from which they are produced, rather than by their legal merits.

Both insider and outsider political tactics are being utilized in NGO campaigns to promote environmental human rights. That is to say that in addition to the formal channels of political influence being utilized by advocacy NGOs to lobby for the recognition of environmental human rights, protest campaigns are being organized in the social base to demand such implementation. These protest campaigns were exemplified in two case studies relating to Nigeria and Irian Jaya. The conclusion reached from the examination of these studies is to draw attention to the economic context within which claims to environmental human rights are made. Specifically, both of the environmental human rights claimed by NGOs conflict with the corporate interests that dominate the capitalist political economy. The possibility for the legal implementation of environmental human rights within the policy constraints imposed by the political economy therefore becomes the focus of attention for the next chapter.

Notes

1   Response to research questionnaire received from Lewellyn Belber, Earth Share, 26 October 1998.
2   Responses to research questionnaire received from Bonnie Harnden, Management Assistant, Amnesty International, 11 December 1998 and from Art Farrance, Ozone Action, 1 December 1998.
3   Response to the research questionnaire received from the Tibet Foundation, 7 January 1999.
4   Response to the research questionnaire received from Joan L Wade, Kate Sherman Fellow for Peace and the Environment, 20/20 Vision, 26 October 1998.
5   Response to research questionnaire received from Earth Sangha, 11 June 1998.
6   Response to research questionnaire received from Borderlinks, 5 November 1998.
7   Response to research questionnaire received from Zoltan Grossman, Midwest Treaty Network, 12 November 1998.
8   Response to research questionnaire received from Darrell Geist, President, Cold Mountain, Cold Rivers, 28 October 1998.
9   Brazil Network, *Brazil Network Newsletter*, March/April 1996, p4.
10 Ibid.
11 Response to research questionnaire received from Liz Campbell, Health and Safety Department, Xerox, 5 May 1999.
12 Principle 1; *Xerox Health and Safety Policy*, received via email from Liz Campbell, ibid.
13 Response to research questionnaire received from Caroline Walcot, Deputy Secretary General, European Roundtable of Industrialists, 29 April 1999.
14 Ibid.
15 Ibid.
16 Ibid.
17 Response from Caroline Walcot, Deputy Secretary General, European Roundtable of Industrialists, 3 May 1999.
18 Response to research questionnaire received from Nathalie Lhayani, Information Division, World Trade Organisation, 30 September 1999.
19 Response to research questionnaire received from the public affairs division, external relations department, International Monetary Fund, 19 April 1999.

20 Response to research questionnaire received from Mark Baldock, Organisation for Economic Co-operation and Development, 18 May 1999.
21 20/20 Vision, Action in Solidarity with Indonesia and East Timor, Asia Pacific Centre for Justice and Peace, Austin, Texas Sierra Club, Bainbridge Ometepe Sister Island Association, Banneker Center for Economic Justice, Border Links, Californians Against Waste, Campaign for Peace and Democracy, Centre for Economic and Social Rights, Centre for Environmental Citizenship, Citizen Alert, Clean Air Society of Australia and New Zealand, Cold Mountain, Cold Rivers, Communication Works, Earth First!, Earth Rights International, Grassroots International, Grassroots World Government, International Labor Rights Fund, Journalists About Children's and Women's Rights and the Environment in Macedonia, Kurdish Human Rights Project, Legal Environmental Assistance Foundation, Midwest Treaty Network, Pacific Institute for Studies in Development, Environment and Security, Peoples Decade of Human Rights Education, Renew America, Rights International, Sacred Earth Network, Training for Change, Wisconsin's Environmental Decade, World Information Transfer, and World Institute for a Sustainable Humanity.
22 Alaska Rainforest Campaign, Alliance for the Wild Rockies, Austin, Texas Sierra Club, CAFOD, Cold Mountain, Cold Rivers, Earth Sangha, Journalists About Children's and Women's Rights and the Environment in Macedonia, Rights International, South and Meso American Indian Rights Centre, Training for Change and Trust for Public Land.
23 Buffalo Nations, Legal Environmental Assistance Foundation, Midwest Treaty Network, Oregon Clearinghouse for Pollution Reduction and Rights International.
24 See chapter 5 for a discussion of environmental justice.
25 Responses to research questionnaire received from Paul Benedek, Action in Solidarity with Indonesia and East Timor, 23 October 1998 and Virginia Schilz, Population Chairperson, Austin, Texas Sierra Club, 23 October 1998.
26 Response to research questionnaire received from Grossman, op cit.
27 Response to research questionnaire received from Benedek, op cit.
28 Response to research questionnaire received from Roger D Stone, Sustainable Development Institute, 18 November 1998.
29 Response to research questionnaire received from Shula Koenig, Peoples Decade of Human Rights Education, 2 December 1998.
30 Response to research questionnaire received from Pharis Harvey, Executive Director, International Labor Rights Fund, 7 December 1998.
31 Response to research questionnaire received from Geist, op cit.
32 Response to research questionnaire received from Mark Ritchie, Institute for Agriculture and Trade Policy, 1 December 1998.
33 Response to research questionnaire received from Francisco Forrest Martin, President, Rights International, 10 June 1998.
34 Response to research questionnaire received from Cynthia Valencic, Vice President for Programs, Legal Environmental Assistance Foundation, 17 June 1998.
35 Response to research questionnaire received from Virginia Schilz, Population Chairperson, Austin Sierra Club, 23 October 1998.
36 Response to research questionnaire received from Geist, op cit.
37 Response to research questionnaire received from Benedek, op cit.
38 Response to research questionnaire received from Campaign for Peace and Democracy, 10 June 1998.
39 Response to research questionnaire received from Doug Israel, Centre for Environmental Citizenship, 1 December 1998.
40 Response to research questionnaire received from Mary Ann Tenuto, Comite Emiliano Zapata, 27 October 1998.

41 Response to questionnaire received from Pam Porter, Wisconsin's Environmental Decade, 2 December 1998.
42 Response to research questionnaire received from Shahbano Aliani, Center for Economic and Social Rights, 30 November 1998.
43 Response to research questionnaire received from Arlene K Wong, Pacific Institute for Studies in Development, Environment and Security, 10 November 1998.
44 Response to research questionnaire received from Journalism About Children and Women's Rights and Environment in Macedonia, 1 December 1998.
45 Response to research questionnaire received from Amos El-Roy Millenium Peoples Assembly, 4 December 1998.
46 Response to research questionnaire received from Earth Rights International, 12 November 1998.
47 Response to research questionnaire received from Paula Palmer, Executive Director, Global Response, 1 December 1998.
48 Responses to research questionnaire received from Mark Murray, Executive Director, Californians Against Waste, 1 December 1998; Richard Nielson, Citizen Alert, 12 October 1998; Amos El-Roy, Grassroots World Government, 4 December 1998.
49 Response to research questionnaire received from Earth First! 1 December 1998.
50 Response to research questionnaire received from Valerie Cook, Grants and Information Systems Manger, Brained Foundation, 23 June 1998.
51 Response to research questionnaire received from Benedek, op cit.
52 Response to research questionnaire received from Communication Works, 10 June 1998.
53 Response to research questionnaire received from Earth Rights International, op cit.
54 Response to research questionnaire received from Aliani, op cit.
55 Response to research questionnaire received from Sue Nackoney, Buffalo Nations, 3 December 1998.
56 Response to research questionnaire received from William Wasch, American Association for the Support of Ecological Initiatives, 24 October 1998.
57 Response to research questionnaire received from Joanne Landy, Campaign for Peace and Democracy, 10 June 1998.
58 Response to research questionnaire received from Martin, op cit.
59 Response to research questionnaire received from Israel, op cit.
60 Response received from Jamie Lennox, Membership Coordinator, Alliance for the Wild Rockies, 10 June 1998.
61 Response to research questionnaire received from Training for Change, 10 June 1998.
62 Response to research questionnaire received from Grossman, op cit.
63 Response to research questionnaire received from Thomas Croft, Campaign Manager, ATD Fourth World (UK), 2 February 1999.
64 Response to research questionnaire received from Porter, op cit.
65 Response to research questionnaire received from Sarah Brown, Campaigns and Press Assistant, Charter 88, 9 December 1998.
66 Response to research questionnaire received from Carolyn T Comitta, Regional Director, North America, World Information Transfer, 10 November 1998.
67 Response to research questionnaire received from Michael Karp, World Institute for a Sustainable Humanity, 10 November 1998.
68 Response to research questionnaire received from Irina Fotieva, deputy director of Altai, 2 March 1999.
69 Response to research questionnaire received from Bill Pfeiffer, Sacred Earth Network, 13 November 1998.
70 Response to research questionnaire received from Earth First!, op cit.
71 Based in Albuquerque, United States.
72 Article 6.

73 Article 7.
74 Article 8.
75 Article 9.
76 Article 11.
77 Parts III and IV.
78 Response to research questionnaire received from Nick Luem, South and Meso American Indian Rights Center, 1 July 1998.
79 Ibid.
80 Response to research questionnaire received from Luem, op cit.
81 See chapter 6 for a discussion of this claimed human right.
82 Response to research questionnaire received from Porter, op cit.
83 Response to research questionnaire received from Wade, op cit.
84 Capital city of the state of Sonora in Mexico; response to research questionnaire received from Borderlinks, 5 November 1998.
85 Response to research questionnaire received from Andrew Wells, Program Director, Asia Pacific Center for Justice and Peace, 14 January 1999.
86 Ibid.
87 Response to research questionnaire received from Fotieva, op cit.
88 Response to research questionnaire received from Luem, op cit.
89 Ibid.
90 Response to research questionnaire received from Diana Rhoades, Alaska Rainforest Campaign, 10 June 1998.
91 Response to research questionnaire received from Grossman, op cit.
92 Response to research questionnaire received from Earth Sangha, op cit.
93 Response to research questionnaire received from Artist Hunger Network, 31 October 1998.
94 Response to research questionnaire received from Frank Sudlow, CAFOD, 18 November 1998.
95 A global institution affiliated to the United Nations rather than an NGO; response to research questionnaire received from Margret Vidar, legal officer, Food and Agriculture Organization, 19 May 1999.
96 The federal agency which insures US companies operating abroad.

Chapter 4

The Formal Response to Environmental Human Rights Claims

> Inequality and domination can only be justified mystically and that is precisely the ideological function of the law.
>
> – Colin Sumner

Introduction

Chapter three examined the demands for the recognition of environmental human rights made by political forces active in the social base. The purpose of this chapter is to analyze how the formal institutions of governments have responded to these claims and to ascertain the limitations of the legal reforms enacted.

This chapter will begin by describing the trend towards the formal legal recognition of environmental rights, differentiating between domestic (constitutional) rights and international human rights law. Structural problems with the legalistic approach to implementing human rights will then be discussed. Law will be argued to be predicated upon a political ideology that reflects and sustains dominant interests in society. This relation between social power and law suggests that constitutional environmental rights which threaten the interests of the holders of capital will remain unimplemented in liberal democratic or capitalist states, a claim verified through a subsequent analysis of the actual record.

The focus then turns to examine international law. Environmental and human rights legislation is argued to conflict with the freedom of global capital and with the ideology of free trade. As in the case of domestic law, the efficacy of international law is broadly based on the interests of the holders of capital, given the capitalist structure of the global political economy. This criterion determines both the enforced status of international trade laws and the lack of enforcement mechanisms for international environmental human rights legislation.

The Trend Towards the Constitutional Recognition of Environmental Rights

Constitutional texts and other legal instruments in approximately forty countries now proclaim some variant of an environmental right (Anderson, 1996; Douglas-Scott, 1996; International Peoples' Tribunal on Human Rights and the Environment, 1998). Most common is the explicit guarantee in a constitution of a right to a 'healthy', 'healthful', 'safe' or 'balanced' environment or to an environment 'suitable for development'.[1] These constitutional guarantees can be criticized for being vague and therefore difficult to legally enforce, since it is, for example, questionable as to when a healthy environment becomes an unhealthy environment. To avoid such confusion, it is necessary to state the specific criteria upon which the meaning of a healthy environment can be established. Chapter 5 for example claims the right to an environment free from toxic pollution. Similarly, the Constitution of Ecuador guarantees 'the right to live in an environment free of contamination'.[2] Ecuador is exceptional in stipulating precise environmental conditions to substantiate an environmental right. Nonetheless, this chapter will later demonstrate that environmental rights remain largely unrealized in that state. In a small number of states, the environmental rights of citizens are not explicitly stated, but have been derived by the courts from the inclusion of environmental protection in the state Constitution.[3]

Domestic rights should not be confused with universal human rights since the former are restricted to the citizens of one state as opposed to being attributed to all people. Notwithstanding this fact, human rights regimes are socially constructed and therefore change over time, rather than reflect an unchanging manifestation of natural justice or natural law (Stammers, 1999). The trend towards the recognition of environmental rights in domestic constitutions is consequently relevant to analysis of universal human rights since widespread changes to constitutional laws may signify the emergence of environmental rights as a norm in world politics. As environmental rights become increasingly prominent in constitutions, so the claim to universal environmental human rights is correspondingly strengthened.

Unfortunately, representatives of only three of the 41 contacted states completed the research questionnaire and such a low response rate prevents reliable conclusions to be drawn as to why environmental rights are being recognized in domestic legislatures. This limitation notwithstanding, from the responses received, representatives of two states reported that environmental rights had been incorporated into domestic law because of (i) changing international norms and (ii) demands from social movements. In response to the question; 'why have environmental considerations been linked to those of human rights?' a representative for the Georgian state replied:

> The legislation of Georgia corresponds with universally recognized norms and principles of international law ... . The people of Georgia, whose strong will is to establish a democratic social order, economic, a social and legal state, guarantee universally recognized human rights and freedoms.[4]

The Argentinean respondent to the same question stated that environmental rights were first incorporated into the 1994 constitution because of the 'influence of international movements regarding [the] environment'.[5] At least two states have therefore perceived a legitimization of claims to universal environmental human rights originating from the recent growth in saliency of environmental concerns in world politics and have altered domestic law in response to such claims. It must however be repeated that the low response rate prevents conclusions to be made as to whether the responses received from Georgia and Argentina are typical of other states or mere anomalies.

The Trend Towards the International Recognition of Environmental Rights

The claim that universal environmental human rights are gaining formal legitimacy in world politics is supported by recent developments in international human rights legislation. However, the vague and non-committal wording in the adopted legislation undermines the efficacy of the environmental rights stipulated in international law. For example, the 1973 Stockholm Conference on the Human Environment stated that 'man has the fundamental right to freedom, equality and adequate conditions of life in an environment of a quality that permits a life of dignity and well-being'.[6] The UN General Assembly declared on 14 December 1990 that all persons have the right to live in an environment which is adequate to ensure their health and welfare.[7] The African National Congress Bill of Rights states that 'all men and women shall have the right to a healthy and ecologically balanced environment and the duty to defend it'.[8] Environmental human rights have also been expressed in Africa through the African Charter on Human and Peoples' Rights that codifies a right to 'a general satisfactory environment favorable to [peoples] development'.[9] The Protocol of San Salvador to the American Convention of Human Rights of 1988 proclaims that:

(1) Everyone shall have the right to live in a healthy environment and to have access to basic public services.
(2) The States Parties shall promote the protection, preservation and improvement of the environment.[10]

Explicit recognition of the linkage between pollution and harm to health has been made in the Convention of the Rights of the Child (Churchill, 1996). This convention expresses the traditional wording of the right to health in providing that each child has the right to enjoy the 'highest attainable standard of health' but unlike all previous treaties adds, 'taking into consideration the danger and the risks of environmental pollution'.[11]

All the stipulations mentioned above declare international environmental human rights but demonstrate vague statements of intent rather than legally enforceable or clearly specified environmental standards. Breaking this mold, in 1994 the Draft Declaration of Principles on Human Rights and the Environment was presented to the United Nations.[12] The draft declaration was the culmination of five years of work conducted by special rapporteur Fatma Ksentini who had been requested to investigate the linkage between human rights and environmental concerns by the Sub-Commission on the Prevention of Discrimination of Minorities (Johnston, 1994). The draft declaration recommends a total of 27 universal environmental human rights, many of which institutionalize uncompromising environmental values (Draft Declaration of Principles on Human Rights and the Environment, 1994). For example, article 14 guarantees the land rights of indigenous communities. Article five states that 'all persons have the right to freedom from pollution, environmental degradation and activities that adversely affect the environment, threaten life, health, livelihood, well-being or sustainable development' (Draft Declaration of Principles on Human Rights and the Environment, 1994). Such radical stipulations that challenge fundamental premises of economic rationality and the capitalist world order have ensured that the draft declaration has been marginalized in formal UN meetings and has, since its completion, evidenced little chance of becoming a legally binding document, and less still for its provisions to be realized.

The latest international attempt to formally recognize universal environmental human rights was the 1999 Declaration of Bizkaia on the Right to the Environment (Basque Institute of Public Administration, 1999). This declaration contains nine articles, all of which are disappointingly vague. Article one for example guarantees the right to 'a healthy and ecologically balanced environment', and article three extends this politically vacuous right to future generations. This declaration was drawn up in co-operation with the Human Rights Institute of the University of Deusto and the UNESCO Centre in the Basque Country and these rather obscure origins combined with its vague wording ensures that this document stands little chance of ever becoming a meaning instrument to guarantee environmental human rights.

A Critical Evaluation of Legal Innovations

On the legislative level, the above analysis documents the present existence of environmental human rights. However, the legal conclusion indicating a positive trend towards the institutionalization of both domestic and international environmental rights is both problematic and misleading when analyzed from a political perspective acknowledging dynamics of social power as influencing the efficacy of law.

It is the assertion in this chapter that the political construction of law prevents legal institutions from addressing violations of human rights and environmental degradation produced by the everyday operations of the capitalist political economy. This claim will be defended in three parts. Firstly, both domestic and international law require individual states to enforce legal stipulations. From the perspective of human rights, state sovereignty is problematic since states acting in defense of powerful interests are in part responsible for structural violations of environmental human rights. Secondly, the legal focus on individual actors reveals a retrospective tendency of law to identify and punish guilty individuals rather than pro-actively address structural, or culturally determined, causes of injustice. Thirdly, and most importantly, the function of law will be argued to be to institutionalize, rather than challenge, existing power relations.

State Sovereignty as a Cause of Environmental Human Rights Violations

Barkun remarks that rules of behavior can properly be called laws only when force or the threat of force stands behind them (Barkun, 1968). International human rights treaties lack a body to enforce them, relying instead for implementation on individual states. In the cases of domestic and international environmental human rights, an evident divergence exists in the stipulations of law on the one hand, and the actual social reality on the other, since states tend to enforce laws in ways that accommodate the interests of powerful actors. As the following examples testify, the state can itself act as a perpetrator of environmental degradation and of human rights violations.

Aleksandr Nikitin, a former captain of the Russian Navy, was arrested by the Federal Russian Security police on 6 February 1996 and accused of high treason in the form of espionage (Gauslaa, 1996; Kudrik, 1998). Nikitin had in fact drawn international attention to the potential environmental catastrophe that was threatened by Russia's poorly maintained nuclear powered submarine fleet and the disposal of spent reactor cores that has been described as a 'Chernobyl in slow motion' (Bellona, 1998). The overt use of espionage laws to silence criticism of the state environmental record led Amnesty International to proclaim Nikitin the first Russian prisoner of conscience since Andrei Sakharov. All charges against Nikitin were finally dropped and two years after the initial arrest took place, a government commission was forced to acknowledge 'serious' radiation levels on a nuclear base on the Kola Peninsula since sites were confirmed to have been used by Russia as a dumping ground for nuclear waste (Gray, 1999). The contempt demonstrated by the Russian state for the civil rights of Nikitin indicates a continuation of policy from the totalitarian era when political rights were dismissed as a political irrelevance. For example, the water inspector Piotr Kozhevnikov was arrested in 1986 and placed in a psychiatric ward for publicizing the dumping of oil wastes by the Soviet Union into the Gulf of Finland (Sachs, 1995).

Disregard for the most basic of human rights is likewise evident in Western states. Ten minutes before midnight on 10 July 1985 two bombs exploded upon the Greenpeace vessel, the Rainbow Warrior, which was moored in Auckland harbor, New Zealand. The second of these killed Fernando Pereira, a Portuguese photographer (Salmi, 1993). The bombs were planted by the French secret service. This instance offers an instructive account of how powerful states systematically violate human rights, not because the state apparatus has engaged in an act of terrorism, which, as Chomsky has comprehensively demonstrated, is a systematic policy of powerful states (Chomsky, 1986; 1987; 1988; 1992a; 1992b; 1993a; 1993b; 1993c; 1993d; 1994; 1995; 1996a; 1996b; 1997a; 1997b; 1998a; 1998b; 1999), but rather because of the reaction of other states following the bombing. The US and British governments refused to condemn the actions of the French even though no warning was given before the explosions, making the bombing more egregious than many of the terrorist operations of the Irish Republican Army which are typically denounced by the same states with moral outrage. President Jacques Chirac has been quoted as saying that 'the French army had every reason to be proud of the two officers involved in the sinking of the Rainbow Warrior' (Rowell, 1996). The French state has never apologized to any member of the Pereira family for the photographer's death (Rowell, 1996). Indeed, in a final demonstration of contempt for the victim's family and the concept of human rights, the French state has since made the man convicted of the manslaughter, Lieutenant Colonel Alain Mafart, a Knight of the Order of Merit (*The New Internationalist*, 1991).

The violation of human rights by states applies to group as well as individual rights. International human rights law attributes group rights to peoples.[13] However, 'peoples' have traditionally been interpreted by statespeople to mean states and to thereby support and legitimize their own power base. The historical record shows that this interpretation often becomes a source of basic human rights violations, particularly regarding the expropriation of environmental resources held by indigenous communities. The Rio Declaration on the Environment and

Development for example declares that 'states have, in accordance with the Charter of the United Nations and the principles of international law, the sovereign right to exploit their own resources pursuant to their own environmental and development policies'.[14] Granting control over environmental resources to states has severe implications for the rights of indigenous peoples. In many states, natural resources cannot be accessed without denying the rights of the indigenous nations that have inhabited and maintained the land (Clay, 1994). The expropriation of communal resources is often given a veneer of legitimacy by states since a whole edifice of law has been constructed to deny the rights of nations to natural resources when they are deemed valuable by and to the state (Clay, 1994). Evidence in support of this claim can be found in the cases of the indigenous Penan and Kelabit tribes in the Malaysian state of Sarawak. Despite possessing recognized land rights, these tribes are unable to use the law to effectualize their opposition to deforestation since the state retains logging rights to the timber (World Rainforest Movement and Forests Monitor Ltd., 1998).

In 1990, the indigenous Huaorani were granted communal legal title to 612,560 hectares of territory in Ecuador.[15] Yet the Constitution,[16] and the Hydrocarbons Law,[17] state that all hydrocarbon deposits in Ecuador are the property of the state (Fabra, 1996). Therefore, although they oppose the process, the Huaroni cannot prevent the mining of oil on their lands when this has been authorized by the state, neither are they entitled to any royalties from the oil extracted. Likewise in Nigeria, although the Ogoni have secure land rights, subsoil resources are owned by the state and oil extraction has continued despite widespread indigenous protests as detailed in chapter three (Sachs, 1996a). Continuing this trend, the Guyanan Indians hold title to their land but not to its mineral wealth. Therefore, the Brazilian government auctions mining concessions without even consulting the indigenous inhabitants (Healy, 1997). Indeed, in Latin America, one commentator argues that governments have undertaken a policy of 'systematic genocide' of indigenous people to clear forest regions for farming, the building of roads, and industrial sites (Gormley, 1976).

Further exemplifying the contempt demonstrated by states for group rights to land, thousands of communal villages were dispossessed in the 1970s by the Marcos regime in the Philippines (*The Ecologist*, 1993). In the Primorski Territory of the Russian Far East the Svetlaya logging firm started harvesting vast quantities of timber in 1990, rapidly encroaching on the traditional lands used by Udegei and Nanai communities for hunting and fishing (Schindler, 1994). In Honduras, communal mangrove swamps were sold by the state to private owners in 1988, denying locals access to the food source that they had previously relied upon for their nutrition (Stonich, 1994).

The identification of state sovereignty as a causal violation of group rights is highlighted through the history of conflicts between states and nations. Clay observes that of the 120 wars being fought in 1993, 75 per cent were between nations and states who define them as citizens (Clay, 1994). The Yanomami territory is split between Venezuela and Brazil, which thereby denies the nation self-determination (Sponzel, 1994). The archipelago scheme, developed by the Brazilian government in 1978, originally planned to reduce Yanomami territory by 75 per cent, fragmenting the population into 20 reserves, with the aim of opening up new lands for logging and mining activities. Under the plan, the area of each reserve would be insufficient to maintain the dependent population. The size of each proposed village unit would be significantly larger than the traditional dimensions leading to disruption of the traditional social dynamics of the Yanomami (Sponzel, 1994). Moreover, the fragmentation of the traditional Yanomami territory would destroy the cultural heritage of the nation since this ancestry is predicated upon a notion of land as sacred space (Sponzel, 1994).

In all these cases cited above, the political sovereignty of states constitutes a major barrier to the realization of the group rights to self-determination and ownership of natural resources which are currently stipulated in international law. Assuming that states can act as vehicles for the implementation of human rights neglects the extent to which the states system itself functions as a contributory cause of ongoing rights violations because human rights and environmental protection measures are subordinated to commercial considerations in the political process. The citing of examples, however numerous, cannot be sufficient to demonstrate the inability to realize environmental human rights within the states system. The problematic nature of the states system for the realization of human rights is instead revealed when the state is understood as an instrument of power, operating in the interests of groups powerful enough to control it (Chomsky, 1992b). Assuming a state framework for the realization of human rights therefore channels the rights discourse towards the formal instruments of state, especially law, where popular mobilization around human rights issues is constrained by the official decision making process and the challenge posed to power relations eviscerated (Stammers, 1995). The remainder of this chapter therefore focuses explicitly upon the role of the state and of law as instruments of power.

The Structural Limitations of Law

Expecting human rights violations to be eliminated through the passing of legislation is unrealistic since law cannot by itself transform social norms (Barkun, 1968). Law can only be expected to codify and institutionalize existing public morality, rather than define or change that morality (Stephens, 1994). It is both the purpose and ability of legal institutions to target individuals that contravene social conventions codified in legislation (Evans and Hancock, 1998). As such, it is capable of providing redress against individuals and organizations who can be readily identified as engaging in deviant behavior (Evans and Hancock, 1998). The focus on agents is however inadequate for the task of implementing human rights when rights violations are produced by the cumulative actions of individuals or institutions that together constitute structural processes which have been internalized as normal by members of society. Law can only identify 'evil' in the unusual and the actor-specific, not in the normal and the actor-invariant built into the everyday operations of the overall structure (Galtung, 1994). Galtung identifies exploitation, repression and starvation as structural processes responsible for systemic human rights violations; processes that existing laws do little to prevent and much to facilitate (Galtung, 1994). As has been argued elsewhere, the efficacy of human rights law is circumscribed by the fact that:

Violations of human rights owe as much to current economic and political structures and practices as they do to the self-interested, willful individual. The international law approach to human rights relies upon the assumption that violators can be identified, made to answer for their actions and punished. However, this overlooks the fact that economic structures cannot be juridical persons with intentions and capabilities (Evans and Hancock, 1998, p. 16).

The requirement for law to identify and punish individuals prevents law from enforcing pro-active measures that could tackle the cause of human rights violations. Of course, law can influence the actions of individuals through threats of punishment to discourage deviant actions, but it cannot singularly replace the cultural, social, religious, ethical, political and economic institutions that condition the norms and values of individuals. The following section expands on this argument to contextualize law within the wider area of policy formulation. Law is argued to broadly reflect underlying power relations in society, since these relations produce the social norms that laws institutionalize. This claim will be explained with particular reference to the interests of production and finance capital that are argued to dominate social relations in liberal democracies and to subsequently constitute the principal influence on law.

Domestic Law as a Reflection of Social Power Relations

According to dominant theories of political jurisprudence, law acts as an impartial institution to rectify infractions of justice and to use objective criteria to adjudicate between conflictual private interests in society (Feinberg, 1988). Subsequently, the operations of social power are argued to have little bearing on the legal sphere which is insulated from such sources of undue influence. Belief in the autonomy of legal reasoning, combined with equal access and application of law to all, regardless of wealth or power circumstances is perhaps held by most citizens and lawyers in Western democracies (Collins, 1982). This belief both reflects and re-enforces the liberal ideology of the neutrality of the state. In a telling study, Collins concludes that 'Western legal theory has become obsessed with the task of demonstrating the apolitical qualities of judicial reasoning and proving how issues of preference and interest play no part in the legal process' (Collins, 1982).

This view of law is both simplistic and misleading since it obfuscates the operational dynamics of power relations. The assumption that legal reasoning, applied through legislation, can address the causes of environmental human rights violations confuses cause for effect. Law reflects, rather than revolutionizes power relations and codifies, rather than creates, social practice (Watson, 1979; Donnelly, 1984; Vincent, 1986). Theorizing a legal sphere independent of either political context or cultural content neglects the very real role played by the law for the legitimization and recreation of existing power relations.

Judicial institutions constitute an arm of the state, and the state is both a reflection of, and an instrument for, social power. As Chomsky reminds us, power is sharply skewed and those who hold power also use the state to defend their interests (Chomsky, 1993d). Economic power is particularly important in influencing political policies in liberal democracies (Russell, 1948; Lukes, 1986; Morriss, 1987;

Hoffman, 1988; Chomsky, 1993d). Galtung explains that there may well be situations when the state can do without popular approval, but there are few occasions when a liberal democratic state can survive the loss of consent of corporations in general and of the banking sector in particular (Galtung, 1994). Dryzek likewise notes the unbalanced influence of powerful economic structures in shaping the political agenda:

> the distribution of power in liberal democratic systems is inevitably skewed. Business always has a privileged position due to the financial resources available to it, government officials' need for business co-operation in implementing policies, and government's fear of an investment strike and economic downturn if it pursues anti-business policies ... . The capitalist market imprisons both liberal democracy and the administrative state by ruling out any significant actions that would hinder business profitability (Dryzek, 1992, p. 22 and p. 26).

In the UK, David Alton MP referred to 'the merging of the interests of the big corporations and the parties [which] reaches deep into Parliament itself' as the 'insidious form of corruption ... which breaches no law but is part and parcel of the system' (quoted in Rowell, 1996). In the US, politics is, in the words of John Dewey, 'the shadow cast on society by big business, and as long as this is so, the attenuation of the shadow will not change the substance' (quoted in Chomsky, 1995). Supporting this assessment, Greider notes that for 'Republicans and Democrats alike, the government took its cues ... from the multinationals' (Greider, 1997). In short, the state is an instrument of power acting in the interests of groups powerful enough to dominate it, rather than the neutral adjudicator of private interests in society suggested by liberal theorists.

This influence of corporate interests on the state extends to the judiciary. The politics of power determines that the legislative, executive and judicial arms of the state all tend to reflect, express and support the interests of the powerful. Eckersley reminds us that the legal system in liberal democracies 'tends to favour those with money, power, education and position' (Eckersley, 1996). This pertinent observation refutes the assertion that the different institutions of the state 'balance' each other (de Toqueville, 1979). Far from being insulated, law reflects the power relations of the society in which it is located. Bertrand Russell correctly concludes that economic power 'easily acquires a certain independence. It can influence law' (Russell, 1948). Coleman explains that controversial legal cases are typically resolved by judges 'appealing to principles of political morality' rather than by citing the practice of other judges (Coleman, 1988). This observation identifies the way in which legal outcomes tend to reflect the dominant ideology of political ethics of the society where the courts have jurisdiction. Marx demonstrated that property law defends unequal property ownership and that contract law institutionalizes existing relations of exchange, thereby protecting capitalism from external challenges (McLellan, 1977; Sumner, 1979).

The use of law as a political instrument is most blatant in the control of political protests by a state. This is self-evident in totalitarian states such as Nazi Germany or the Soviet Union, where law was overtly used to ban any form of public protest. Social control is also an evident feature of law in liberal democratic states. Penny

Green concluded in her study of the 1984–5 miners strike in the UK that 'both criminal and civil law provided a significant aspect of the overall strategy employed by the state to prevent the union engaging in effective picketing' (Green, 1990). Moreover, law under the Thatcher governments was argued to have 'played an important role both in curbing the growth of working-class organisation and in criminalising workers engaged in conflict with their employers' (Green, 1990).

Much of the political component of law is made evident not through the overt criminalization of political challenge but is rather expressed in a more subtle manner through the underlying ideological premises upon which law is constructed (Sumner, 1979). Gramsci significantly refined the Marxist position on law by focusing on the effect of law on popular understanding, or notions of common sense (Hoare and Smith, 1971). In particular, Gramsci argued that law combines elements of repression, ethics and social codes of conduct in order to construct consciousness and institutionalize a system of popular ideological belief and social conformism useful to the hegemonic bloc (Sumner, 1979). By ideological belief, Gramsci was referring in particular to respect for authority, private property and the normalization of exploitative practices.

Analyzing law through a Gramscian focus on hegemony and underlying ideology explains why law rarely explicitly stipulates the interests of the powerful. The need to ensure order and compliance with statutes means that law must be presented as impartial and politically neutral rather than overtly promoting the interests of one group. As Hay puts it:

> the courts deal in terror, pain and death, but also in moral ideals, control of arbitrary power, mercy for the weak. In doing so they make it possible to disguise much of the class interest of the law (Hay quoted in Sumner, 1979, p. 264).

The political nature of law as a defense of the powerful is therefore obfuscated by the inclusion of ethical codes that are also expressed in statues. Under the framework of hegemony, law is simultaneously an instrument of party politics, an enforcer of revered ideas and an agency for the regulation and maintenance of a social order (Sumner, 1979). The state and the courts alike have scope for agency and change, but only within the narrow framework given by (i) the dominant ideology and (ii) the interests of the hegemonic bloc (Collins, 1982). Law-creation is, by definition and both in process and outcome, influenced principally by the powerful (Sumner, 1979). Law reflects the interests of the political forces behind legislation, the choice of problems that these forces prioritize and seek to solve and the ideologies through which these problems are identified, perceived and understood (Sumner, 1979).

There is therefore an evident paradox in expecting human rights to be implemented through existing laws for, as Stammers argues, 'ideas of human rights can only be justified insofar as they challenge rather than sustain existing relations of power' (Stammers, 1995). Yet the above analysis has argued that law reflects, supports and institutionalizes existent relations of power in society, problematizing the use of law as an instrument for the realization of human rights. The nature of law as a defense of power and privilege is exemplified in the 'floodgates' principle. Here, the courts dismiss a case not upon its merits, but rather according to the need to prevent setting a precedent for the opening of the 'floodgates of litigation' that would allow a vast increase in cases, placing unworkable demands on the courts (Hayward, 2000). The floodgates argument reflects the tacit acknowledgment of the legal establishment that it either cannot, or will not, make decisions requiring radical social change.

Locus Standi

The privileged position assigned to private capital interests over the general protection of the environment is institutionalized in liberal democratic legal systems through the legal concept of locus standi, or standing. Before courts can hear cases, potential litigants must establish standing, which is to say that a private party bringing a case to the courts must first demonstrate that they are suffering or will suffer injury, damage or an invasion of their rights over and above that incurred on the members of public in general (Glazewski, 1996). From the perspective of environmental protection, this stipulation is exceptionally problematic since factors such as climate change and toxic pollution harm not isolated and identifiable individuals but rather the whole of the biosphere. The possibility of individuals using legal instruments against indiscriminate ecological damage is arbitrarily foreclosed since claims cannot be heard from citizens unless they can demonstrate a personal stake in the outcome over and above that of the general population (Eckersley, 1996). Corriveau for example notes in the case of Quebec that environmental protection groups do not have the locus standi to resort to the judicial system unless they are directly and materially injured (Corriveau, 1995). In the case of standing in England, Reid notes that:

> the difficulty can be demonstrated by considering the position in relation to wild birds. As wild creatures, they are not the property of anyone, and therefore nobody's legally recognised rights or interests are affected by anything that causes them harm. Many people may be very concerned about the fate of the birds, but in the past such concern has not been regarded as sufficient to justify permitting access to the courts when no legal interests are at stake (Reid, 1995, p. 42).

Blackstone summarizes that, 'one can sue individuals or corporations if they damage one's private property but not if they damage the public environment' (Blackstone, 1974). Reflecting the institutionalized priority of private economic interests over public environmental concerns in liberal democratic states, the law recognizes only a limited range of interests, focused on property rights, without paying equal regard to the environmental rights of the public that are violated when ecological harm is incurred (Reid, 1995).

The institutionalization of standing as a preliminary requirement to establish access to the courts can therefore be viewed as one manifestation of how the legal system favors a focus on private interests at the expense of overall environmental protection. This ideological position permeates the law in liberal democracies. In the case of English law, Alder states that:

> there is an underlying bias in favour of financial interests. This was formed in the laissez faire era of the nineteenth century upon the foundations of property rights and freedom of

contract and was incorporated by judicial interpretation into the post World War II planning system. Within this framework, environmental interests are not recognised as rights and must therefore be protected, if at all, by specific legislation (Alder, 1993, p. 72).

According to English jurisprudence, damage sustained by the environment is to be prevented by the Attorney-General and other political figures acting ex-officio as guardian of the public interest (Eckersley, 1996). The following example typifies how this environmental responsibility is consistently subordinated to the same commercial considerations that are privileged by the courts in liberal democracies. In October 1993:

> Environment and Countryside Minister Tim Yeo MP, announced that the Government opposed groups such as Friends of the Earth being given a legal right under European Community law to sue those responsible for damaging the "unowned" environment to recover the costs of clean up or remediation. The prospect of such a right, proposed by the European Commission in its Green Paper on Civil Liability for Environmental Damage, was of particular concern to banks, insurance companies and other businesses in the financial sector (Friends of the Earth, 1993, p. 6).

Legal Ineffectuality

The claim that law tends to reflect private commercial interests in implementation as well as in formulation is substantiated by an examination of the ineffectuality of domestic environmental rights. It will now be argued that environmental rights are given a low political priority in liberal democracies and are systematically violated with relative impunity from the courts.

The 1988 Brazilian Constitution granted land rights to indigenous people defined in terms of land 'used for their productive activity, those necessary for the preservation of their natural resources and those which are important for their physical and cultural reproduction, according to their customs and traditions' (*Brazil Network Newsletter*, 1996a). Examining the effectiveness of this legislation, one commentator summarized that the legal development, 'has not solved the environmental problem, and the Brazilian environmental reality has not greatly improved since then' (Fernandez, 1996). The Xavante Indians in the Brazilian Amazon have, for example, had their land rights violated by illegal logging and cattle ranching without redress being provided by either the political or the judicial arms of the state (Albert, 1994). Yanomami Indians in Brazil who have had the economic and social fabric of their communities destroyed by gold miners exploiting the Amazon have been similarly ignored by the bodies charged with upholding the law.[18] One of the political decisions most disastrous to the Yanomami nation was the construction between 1973 and 1976 of the Perimetral Norte highway, 225 km of which passed through Yanomami lands. Disease, epidemics, gold diggers, settlers and logging corporations followed the new road despite vehement protests from the Yanomami (Sponzel, 1994). The Inter-American Commission on Human Rights found that the Brazilian government had violated the rights to life, liberty and personal security of the Yanomami Indians after members of the tribe alleged that the highway construction had breached the American Declaration of the Rights and Duties of Man (Desgagne, 1995). Yet, questioning the significance of legal stipulations, the ruling failed to significantly empower the Yanomami in their struggle against the invasion of their lands and the aggregate effect of the road on the indigenous nation has been subsequently described as 'ecocide, ethnocide and genocide' (Sponzel, 1994).

In the Malaysian state of Sarawak, the land rights of indigenous groups are legally recognized. However an environmental report found that these rights to land and resources have been 'systematically ignored' by the logging industry (World Rainforest Movement and Forests Monitor Ltd., 1998). Breaches of native peoples property rights have furthermore gone 'largely unpunished' by the state, despite an increasing number of court cases brought on behalf of community representatives and individuals (World Rainforest Movement and Forests Monitor Ltd., 1998). The ineffectiveness of legal environmental rights in the current political economy led Harding to conclude that 'emphasis on formal constitutional rights is likely to result in the dismal conclusion that neither environmental rights nor human rights in general have anything more than theoretical potential' (Harding, 1996). In the case of the environmental right guaranteed under the African Charter, Churchill points out that 'it is difficult to gauge what impact, if any, the environmental right which it contains has had in practice' (Churchill, 1996). Douglas-Scott similarly concludes that 'experience drawn from constitutionally entrenched environmental rights tends to show that such rights can provide a false hope' (Douglas-Scott, 1996). In Hungary, this trend continues, for the 'Constitution provides for a right to a healthy environment, and all citizens are accorded a statutory right to participate in environmental protection, but neither of these have been much utilized' (Anderson, 1996). Similarly in Mexico, strict environmental legislation exists in statutes, but has rarely been enforced against endemic infractions (Shea, Elguea and Bustillo, 1997).

In Nicaragua, the government has granted logging concessions for mahogany in the North Atlantic Autonomous Region to corporations. The region is inhabited by the Miskito, Sumu and Rama indigenous peoples. One indigenous community has already been forcibly evicted from its communal lands by the activities of a logging corporation (Shea, Elguea and Bustillo, 1997). The logging concessions violate Nicaraguan law since, according to statue, the people of the autonomous region have ownership rights over the land and resources (South and Meso American Indian Rights Center, 1998). The Nicaraguan government has a ban on mahogany exports, but claims that it lacks the resources to enforce it. Despite a Supreme Court ruling that logging concessions are illegal, the Ministry of Natural Resources has created loopholes to allow logging to continue (South and Meso American Indian Rights Center, 1998). This situation suggests that the state prioritizes revenue receipts from logging concessions over protecting the land rights of indigenous communities. Examining the impact of development in remote areas of Indonesia from an anthropological perspective, Aragon describes a civil service report from a region of South Kalimantan that advised the Forestry Commission to ignore formal rules on selective cutting on the grounds that the logging company concerned was in any event going to ignore regulations 'in order to obtain a sufficient profit' by clear-cutting the affected forested areas (Aragon, 1997). These examples all draw attention to the political context within which environmental and human rights law operates and to the economic interests that influence the efficacy of legal stipulations.

The ineffectuality of the law to provide redress for marginalized groups suffering the structural violation of environmental rights will now be exemplified through the particular case of Ecuador. Ecuador has been chosen for inquiry since the state is unique in constitutionally guaranteeing a right to an environment free from contamination.[19] As such, specific and strict criterion is stipulated in Ecuador's environmental right as opposed to the more common reference to a 'healthy' environment. The degree of environmental degradation faced by certain communities in Ecuador is nonetheless disastrous by any standard and the opportunities available for legal redress are virtually non-existent. The indigenous Huaorani are, for example, suffering extensive toxic contamination of their lands due to the activities of oil companies. The Huaorani have been unable to utilize their legal right to an environment free of contamination because, as Fabra explains:

> for the Huaorani, the difficulties of obtaining effective access to justice are insurmountable because their distinct culture and limited contact with mainstream society hamper adequate defence of their rights: most Huaorani have no knowledge or understanding of the Ecuadorian legal system, do not speak the language in which the laws are written, and have a completely different set of values than most other Ecuadorians. In addition, indigenous groups do not generally have the financial resources to engage in any legal actions against development projects on their land (Fabra, 1996, p. 254).

Despite firm and explicit legislation stipulating environmental rights in Ecuador, there is no enforcement apparatus to prevent environmental pollution or natural resource depletion (Sachs, 1995). As a result of the lack of enforcement of environmental legislation, oil companies operating in the Ecuadorian Amazon have burnt approximately 53,000,000 cubic feet of gas daily, been responsible for numerous oil spills and have despoilt the natural resource base of several indigenous groups (Rowell, 1996). Since the arrival of petrochemical MNCs in the Oriente region of Ecuador in the 1970s,[20] the populations of the Cofanes and the Siona-Secoya indigenous groups have been reduced substantially in number,[21] and the Tetetes and Tagiere have been entirely exterminated (Fabra, 1996). A spokesperson for the local environmental NGO Acción Ecológica claims that in the Oriente, 'Texaco is viewed as the chief human rights violator' since the company 'invaded the forests, killed the rivers and animals, created a health disaster and destroyed indigenous groups' (quoted in Jochnick, 1995).

The environmental impacts of oil operations in the Oriente are catastrophic by any standard. Over four million gallons of toxic wastes were released into the Oriente's environment in 1990 alone, with 90 per cent of the oil operations responsible for the pollution being run by Texaco (Kimerling, 1991; Jochnick, 1995). Toxic contaminants in the drinking water measure up to 1,000 times the levels allowed by the Environmental Protection Agency (EPA) in the US (Jochnick, 1995). Local health workers have subsequently reported increased rates of gastrointestinal problems, skin rashes, respiratory diseases, headaches, birth defects and cancers amongst the local inhabitants of the Oriente (*McSpotlight*, 1997). The contamination of the rivers has destroyed local fish stocks to the extent that malnutrition rates among primary school children average between 65 and 70 per cent (Kimerling, 1991). Kimerling reports that locals 'complain that Texaco will give them T-shirts and satchels with its emblem, but won't spend a sucre to prevent contamination to protect their health' (Kimerling, 1991).

Jochnick provides further evidence both for the corporate violations of environmental rights and for the connections between corporate, political and judicial power in Ecuador (Jochnick, 1995). In the case of several MNCs beginning oil production in the Yasuni National Park, a designated World Biosphere Reserve in Ecuador:

> lawyers initially succeeded in blocking the Conoco-Maxus operation under a constitutional provision providing for the right to a contamination-free environment and under laws prohibiting exploitation of protected areas. However, one month after ordering a stop to the Conoco-Maxus plans, the constitutional court reversed itself in the face of what one judge later described as intense pressure from government and the oil industry (Jochnick, 1995).

Ecuador exemplifies the limitations of legal environmental rights since this state alone states specific criterion for the implementation of the right to a pollution free environment. Yet, even when the problem of vagueness is overcome by an uncompromising defense of environmental protection and prohibitions on toxic contamination, legal rights are neglected by state institutions keen to accommodate the interests of corporate investors.

In summary, power relations have been argued to be crucial in both (i) legal formulation, (defining new laws) and (ii) legal implementation, (determining the efficacy of existing laws). The above focus on social power interests and law endorses the observation made by Anderson that 'legal recognition of environmental rights will not necessarily change anything unless disadvantaged groups possess economic and political power to mobilize legal institutions' (Anderson, 1996).

International Law as a Reflection of Social Power Relations

It has been argued above that the domestic legal sphere exists in a political context and tends to institutionalize the predominant power relations in society. This claim applies equally in the case of international law. International laws and treaties on human rights can be signed for many reasons, many of which are overtly political. For example:

> agreeing to international human rights law offers an opportunity for governments to be seen as decisive and responsible, to garner public support and to re-enforce traditional thinking on sovereignty and international society. By entering into human rights treaties, states are seen as responding to the concerns of their citizens on human rights issues while making few, if any, fundamental changes to the structures that are the cause of many violations (Evans and Hancock, 1998, p. 17).

Carr observed that international law, like politics, is a combination of ethics and power and cannot be properly understood independently of the political interests which it serves (Carr, 1939). Similarly focusing on the way in which international law reflects power relations, Barkun remarks that developments in international law are linked to the goal of preserving an international status quo rather than directed toward the rearrangement of political power (Barkun, 1968). The interests of global capital will now be argued to constitute the most important factor in determining the efficacy of international law. Methodologically, this claim dissolves the liberal distinction between economics, politics and law and can be validated through an assessment of the power of global capital and its influence over the political decision-making process. The global capitalist economy operates to ensure that governments prioritize the interests of capital and considerations of economic competitiveness over and above implementing international law relating to universal human rights and environmental protection.

Unlike domestic capital which is fixed in one particular state, global capital can choose in which state to invest. The purpose of this section is to assess the nature of the power that accompanies this capacity. In particular, competition amongst states for limited international investment will be argued to force governments to adopt policies favorable to investors or else risk losing capital to other states. This situation exists at the cost of states sacrificing policies aimed at environmental protection and the realization of human rights.

The growing importance of global capital is exemplified in the 16 fold growth of Foreign Direct Investment (FDI) by US based TNCs between 1950 and 1980, with a corresponding growth of less than half in domestic investment in the US economy during the same period (Ould-Mey, 1994). FDI is 'investment abroad, usually by TNCs, involving an element of control by the investor over the corporation in which the investment is made' (Griesgraber and Gunter, 1996). The flow of private capital from OECD to non-OECD states has increased from $18 billion in 1987 to $225 billion in 1996 (Flavin, 1997). The global turnover of the largest 200 TNCs now accounts for a quarter of all global economic activity (Ramonet, 1998). TNCs now control 70 per cent of world trade, 80 per cent of FDI, and 30 per cent of world GDP (Thomas, 1993; Miller, 1995; Raghaven, 1996; Corporate Europe Observatory, 1997).

Significant political influence accompanies this concentration of economic power (Makhijani, 1992). In his study of the global political economy, Korten concludes that the ability to shift production from one country to another weakens the bargaining power of each state and shifts the balance of power from the local human interest to the global corporate interest (Korten, 1995). Gill similarly argues that the globalization of productive and financial capital confers privileged rights of citizenship and representation on corporate investors and thereby constrains the democratization process (Gill, 1995). The political influence held by economic actors that confers such privileged rights resides in the desire of states to acquire the employment, transfer skills, greater revenues and information technology that MNCs provide (Lake, 1993). Corporate power constrains the choices open to governments since policies must favor capital interests or else risk an outflow of finance capital and FDI and face a possible economic crisis. In this sense, liberal democratic states are dependent upon corporations for their economic survival. Corporations naturally use this considerable political power to minimize their tax payments and to extract the maximum in incentives to invest in a particular state. This capability ensures that should any state undertake policies that work against the interests of production or finance capital, investors will respond by withdrawing their assets. It is in this sense of dependency that Cox observes that competitiveness in the global economy is the ultimate criterion of public policy (Cox with Sinclair, 1996).

One lucid example of the way in which global markets increasingly determine the policy agenda is provided by the election of the Liberals in Canada in 1993. The Liberals were elected on the platform of a spending program to create jobs (Weinberg, 1998). However, increased government spending is an anathema to international investors since it introduces inflationary pressures (Weinberg, 1998). Due to the concerns of the financial markets, and contrary to the platform upon which his government was elected, Prime Minister Jean Cretien instead cut spending on social programs (Weinberg, 1998). In the global economy, financial markets now set de facto limits on policy choices of even the most powerful states, preventing the adoption of policies that would conflict with the competitiveness of capital. Global financial markets can now cause currency devaluations, force up interests rates, prompt capital flight, increase government borrowing and can even prompt bank failures in states whose governments do not prioritize pro market policies (Cox with Sinclair, 1996; Korten, 1997).

The power of global capital constitutes a decisive political consideration in an age of globalization. Capital flows into those states most successful in increasing competitiveness and punishes those that work against corporate interests with the very real threat to relocate abroad. A spokesperson for the European Roundtable of Industrialists has for example asserted that 'governments must recognise today that every economic and social system in the world is competing with all of the others to attract the footloose businesses' (quoted in Corporate Europe Observatory, 1997). Exemplifying this process, McDonnell's president of operations in China, Peter Chapman, explains that 'we're in the business of making money for our shareholders. If we have to put jobs and technology in other countries, then we go ahead and do it' (quoted in Greider, 1997).

To maximize their competitiveness, corporations are keen to minimize private costs, such as those relating to labor and environmental controls and fiscal payments (Cox, 1987). The political power held by corporations as outlined above forces the adoption of pro-corporate policies by governments around the world at the expense of environmental human rights. Typifying the trend of adopting political policies that prioritize the interests of foreign capital producers, the Philippine government has placed advertisements in the global business press reading 'to attract companies like yours ... . we have felled mountains, razed jungles, filled swamps, moved rivers, relocated towns ... . all to make it easier for you and your business to do business here' (quoted in Korten, 1995). Korten notes that this claim was not mere hyperbole (Korten, 1995).

The recent history of the tuna-canning industry illustrates how globalization accommodates the interests of corporate investors. The wages in California averaged $17 an hour when the tuna-canning industry was located in that state, so the industry moved to Puerto Rico, where the wages were only $7 an hour. Then the industry moved to American Somoa, where wages were $3.50 an hour, then to Equador where workers receive $1 an hour and finally to Thailand, where the wage rate averages $4 per day (Brazier, 1998). Sweatshops epitomize capital mobility and free trade in the global economy. As in the case of the tuna-canning industry, garment industry giants often locate according to the lowest labor costs (*Sweatshop Watch*, 1998). Many garment workers in the Third World subsequently work in oppressive conditions for less than a living wage, for example, in Vietnam garment workers average US \$0.12 per hour (*Sweatshop Watch*, 1998). Therefore, the structure of global capitalism determines that wages in the periphery of the global economy remain below the poverty line. Goldsmith explains that:

> In most developed nations, the cost to an average manufacturing company of paying its workforce is an amount equal to between 25 per cent and 30 per cent of sales. If such a company decides to maintain in its home country only its head offices and sales force, while transferring its production to a low-cost area, it will save about 20 per cent of sales volume. Thus, a company with sales of 500 million dollars will increase its pre-tax profits by up to 100 million dollars every year. If, on the other hand, it decides to maintain its production at home, the enterprise will be unable to compete with low-cost imports and will perish (Goldsmith, 1994).

Low wages in the global economy serves the interests of global capital at the expense of workers who suffer continued poverty and the denial of economic rights (Weissman, 1997). Corporate profits depend increasingly on keeping wages low and polluting the environment (Woollacott, 1995). To attract foreign investors, governments have suppressed unions and held down wages, benefits, and labor standards (Korten, 1995). The incentive to minimize costs can be seen to lead directly to violations of human rights. For example, in May 1995, banana workers in the Cowpen region of Belize established the United Banners Banana Workers' Union (UBBWU) in response to the working conditions on Fyffes farms where workers had no access to medical care and drew water from a source contaminated with pesticide residues (Doyle, 1996). Fyffes responded by firing 15 union executives (Doyle, 1996). The general irrelevance of human rights to corporations is illustrated in a Boston based survey that found only 10 per cent of US TNCs had any guidelines at all on overseas human rights (Forcese, 1997).[22]

The corporate interests that determine violations of economic human rights also ensure deepening environmental degradation. Williams claims that 'direct foreign investment is influenced by a range of factors, and the share of environmental costs in output value is too small to be an important component in firms' decision-making' (Williams, 1993). In contrast to this assertion, Agarwal and Narain argue that 'increasingly strong pollution control measures in the West have resulted in numerous industries, which are extremely polluting and dangerous, moving into the Third World' (Agarwal and Narain, 1992). The following argument contends that, of these conflicting two positions, Agarwal and Narain are correct in their assessment and that the tactic of externalizing costs to maximize profit is indeed an important consideration for corporations making location decisions.

Knight notes that to accommodate the best interests of foreign producers in India, forestry regulations 'appear to have been loosened' for the pulp and paper industry and mining laws 'watered down' to benefit mining corporations (Knight, 1997a). Also in India, the chairperson of the dyes and pigments manufacturers association acknowledged that MNCs are now moving into India because of stronger pollution control laws in the West (Agarwal and Narain, 1992). Rowell reports that in its negotiations on terms of investment with the state of Goa in India, Du Pont drew up a contract that specifically exonerates the company from any liability should its industrial operations result in damage to either the environment or worker's health (Rowell, 1996). In his study into business investments in Nigeria, Frynas concluded that, 'governments have often sought to attract foreign investors by permitting ecological dumping, in other words, lower environmental standards' (Frynas, 1998). The Rare Earth company relocated to Malaysia after it was prevented from operating in Japan due to a tightening of Japanese environmental laws. Its factory processed monazite for electronic components from chlorides and carbonates. Radioactive thorium hydroxide is produced as a by-product of this process and as the least costly option, this has been dumped near to villages in the Malaysian state of Perak where the company plant has been relocated (Harding, 1996). The Australian mining company BHP is responsible for the daily dumping of 80,000 tons of tailings into the Ok Tedi and Fly rivers at the Ok Tedi copper and gold mine in Papua New Guinea (Imhof, 1996). Responding to compensation writs for environmental damage filed in August 1995 by 30,000 inhabitants of the Fly River Basin, BHP drafted legislation for the Papua New Guinea Parliament that subjected anyone who sued BHP to fines of up to $75,000 (Imhof, 1996).

Graf summarizes that 'hundreds of Northern plants have been relocated to the Third World specifically to avoid the costs of higher safety and health standards in the North' (Graf, 1992). Tetreault similarly concludes, 'the incentive to reduce costs creates a trend for MNCs to pick up and locate anywhere that it can maximize its ability to externalize costs' (Tetreault, 1988). At a time when the value and extent of FDI was a fraction of what it is today, the Brundtland Commission estimated that MNCs would have to spend $14 billion on pollution controls on their plants located in the Third World to raise them to the environmental standards stipulated in the US (*The Ecologist*, 1993).

The citing of examples, however widespread, is methodologically insufficient to demonstrate that the political power held by global capital is the structural feature of the global economy that derogates environmental human rights. To demonstrate that the capitalist organization of the global economy allows capital to pursue its own interests at the expense of the claimed universal environmental human rights, it is necessary to identify the specific traits of capitalism that cause corporations to violate such rights. The method now adopted to undertake this task is to isolate and examine the record where capitalism operates in its purest form. Such an examination reveals that it is inherent to the ontology of capitalism to cause structural violation of environmental human rights.

Global capital is accorded almost complete freedom in Export Processing Zones (EPZs). EPZs are free trade areas that are exempt from tax, labor and environmental regulations. EPZs therefore reflect the corporate interest to minimize government regulations, perceived as an anathema by industry. For example ERT secretary-general Keith Richardson claimed in relation to environmental protection; 'the wrong thing to do is to just go around and publish new taxes and new regulations. It causes a lot of trouble' (quoted in Corporate Europe Observatory, 1997). Operating in EPZs, foreign investors are free to choose their own level of wages and pollution. This most closely resembles a pure capitalist structure since restraints on the process of production and accumulation are entirely absent. The following discussion argues that the minimization of private costs under conditions of capitalism necessarily results in the violation of the claimed environmental human rights.

To attract foreign investors, Kenya provides EPZ investors with a ten year tax holiday (Weissman, 1996a). Egypt offers investors complete exemption from all taxes (Weissman, 1996a). In addition to a 10 year complete exemption from taxes, investors in Cameroon's EPZ are given flexibility in hiring and firing workers (Weissman, 1996a). The maquiladora is an EPZ in Mexico, just to the South of the US border, that contains over two thousand TNC plants. It was created by the 1965 maquila program between the US and Mexican governments that was designed to develop the border region. Corporate relocation to the maquiladora is encouraged through providing exemptions from environmental and workers rights legislation (Korten; 1995; Rounds, 1995). TNCs operating in the maquiladora are, for example, allowed to fire and blacklist trade union leaders. Korten describes the subsequent context of human rights violations:

> To maintain the kind of conditions transnational corporations prefer, the Mexican government has denied workers the right to form independent labour unions and has held wage increases far below productivity increases. In the summer of 1992, more than 14,000 Mexican workers at a Volkswagen plant turned down a contract negotiated by their government-dominated labour union. The company fired them all, and a Mexican court upheld the company's action. In 1987, in the midst of a bitter two-month strike in Mexico, Ford Motor Company tore up its union contract, fired 3,400 workers, and cut wages by 45 per cent. When the workers rallied around dissident labour leaders, gunmen hired by the official government-dominated union shot workers at random in the factory (Korten, 1995, p. 129).

The rights of workers are at best neglected and at worst systematically violated by the focus on allocative efficiency institutionalized in the global capitalist economy. Corporations have a similarly poor record in the case of environmental protection in the maquiladora. Firms located in the maquiladora have been criticized for failing to provide their work force with basic health and safety precautions (Korten, 1995). Exempt from environmental regulations, toxic waste has been 'indiscriminately dumped' in the maquiladora area, and '75 per cent of the industries were dumping toxic wastes directly into the public waterways' (Johnston and Button, 1994; Herrmann, 1995). Residents in the maquiladora region are living in 'a virtual cesspool', suffering high rates of infectious diseases, cancers, neurological disorders and birth defects caused by the toxins (Herrmann, 1995). Clusters of communities afflicted by unusually high rates of congenital disease, such as anencephaly, a fatal birth defect in which a child is born without a fully developed brain, have been reported in specific neighborhoods (Herrmann, 1995).

Assessing the full impact of the physical damage to health caused by the systematic pollution is hampered by the absence of right-to-know laws in Mexico, problematizing efforts to establish accurate details of amounts and types of toxic chemicals in the environment (Nusser and Haurwitz, 1998). The scale of this phenomenon should not be underestimated. In December 1996 the maquiladora assembly sector was second only to oil in generating foreign income for Mexico (Hall, 1996). The examples cited above cannot be discounted as rogue commercial actors acting on the periphery of the global economy. They indicate the choices made by business freed from social responsibilities and able to follow their own private interest defined in terms of competitiveness and efficiency, that is the 'pure' form of capitalism. Should any corporation prioritize social or environmental concerns over profit maximization they would be penalized or eliminated by the structural forces of the market that rewards allocative efficiency. For example, the AmeriMex Maquiladora Fund was formed specifically to acquire US companies that have resisted relocation to the maquiladora (Korten, 1995). As explained in the prospectus of the AmeriMex Maquiladora Fund:

> The Fund will purchase established domestic United States companies suitable for maquiladora acquisitions, wherein a part or all of the manufacturing operations will be relocated to Mexico to take advantage of the cost of labor ... . We anticipate that manufacturing companies that experience fully loaded, gross labor costs in the $7–$10 per hour range in the US may be able to utilize labor in a Mexican maquiladora at fully loaded, gross labor cost of $1.15–$1.50 per hour. Though each situation may vary, it is estimated that this could translate into annual savings of $10,000–$17,000 per employee involved in the relocated manufacturing operations (quoted in Korten, 1995, pp. 213–14).

The Interest of Capital Accumulation as the Criterion for the Efficacy of International Law

The foregoing discussion has claimed that the nature of the political power wielded by global capital encourages states to allow low cost production at the expense of continuing human rights violations and the socialization of costs through pollution. It will now be argued that power relations determine the efficacy of international law. In particular, the interests of capital determine the generally ineffectual enforcement of international environmental law and human rights law relative to the strict enforcement of international trade, commerce and property laws. The strict enforcement of global investment rights suggests that international law can be vigorously enforced in specific circumstances, a possibility that refutes the realist argument that international law *per se* is ineffectual.

Infractions of the provisions of international human rights law are notoriously endemic and those responsible for violations rarely face any sanctions. Similarly, in the case of global environmental politics, legally binding treaties are seldom agreed and are more rarely still backed by sanctions or enforcement mechanisms, as will now be exemplified in the international response to the problem of climate change.

In August 1990 the Intergovernmental Panel on Climate Change (IPCC) released its *First Assessment Report* that estimated 60–80 per cent cuts in carbon dioxide emissions would be required to stabilize atmospheric carbon dioxide levels (Greenpeace, 2001). The international community of states has since conspicuously failed to agree legally binding reductions in greenhouse gas emissions remotely resembling this figure despite holding a number of high profile conferences on the subject. The 1992 UN Framework Convention on Climate Change (UNFCCC) committed 154 states to reduce carbon dioxide emissions to 1990 levels by the year 2000 (Corporate Europe Observatory, 1998). Subsequent Conference of Parties (CoPs) in 1995, 1996, and in 1997, saw numerous unsuccessful attempts to set these commitments in a legally binding treaty. In December 1997 the Kyoto Protocol was agreed. Under the (non-legally binding) terms of the protocol, states signed up for overall nominal reduction in carbon dioxide emissions of 5.2 per cent by 2010 against 1990 levels (Greenpeace, 2001). A climate conference was held in the Hague in November 2000 with the intention of making the provisions of the Kyoto protocol legally binding (McKie, 2000). However, talks broke down on the 25 November when European delegates rejected a US proposal that would have allowed the US a smaller reduction in carbon dioxide emissions than that which they agreed to make at Kyoto (McKie, 2000). The seventh CoP, held in Marrakesh between 29 October and 10 November 2001 finally resulted in a 245 page compilation of rules and procedures through which to incorporate the Kyoto protocol in international environmental law (Australian Greenhouse Office, 2002).

The effects of the Kyoto protocol and Marrakesh agreement are practically irrelevant in terms of climate change science. Models typically project an expected temperature increase of 2.1 degrees by 2100 to be mitigated to an increase of 1.9 degrees if carbon dioxide emissions are reduced in line with the Kyoto protocol (Lomborg, 2001). The net effect of this is to postpone an increase of 2.1 degrees by six years (Lomborg, 2001). This achievement, if it can be called an achievement, is more than negated by the decision of George Bush to pull the US out of international legal commitments on carbon dioxide reductions (Brown, 2002b). Consumerism has been defended with almost religious fervor by successive political administrations in the US. Emitting 24 per cent of global carbon dioxide emissions, the US has only 4 per cent of the world's population (Greenpeace, 2001). Between 1990 and 1997 US greenhouse gas emissions had risen by 8 per cent, compared to the 5.2 per cent reduction between 1990 and 2000 that was agreed in the Framework Convention of 1992 (Karacs, Dejevsky and Schoon, 1997). This dismal record is likely to further deteriorate under the Bush administration. The senior US climate negotiator Harlan Watson, has recently stated that it is wishful thinking to believe that the US would 'trash its economy' to take action on climate change (Brown, 2002b). Recent figures report that the US government expects a 30 per cent increase of carbon dioxide emissions on 1990 levels by 2010 (Brown, 1998f). This figure will almost certainly have to be revised further upwards since the announcement from President George Bush that hundreds of new fossil fuel power stations will be constructed in response to the energy shortages produced by the consumerist way of life.

International law has not been effective in addressing climate change since such a result contradicts the power relations that operate in the global political economy. In particular, cuts in fossil fuel usage would constrain economic growth and the opulent lifestyle of the present beneficiaries of capitalism, the very ideological goals economic rationality is predicated upon. The dismal record of international human rights and environmental law stands in direct contrast to the broadly successful enforcement of international trade and property laws (Evans, 2000). Exemplifying the privileged position accorded to trade related international law compared to international human rights law, the US Clinton Administrations put pressure on state legislatures not to pass pro human rights laws that might conflict with World Trade Organization (WTO) rules (*Public Citizen*, 1998a). This development followed the imposition by Maryland of investment and trade sanctions against the then military dictatorship in Nigeria and measures imposed by Massachusetts against the dictatorship in Burma (*Public Citizen*, 1998a). In both of these cases the sanctions were introduced in a response to the egregious use of torture and violations of the right to life in the targeted states (*Public Citizen*, 1998a). The evident prioritization of trade based international law over human rights legislation by the US in this instance is especially notable because of the privileged position enjoyed by this particular state in determining the priorities and direction of the world order (Evans, 1996).

International laws defending the interests of business have been successfully enforced to protect market access for global corporations. Indeed, free trade laws have been used to force developing states to allow imports of Western goods that are even known to damage health, such as tobacco products (Chomsky, 1992b). In 1991 free trade laws were used by the multinational chemical company Hoechst to force a reversal of the Philippine government's ban on the pesticide endosulfan, even though use of the pesticide is banned in the US due to its known deleterious effects on health (Sachs, 1995). In 1989, the US General Accounting Office estimated that a quarter of the pesticides exported by US MNCs were banned domestically (Sachs, 1995).

A further example of the successful implementation of free trade laws at the expense of the human right to health is provided in the case of baby foods in Guatemala. In 1983, Guatemala adopted the International Code of Marketing of Breast Milk Substitutes into its law. The code was designed to protect the lives of infants by promoting breast-feeding over breast-milk substitutes. The law forbids the use of pictures of babies on baby food labels. The food manufacturer Gerber threatened Guatemala with trade sanctions under GATT rules for not allowing it to use its trademark of the Gerber baby in the marketing of its baby food products. In 1995 the government stopped enforcing the law and the following year the Guatemalan Supreme Court ruled that imported products were exempt from the ban on the use of baby photos on foods (Mokhiber, 1996).

Unlike the human rights regime and international environmental laws, international economic institutions, specifically the NAFTA, the GATT and the WTO, have been specifically designed and resourced to ensure compliance through the imposition of graduated sanctions against transgressors. Japan has, for instance, successfully used GATT provisions to reverse national bans on the export of unprocessed timber from Indonesia, Malaysia, Brazil, Thailand and the US (Agarwal and Narain, 1992). These exports bans were introduced to protect forested areas from unsustainable logging practices and their repeal has directly contributed to continued deforestation in the affected states (Agarwal and Narain, 1992). The WTO has institutionalized rule compliance through a dispute settlement system (DSS) backed by a graduated system of sanctions (Chimni, 1999). As Chimni points out, the lament that international law is not law as it lacks enforcement mechanisms, categorically does not apply in the instance of the WTO (Chimni, 1999).

NAFTA institutionalizes the privileged position of capital interests over human rights or environmental concerns since under its provisions there are no transnational rights other than those accorded to capital (Gill, 1995). Although NAFTA incorporates side agreements protecting workers rights and environmental considerations, these have been properly criticized for being underfunded and lacking adequate enforcement mechanisms juxtaposed to the provisions relating to free trade (Thomas and Weber, 1999). The ability of NAFTA to enforce, through law international, corporate interests is illustrated in a case brought to a NAFTA panel by the Ethyl corporation. In April 1997 Canada imposed a ban on the import and inter-provincial transport of the petrochemical additive MMT. MMT is a manganese-based compound that is added to gasoline to reduce engine knocking. However, the primary ingredient of MMT is manganese, a known human neurotoxin that prompted the Canadian ban. Ethyl is the only manufacturer of MMT (*Corporate Watch*, 1998g). As *Public Citizen* reports:

> Ethyl responded to Canada's public health law with a $250 million lawsuit claiming the law violated its investor protections under NAFTA. Ethyl argued that the law was an "expropriation" of its assets or an action "tantamount to expropriation" because it would eliminate profits Ethyl expected to earn through Canadian sales of the additive. The Canadian government settled the NAFTA suit ... agreeing to pay Ethyl $13 million in damages and to cover the company's legal costs. It will also proclaim publicly that MMT is "safe" – in direct contradiction of the view of its national environmental protection agency (*Public Citizen*, 1998b).

This case illustrates the way in which corporate interests have been privileged in NAFTA rules (Weissman, 1996b; Chomsky, 1998a). The Ethyl lawsuit is also instructive since it demonstrates that international law can indeed be enforced, provided that this is conducive to business concerns. International human rights law and international environmental legislation that threaten business interests can be violated with relative impunity not because of an inherent inability to enforce international laws but rather because the efficacy of international law is determined by power relations. In particular, international trade laws have been successfully enforced, even when these conflict with domestic environmental health legislation (*Public Citizen*, 1998b).

The week following the settlement of the Ethyl case the Canadian government faced another lawsuit that similarly illustrates the ability of corporate interests to use the economic provisions of NAFTA to force the reversal of environmental protection laws. In an attempt to reduce the pollution resulting from the trade in toxic wastes, Canada banned the export of Poly-chlorinated Biphenyl (PCB) contaminated waste in 1995. In early 1997 the ban was revoked after US firms announced they would challenge the validity of the law under NAFTA provisions. The US based PCB treatment company, Myers Inc., also demanded an undisclosed sum from the Canadian government for profits lost during the 15 month period of the ban. This case exemplifies how NAFTA empowers a company to demand compensation from states for environmental protection legislation that restricts sales (Rangnes, 1998).

A juxtaposition of international trade law on the one hand with international environmental and human rights law on the other, demonstrates that the criterion determining whether international legislation is effectively implemented in practice is that of power relations. Reflecting upon the centrality of capital interests in global society, Chimni accurately summarizes that 'changes in international law over the past two decades have made it an instrument for safeguarding transnational capital' (Chimni, 1999).

Conclusion

The evident trend towards the formal acknowledgment of environmental human rights in domestic and international legislation starkly contrasts the continuing environmental degradation, toxic pollution of eco-systems and iniquitous land ownership determined by the global political economy. Examining the political component of law, it has been argued in this chapter that environmental human rights have been largely formulated in vacuous terms. By officially recognizing environmental rights, formal political institutions have promoted the veneer of responding to environmental concerns whilst simultaneously facilitating a continued focus on economic efficiency by eviscerating the rights of any effective impact. Isolated but noteworthy exceptions notwithstanding, environmental human rights have been devised and implemented by courts and politicians in ways that accommodate existing economic relations. The evisceration of environmental rights has been compounded by the lack of enforcement mechanisms and sanctions against individual and structural transgressors (Johnston, 1997).

This chapter has argued that law is an integral aspect of the hegemonic power apparatus rather than an impartial rules-based mechanism that it is characteristically and mistakenly understood to be. In both domestic and international manifestations, law has become a mechanism to safeguard and promote the interests powerful corporate groups in civil society. This claim has been exemplified by juxtaposing international trade laws on the one hand with environmental and human rights law on the other. Whereas law is increasingly being expanded in response to environmental problems and human rights contraventions, wording is typically vague, sanctions noticeable by their absence and enforcement mechanisms can be accurately categorized as wholly inadequate. Consequently, the efficacy of international human rights and environmental law to prevent ongoing violations of human rights and ecological degradation must surely be questioned. This stands in stark contrast to the effective use of international trade law to protect the vested interests of powerful Western corporations. Trade rules safeguard the massive agricultural subsidies provided to agribusinesses based in the developed world whilst simultaneously providing a mechanism through which to force open markets in developing states to Western corporations and investors.

An examination of the subject of environment human rights that is restricted to analysis of legislation is misplaced since it confuses cause for effect. Whereas a methodological approach based on legal analysis presupposes that considerations of jurisprudence and the drafting of new legislation can determine social relations, the analysis conducted in this chapter argued that the converse is the case. It is not only the assertion here that legally stipulated environmental human rights are not being implemented in practice, it is rather that they cannot be realized in the global political economy given (i) the current configuration of power in civil society that favors economic values over ecological protection and (ii) the ideological and functional nature of law as a hegemonic instrument reflecting powerful social interests.

The criticisms made on the ability of law to implement environmental human rights must be properly differentiated from the values embodied in the legal rights themselves. The concepts expressed in legally existing environmental rights suggest an alternative social order that rejects the supremacy of economic rationality. The problems encountered in realizing environmental human rights reside in the vague wording of both domestic and international environmental rights and in the subsequent inadequate implementation that subordinates environmental human rights to economic considerations. For both domestic and international environmental human rights to be realized it is necessary to first address the power relations that determine the capabilities of law. The effective implementation of environmental human rights law is conditional upon a general change in the social values upon which political cultures are constructed. Rather than petitioning political and legal institutions to enact pro-environment changes, the focus of attention of anti-systemic forces could instead be placed on campaigning for greater recognition of ecological values in society. Until this is achieved, the courts and policy-making forums alike will remain the juridical and political expressions of the capitalist economy.

The following two chapters articulate the perspective of ecological rationality to offer an alternative interpretation of existing human rights legislation and to thereby establish the political foundations of the two claimed environmental human rights.

Notes

1   Ontario Environmental Bill of Rights Act (Bill 26, December 1993); article 123, 1979 Peruvian Constitution; article 2, section 16, 1987 Philippines Constitution; section 18, Hungarian Constitution; article 69, Croatian Constitution; article 66, Portuguese Constitution; article 32, Italian Constitution; article 42, Russian Federation Constitution; section 18 of 1995 ammendment to the Swedish Constitution; article 46, Constitution of Belarus; article 26, Constitution of Kazakhstan; article 45, para 1, 1978 Spanish Constitution; article 110b, Norwegian Constitution.
2   Article 19, para 2.
3   Article 24, Greek 1975 Constitution. In 1983 Austria amended its Constitution to include the protection of the environment as a task of the state, as did Austria in 1984, Belgium and Germany in 1994 and Finland in 1995.
4   Response to research questionnaire received from Gia Abramia, Georgian Center for Environmental Research, 8 May 1999.
5   Article 41 of the 1994 reformed Argentinean constitution, response to research questionnaire received from Gustavo Saltiel, Ministry of Justice, Argentina, 4 October 1999.
6   Principle 1, 'Declaration on the Human Environment', *Report of the United Nations Conference on the Human Environment*, New York (United Nations, 1973), UN Doc. A/CONF.48/14/Rev.1.
7   Resolution 45/94.
8   Article 12, para 2.
9   Article 24, *African Charter on Human and People's Rights*, 27 June 1981, Organisation of African Unity, Document CAB/LEG/67/3/Rev.5.
10 Article 11, para 1, 'Protocol of San Salvador', *Additional Protocol to the American Convention on Human Rights in the Area of Economic, Social and Cultural Rights*, 17 November 1988, San Salvador, OAS Doc OEA/Ser.A/44.
11 Article 24, 1989.
12 Final Report of the Special Rapporteur, *Human Rights and the Environment*, UN Doc. E/CN.4/Sub.2/1994/9 (6 July 1994).
13 See, for example, ICESCR (1966) and ICCPR (1966).
14 Principle 2.
15 The Instituto Ecuatoriano de Reforma Agraria y Colonizacion granted the land title by Order of 3 April 1990.
16 Article 46, (1).

17 Article 1.
18 Amongst other instances, gold miners pollute rivers, scare away game and introduce epidemics of flu and malaria into Yanomami communities.
19 Incorporated into the Ecuadorian constitution in 1983.
20 13 million hectares of tropical rainforest lying at the headwaters of the Amazon river network.
21 The number of Cofan Indians has reduced from 70,000 to 3,000 between 1975 and 1995.
22 The study focused on major US retailers and brand name goods manufacturers.

Chapter 5

The Human Right to an Environment Free from Toxic Pollution

Airy-fairy environmentalists were attacked by Mrs Thatcher yesterday in a strong call for realism over pollution ... . There was no way we could do without "the great car economy" she warned, because the economy would collapse if we did.
– Kate Parkin, *Daily Express*, 17 March 1990

Introduction

Chapter 3 described how a number of environmental activists and advocacy groups have claimed that toxic pollution violates human rights. The same connection has also been made by several academics. Blackstone states for example that 'none of our rights can be realized without a livable environment' (Blackstone, 1974). Shue identifies access to clean air and water as a basic subsistence right (Shue, 1980). It is therefore evident that both activists and academics have identified a capacity for violations of human rights to be mediated via environmental degradation. Yet it is also evident that the precise nature of this form of violation tends to be implicitly presupposed as axiomatic, rather than being explicitly demonstrated. This is a notable shortcoming given the legal position that toxic pollution neither constitutes harm nor necessarily causes human rights violations.

This chapter makes the case for recognizing the human right to an environment free from toxic pollution. This right will be derived from analysis of (i) political philosophy and (ii) the politics of law. The section on political philosophy focuses on differentiating capitalism from liberalism. Whereas capitalism condones the routine production of toxic pollution when this is required to achieve conditions of allocative efficiency, liberalism must necessarily oppose this process because of the centrality of the harm principle to liberal political philosophy. If an action is defined as harmful, it must logically be opposed by liberal thinking in order to protect those individuals who would otherwise suffer. This so called harm principle, also known as non-malfeasance, sanctions collective action to prevent individuals from being injured by others, even when the 'others' involved are a large majority of the population. The body of an individual is, by definition, harmed by exposure to toxic pollutants. If a pollutant were not harmful, then it would logically be categorized as non-toxic rather than as toxic. A person exposed to toxins produced by the actions of another can logically be said to have been harmed since the person's health and well-being is not as good as it would have been in the absence of that intervention.

The epidemiological evidence demonstrates that toxic pollutants violate human rights to life; to the security of the person (non-intervention); and to health (ICCPR articles 3,6,9; Universal Declaration article 3). It is necessary to recognize the claimed right to an environment free from toxic contamination to realize these legal human rights since exposure to certain pollutants are known to damage cellular structures. Damage incurred on cells can result in the development of subsequent illnesses such as cancer. Increased air pollution in Chinese cities has, for example, been responsible for raising the death rate from cancer by 6.2 per cent and from lung cancer by 18.5 per cent between 1988 and 1995 (Swope *et al.*, 1997). It is because of the ability of pollutants to harm human physiology that environmental conditions are specifically covered by health and safety employment rights (European Social Charter part 1, article 3; American Protocol article 7; International Covenant on Economic, Social and Cultural Rights article 7c). It is paradoxical that exposure to dangerous substances at the workplace is now strictly controlled by workers rights, while the exposure of the general population to the same pollutants has hitherto been generally disregarded as a human rights issue.

The analysis of the politics of law in the second part of the chapter examines why toxic pollution continues to be classified as 'public nuisance' and 'risk' rather than as 'harm' under law. This classification is argued to have been constructed to accommodate the systematic degradation of the environment that is required to achieve sustained economic growth and conditions of allocative efficiency.

Only those activities classified as harm need to be prohibited under law. Categorizing pollution as risk and public nuisance therefore accommodates ongoing toxic pollution within legally specified limits. This research demonstrates that toxic pollution does constitute harm, legal denials to the contrary notwithstanding. This conclusion is reached by employing Feinberg's definition of harm (Feinberg, 1984). Although Feinberg himself strongly denied that toxic pollution constitutes harm, this assertion is found to be in logical contradiction to the impartial implementation of his stated definition. The epidemiological evidence demonstrates that for the principle of non-malfeasance and existing human rights stipulations to be realized, the toxic pollution of the environment must be prevented. Herein lies the paradox for law since this outcome would contradict conditions of capitalism. This paradox is argued to explain the continuing refusal of the courts to acknowledge toxic pollution as constituting harm and to thereby accommodate the damage to ecosystems and human health alike that result from capitalist modes of production and the consumerist lifestyle.

An environment free from toxic pollution differs from an environment free from toxic chemicals since a number of toxins found in the environment are produced from natural, rather than anthropogenic sources (Simpkins and William, 1992). The argument that, since toxic chemicals occur naturally in the environment, the anthropogenic production of toxic pollution is exempt from violating human rights is an invalid claim. Nature cannot cause violations of rights since human rights are restricted to considerations of political organization in human societies. By way of analogy, thousands of people suffer injury or deaths in hurricanes each year. The claim that the weather had violated their rights to life and non-interference is however nonsensical. In the following discussion of toxic pollution, the focus of attention is therefore restricted to anthropogenically produced, rather than naturally occurring, toxic substances since these alone can be termed pollutants and sanctioned or prevented by political choices.

It is important at the outset to differentiate between various pollutants. Non toxic pollutants such as carbon dioxide may pose great risks for climate change and habitat change but have no deleterious effects on human health and consequently emissions could continue with no violation of liberal principles. A focus on the well being of biodiversity could draw attention to non-toxic pollution as a source of harm. However this extended notion of harm takes into account the interest of non-human life and would consequently not even be considered by a legal system principally constructed to protect the rights of individual people, especially rights to private property. As such, a theoretical defense of the environmental human right from a position of ecological ethics is not attempted here.

A second category of pollutants only harms human health when a threshold level is reached. Exposure to amounts of such pollutants under the threshold level does not constitute harm. The non-interference and harm principles are only violated when exposure levels exceed threshold levels.

The third category of pollutants relates to toxic substances to which there is no safe exposure level. It is this category of pollutants that must be eliminated for the liberal principles of harm and non-interference to stand since these toxic chemicals are harmful to human life by virtue of their ontological property to cause cellular damage. It is this third category of pollutants that is focused upon in this chapter and a particular emphasis will be placed on toxic air pollutants emitted in vehicle exhaust fumes.

The Differentiation of Capitalism from Liberalism

A juxtaposition of capitalism with liberal political theory will now isolate the former from the theory of justice that is commonly, and erroneously, given in its defense. Capitalism is examined here since the capitalist economy requires systematic environmental degradation and toxic pollution to achieve sustained economic growth and allocative efficiency. The focus on the liberal paradigm for the comparison with capitalism has been chosen for two reasons; (i) the ongoing prominence of liberalism in political philosophy and (ii) common confusion between liberalism and capitalism. Whereas capitalism will be identified as necessarily advocating violations of the claimed human right to an environment free from toxic pollution, liberalism will, in contrast, be found to necessarily support the right.

Liberalism and capitalism can be differentiated through the perceptions of rights and responsibilities promoted by each theory. Liberalism embodies a vision of a polity comprised of citizens equal in political power, rights and duties. Characteristically focusing on market relations, capitalism in contrast identifies individuals as consumers rather than as citizens. Capitalism subsequently elevates private property rights over human rights. Capitalism furthermore accommodates the unequal distribution of wealth and power through endorsing a narrow notion of equal opportunity rather than any more substantive version of equality (Lentner, 2000). Whereas liberalism is a (albeit broad and varied) philosophical theory that conceptualizes a notion of just conduct in social relations between individuals based on autonomy, consent and non-malfeasance, capitalism is predicated upon the pursuit of private interest at the expense of harming others, as accommodated by law.

The tradition of political liberalism spans a wide range of nuance positions that can be categorized into two broad variants, (i) utilitarian liberals inspired by Mill's focus on general welfare and (ii) deontological Kantian liberals who focus on justice as universal rights (Postema, 1994). Both variants proscribe actions that result in harm to others in society. This principle of liberalism was established in 1672 when Pufendorf ranked 'first and noblest' the requirement 'that no man (sic) hurt another' (quoted in Goodin, 1985). Thereafter, liberal theory has advocated clear limits to the liberty of each individual to protect others from harm. Mill for example concluded that:

> The sole end for which mankind are warranted, individually or collectively, in interfering with the liberty of action of any of their number, is self-protection. That the only purpose for which power can be rightfully exercised over any member of a civilized community, against his will, is to prevent harm to others (Mill, 1994, p. 9).

According to Mill, not only is it permissible for society to prevent an individual from engaging in an activity that harms others, but there exists a *primâ facie* case for criminalizing such actions and for punishing the transgressor (Mill, 1994). This defense of non-malfeasance is noteworthy since Mill is often cited in defense of a utilitarian interpretation of liberalism which focuses more on the overall good of society rather than on individual rights. Yet even here, acts that harm others are clearly categorized as illegitimate. Such a categorization resonates the Lockean imperative that 'no-one ought to harm another in his Life, Liberty or Possessions' (Mill, 1994). Goodin points out that this principle has subsequently been institutionalized in Western jurisprudence: 'Non-malfeasance-the duty not to harm others-constitutes the common thread linking criminal and civil law, both historically and analytically' (Goodin, 1985). There is consequently general agreement amongst liberal political theorists that the need to prevent harm to other parties is always an appropriate reason for legal coercion (Feinberg, 1984). This harm principle actualizes the conceptual autonomy of individuals that lies at the heart of liberal claims to rights. Exemplifying such claims to autonomy, Robinson justifies those rights that ensure mutual respect for a principle of non-interference (Robinson, 1995). Hart similarly defends the equal right of all people to be free and characteristically for a liberal rights theorist, defines freedom in negative terms, thereby advocating the right not to be interfered with so long as actions performed do not harm anyone else (Hart, 1984).

Capitalism is, in stark contrast to liberalism, characterized by an inability to advance any theory of justice beyond a dogmatic advocacy of private property rights, the market mechanism and an account of individual identity that reduces people to the status of workers, traders and consumers. The desire for economic growth in general and personal material gain in particular replaces impartiality as the central imperative for structuring society. The subsequent damage incurred by capitalism is imposed on both the environment and fellow citizens (Greider, 1997).

The distinction between capitalism and liberalism can be vividly illustrated through examining the issue of toxic pollution. A certain degree of confusion currently exists in relation to the status of toxic pollution in liberal and capitalist systems. Machan for example contends that health-damaging pollutants contravene the rules of capitalism:

Under capitalism any pollution which would most likely lead to harm being done to persons who have not consented to being put at risk of such harm would have to be legally prohibited ... . This may lead to an increase in the cost of production or to the elimination of some production processes, and, in either case, to increased unemployment and increased hardship. Still, that would be the consistent way to apply the capitalist-libertarian principle in the legal system. The international or negligent violation of individual rights, including the rights of life, liberty and property, must be legally prohibited. To permit the production to continue on grounds that this will sustain employment would be exactly like permitting the continuation of other crimes on grounds that allowing them creates jobs for others ... . No one has a right to benefit from acts or practices that violate the rights of others (Machan, 1984, p. 97).

To endorse this interpretation is, however, to confuse capitalism with liberalism. Liberalism requires the cessation of pollution for the reasons which Machan mistakenly ascribes to capitalism. Whereas both systems promote private interests, liberalism necessarily restricts this pursuit according to (i) the rights of other individuals and (ii) the harm principle. In contrast, capitalism condones a focus on private interest at the expense of harming other individuals when this achieves the desired goals of allocative efficiency and economic growth that together constitute the core principles of economic rationality (chapter 1). The capitalist economy not only accommodates the corporate interest to pollute but indeed rewards such action as a method of maximizing profits by externalizing costs, that is by imposing the costs arising from the production process onto others in society (*The Ecologist*, 1993). The externalized costs relate for example to (i) the damaging effects of toxins on the health of exposed people; (ii) the associated increase in health costs incurred to redress this harm; (iii) the cost of cleaning up pollution and (iv) damage to crops, buildings and individuals caused by pollution. This list is limited to the economic costs of pollution and is in addition to the many ecological costs caused by pollution. Most pressing amongst the ecological costs of pollution are the changes to habitats associated with climate change that poses an unquantifiable threat to future biodiversity on the planet.

Reducing or eliminating releases of pollution would raise production costs for corporations. Companies have characteristically used their considerable power to protect their private interests to pollute at the expense of transferring costs onto the rest of the community (Miller, 1995). Corporate guru William Dugger draws attention to the social damage incurred by the capitalist pursuit of private interest by reminding us that the corporation has evolved to serve the interests of whoever controls it, at the expense of whomever does not (Dugger, 1989). In facilitating the externalization of costs by accommodating the pollution of the environment, the capitalist political economy encourages pollution, mitigated only by the increasingly limited extent to which governments are willing and able to use laws and regulations to control the pursuit of private material interests.

Individuals attempting to reduce their impact on the environment in a capitalist society are what game theorists would refer to as 'suckers' (Axelrod, 1990), that is choosing options that benefit the community in general at the expense of their own particular interests. Overall pollution levels will remain virtually the same whatever activity any one individual engages in. In the case of transport for example, individuals choosing to minimize their environmental impact by walking or cycling will nonetheless suffer the social ills of cars. These ills include noise pollution, exposure to toxic (harmful) exhaust fumes and threats to physical injury posed by cars, without enjoying any of the private benefits that lead people to use cars in the first place. In this sense individuals are encouraged to pollute the environment as in their own self interest since environmentally responsible behavior is discouraged by the cultural and economic structure (Gorz, 1988; Bojo, Maler and Unemo, 1990; Opschoor, 1994). Similarly, corporations operating in a manner that prioritize environmental concerns over cost considerations will be forced out of the market by less scrupulous competitors who can undercut their prices (Greider, 1997).

Although advocates of economic rationality may logically demand that the social costs of pollution be internalized through the application of the polluter pays principle, the elimination of toxic pollution on grounds of human rights would necessarily be dismissed as irrational since this subordinates 'objective' economic calculations of allocative efficiency to 'normative' environmental values.

Although toxic pollution is normalized and, as we have seen, encouraged by the capitalist political economy, it is at the expense of (i) degrading the general environment and (ii) harming others in society, thereby directly contradicting the harm (non-malfeasance) principle of liberalism.

Liberalism as a Higher Order Theory

Liberalism has been identified as a 'higher-order theory' as opposed to being just another sectarian doctrine (Nagel, 1994). This claim rests upon a definition of liberalism as impartiality between the many different accounts of the good that exist under conditions of modernity (Kernohan, 1998). Rather than it being the purpose of governments and laws to define and promote the good life for citizens, liberalism promotes the toleration of a plurality of diverse versions of the good in society, limited only by the harm principle. Nagel correctly observes that:

> If liberalism is to be defended as a higher-order theory rather than just another sectarian doctrine, it must be shown to result from an interpretation of impartiality itself, rather than from a particular conception of the good that is to be made impartially available (Nagel, 1994, p. 66).

In making this assertion, Nagel joins Rawls and Barry in emphasizing impartiality as a defining characteristic of liberalism (Rawls, 1972; Barry, 1995). Under this assessment, the state cannot promote any one version of the good but must rather ensure that one interpretation of the good is not conducted by one section of society at the expense of harming other citizens. Extending this discussion to cover environmental ethics, Baxter points out that any notion of justice as impartiality must have compelling reasons to exclude communities, including non-human life-forms, from moral considerability or else will constitute an arbitrary form of discrimination (Baxter, 2000). Agar demonstrates through his use of bio preferences that delineating the morally relevant community to Homo sapiens may be both arbitrary and overly simplistic (2001). The implications of a focus on environmental ethics suggests that ecological rationality attains an elevated status in the notion of ethics as impartiality by virtue of the fact that only this ethical paradigm takes into account the needs of all life-forms. This argument is however not pursued further here since the focus is on understanding the philosophy and political interests that underlie the legal construction of human rights.

The contemporary legal system promotes not political impartiality but rather a particular account of the good. Specifically endorsed is a vision of capitalism based on the pursuit of economic growth, allocative efficiency and consumerism as axiomatic political 'goods'. Achieving these goals requires accepting toxic pollution. (Any half-competent economist can demonstrate that the elimination of toxic pollution is an economically inefficient use of resources.) This capitalist utopia therefore entails exposing citizens to toxic pollution which damages their health and is therefore by definition harmful. Since (i) a particular political ideology is being promoted as a universal good (the values of economic growth and efficiency) and that (ii) this vision entails harm to other individuals (through toxic pollution), capitalism cannot be logically compatible with liberal political philosophy.

The status of liberalism as a higher order theory requires that it cannot condone an activity that entails harm even when the political predilections of the majority of a population desire that it should be allowed. Take for example the issue of car use. The use of cars is (i) popular among a majority (as a means of personal mobility and freedom) and (ii) viewed with contempt by a minority who refuse to internalize the dominant materialist values that characterize capitalist societies. Herbert Read articulates the view of the latter group:

> Some of the Greek philosophers rightly associated thought with walking, and they were for that reason called peripatetic. But walking in our time, like philosophy in our time, has declined to a state of paralysis. The paths across the fields have long since been ploughed away; even bridle-paths which in my childhood were busy with human traffic have completely disappeared. The cause of this rapid obliteration of pathways: the internal combustion engine ... The price that has been paid is the end of a way of life out of which whatever poetry and intelligence we possess arose as naturally as poppies and cornflowers from the undisciplined earth, and the alienation of sensibility that is the inevitable consequence of mechanization. We have lost the physical experience that comes from a direct contact with the organic processes of nature ... elementally human experiences that to be deprived of them is to become something less than human (Read quoted in Williams, p. 138).

Less articulate, if more demonstrative in his dislike of the car culture, Kudno Mojesic was arrested in the road outside his Belgrade home attacking cars with an axe, shouting 'away with all cars' and 'cars are the devil's work' (quoted in Williams, 1991).

If liberal political theory is indeed to be predicated upon a notion of impartiality between divergent accounts of the good, toxic pollution cannot be excused from constituting harm on the grounds that the trade-off enjoys widespread support in liberal democratic states. Many people enjoy watching or participating in motor racing and find cars a comfortable and convenient mode of transport. Another group of people disapproves of this trade-off and considers it a social evil to put up with toxic pollution in return for a more efficient economy. The questionnaires conducted for the purpose of this research for example demonstrate significant support for the human right to an environment free from toxic pollution amongst environmental

NGOs (chapter 3). Therefore, one section of society can be identified to approve of the car culture and another can be identified to disapprove of the car culture. As Gray reminds us, it is the position of liberal political theory to defend autonomy and minority rights over majoritarian pressure to infringe those rights (Gray, 1989). Even the utilitarian strand of liberalism promoted by Mill holds that physical security be accorded the status of a weighty moral right, in ordinary circumstances indefeasible by considerations of general welfare (Gray, 1989). A majoritarian decision to produce toxic pollution in return for more consumption and convenience represents a majority choosing an option that entails harm for everyone, including a dissenting minority. Since harm is necessarily imposed on unconsenting individuals liberal political theory cannot legitimize toxic pollution. Consent in any case provides no legitimate basis for existing criminal activities that cause physiological harm such as assault, battery, mayhem and homicide which 'remain unexcused and unjustified even when there was a perfectly willing victim' (Feinberg, 1988). Again, the centrality of the harm principle requires that liberalism oppose harmful acts, regardless of the disposition of the victim.

Another way in which toxic pollution violates conditions of impartiality is through its tendency to affect impoverished and politically marginalized communities. The reason for this is clear, whereas no one likes living next to a toxic waste dump, only the rich can afford to choose where to live. Subsequently, civil rights have been adversely affected by toxic pollution. In the United States, Earth Rights International for example points out that 'poor and minority communities are common sites for nuclear power plants, incinerators and other potentially harmful development'.[1] This trend has resulted in the creation of the environmental justice movement that interprets the tendency as a form of environmental apartheid. In particular, the movement claims that civil rights to racial equality (ICCPR article 26) are being violated, since communities of color are 47 per cent more likely than average to be exposed to industrial pollution (Grossman, 1995; Sabir, 1995; Sachs, 1995). One study of hazardous waste landfills conducted by the US General Accounting Office lends further weight to this trend by concluding that three quarters of waste sites were located in low income or minority communities (Johnston, 1994). The Oregon Clearinghouse for Pollution Reduction 'observe patterns of disproportionate environmental degradation occurring in areas with lower incomes and less ability to protect lifestyle'.[2] Explaining this modality from the corporate perspective, Cerrell Associates stated in a 1984 report that:

> all socio-economic groupings tend to resent the nearby siting of major facilities, but middle and upper strata possess better resources to effectuate their opposition. Middle and higher socio-economic strata neighborhoods should not fall within the one-mile and five-mile radius of the proposed site (quoted in Mishan, 1993, p. 23).

This leaked report exemplifies the structural tendency to impose environmental hazards onto economically marginalized groups. The capitalist political economy disproportionately responds to the demands of powerful interests and demonstrates contempt for impartiality.

It is not the liberal but the capitalist position that dismisses the eradication of toxic pollution as irrational since moving away from an optimal level of pollution reduces allocative efficiency and economic growth. Individuals opposing toxic pollution on environmental or health grounds are harmed not once, but twice. Firstly by the deleterious effects of toxic pollution on health and secondly by a legal system defending the private property rights of polluters to pollute over and above the harm principle and the right to be free from toxic pollution.

The political parameters that define economic rationality rule out policy options that are allocatively inefficient, irrespective of the harm principle and impartiality. Since organising the economy to maximise efficiency requires the production of toxic pollution, proponents of economic rationality conclude that the subsequent harm incurred is unavoidable. The argument that toxic pollution is unfortunate but unavoidable is as devoid of logic as it is of creative thinking. No one 'needs' a private jet or a luxury yacht, or the plethora of other unnecessary goods routinely churned out by modern industry. There is however a very real need to reduce wasting resources on such superfluous items to ensure that economic activity is diverted to satisfy basic human needs and to conserve resources for the essential needs of future generations and non-human life. There is a similar need to phase out use of fossil and nuclear fuels and to invest in renewable energy to ensure that atmospheric carbon dioxide levels do not destroy the Earth's biodiversity. Non-polluting alternative sources of energy are not implemented because of the efficiency and cost considerations that define capitalism (chapter 1). A combination of hydro, solar, wind and tidal power energy could replace reliance on fossil fuels and nuclear energy. Given sufficient investment offshore wind farms alone could provide more than enough electricity to meet Britain's current energy needs (Carrell and Lean, 2001). Due to high initial costs and the theory of discounting, economic rationality deems it efficient to continue relying on fossil fuels for energy generation (chapter 1). Although the economic logic is internally consistent in focusing on efficiency considerations, the trade-off is the systematic violation of the harm principle and endorsing unknown risks with regard to future climate change.

State support of the car industry in the UK exemplifies the capitalist prioritization of economic growth over the liberal principle of impartiality. The public subsidizes vehicle users through government expenditure on road construction and maintenance. Each lorry in the UK for example causes on average £28,000 of damage to roads per year but generates just £25,000 in revenue from fuel tax and vehicle excise duty. These costs only cover road damage and take no account of the significant costs caused by congestion, or of policing the road network, or of traffic accidents, or of the costs to human health or of pollution as a contributory factor in acid rain and climate change (Clement, 2000). Therefore the public subsidizes every lorry operator to the tune of at least £3,000 per year (Clement, 2000). A strong car industry has been central to the capitalist political economy, as explained by Paterson:

> state promotion of cars is perhaps best understood in terms of the state's structural role in capitalist societies, its general imperative to support the conditions for capital accumulation ... The acceleration of the movement of goods, the transformation of production by car manufacturers in what became known as Fordism, and the most direct stimulation of the economy by the car industry, all meant that the car has played a key role in promoting accumulation in the twentieth century, and thus in reproducing capitalist

society on a global scale. It has also played an important role in integrating the economy globally as car manufacturers have led the way in organizing production transnationally. As a consequence of its role in reproducing capitalism, it also became a part of state managers' strategies for reproducing their own state power, legitimizing their rule through promoting the car and thus economic growth (Paterson, 2000).

The structural centrality of the car industry to capitalist economies requires that the harm incurred by the industry be denied, rejected, downplayed, dismissed, discredited or ignored. As Thatcher put it, we cannot do without 'the great car economy' because the economy would collapse if we did (Williams, 1991). This statement illustrates how economic considerations determine policy in capitalist societies at the necessary expense of both the harm principle and of liberal impartiality.

Utilitarianism and Toxic Pollution

The above analysis has argued that a capitalist defence of toxic pollution necessarily contradicts liberalism because it requires a disregard for the harm principle and advocacy of one particular version of the good (the quest for accumulation and allocative efficiency). Furthermore, it will now be demonstrated that a utilitarian theory of justice demonstrates fundamental contradictions with the private interest focus of capitalism. Individual rights to autonomy and property, rather than calculations of overall utility, have characteristically been central arguments for beneficiaries of capitalism to prevent economic redistribution. This is precisely why liberal individualism has often (and as we have seen erroneously), been given in defense of capitalism.

A utilitarian defense of capitalism is contradicted by the polarized distribution of resources in the capitalist world order. The global political economy institutionalizes a plutocratic rather than a utilitarian model of governance (Cox, 1983; George, 1984; Gill, 1995). Wallerstein points out that 'the capitalist system is and always has been one of state interference with the freedom of the market in the interests of some and against those of others' (Wallerstein, 1979). Whilst the capitalist advocacy of the free market is a useful tactical instrument to discredit and marginalize concern for the impoverished, it is soon abandoned, 'when one suggests that governments stop printing money, protecting property, guaranteeing bank accounts and purchasing large quantities of privately produced goods with money obtained by taxation' (Makhijani, 1992).

No African state has an annual turnover as large as that of Exxon (Timberlake, 1985). The claim that this income generated by corporations benefits all is refuted by an analysis of the increasing polarization of wealth produced within the political economy. A combined net worth of $760 billion is enjoyed by 358 billionaires, an amount equal to the overall wealth of the poorest 2.5 billion of the world's people (Korten, 1995). The United Nations Development Program (UNDP) reports that 'no fewer than 100 countries – all developing or in transition – have experienced serious economic decline over the past three decades. As a result per capita income in these 100 countries is lower than it was 10, 20 even 30 years ago' (quoted in Thomas, 1999; Chanrasekhar, 1997). The same report details that in the last 30 years, the poorest 20 per cent of the world's people saw their share of global income fall from 2.3 per cent to 1.4 per cent, whilst the richest 20 per cent saw their share increase from 70 per cent to 85 per cent (Parkin, 1997). For more than one billion people, absolute poverty is now the reality of this skewed distribution of resources (Muzaffer, 1993). There are 800 million people who eat a diet with less than 90 per cent of their minimum calorific requirements and one and a half billion people are deprived of primary health care (Chatterjee and Finger, 1994; Miller, 1995; Prakash, 1995).

A utilitarian based defense of capitalism is subsequently untenable since the market mechanism denies resources to a large number of human beings who are in the greatest need of resources and who would derive the most utility from entitlements to resources. Since a hundred dollar bill has less utility for a millionaire than a penny has for a child, utilitarian based politics would necessarily prevent extreme inequalities by redistributing income to the impoverished to enhance overall human utility. If capitalist societies were motivated by a utilitarian ideology, redistributive policies would seek to reduce inequality as a basic political priority. Such policies are unequivocally absent from the present global political economy. Indeed, such utilitarian proscriptions are characteristically discredited by defenders of capitalism on the very grounds that the redistribution of wealth is a violation of the right of individuals to own private property.

The focus of our inquiry now turns to understand how the legal system allows the continued production of toxic pollution.

The Paradox of Law

The accommodation of toxic pollution in law illustrates the way in which legal concepts have been selectively interpreted and applied to protect existent relations of production, exchange and consumption. Toxic pollution constitutes an arbitrary source of physiological harm that is more direct than other forms of legally recognized harm. Theft, for example, may certainly be inconvenient and unjust to the victim, but in the absence of any physical violence, does little to harm the actual body of a person. Yet a plethora of property and contract laws exist to define very precisely ownership rights. Any contravention of these ownership rights is subsequently classified as harm against the victim (Feinberg, 1984). The harm incurred by pollution has in contrast been downplayed, indeed denied by law, even though, unlike contraventions of property rights, toxic pollution incurs physical harm that can lead to diseases and even death. Law thereby focuses on and protects exchange relations at the expense of ecological concerns.

The epidemiological evidence that specific pollutants can violate the right to life has been acknowledged in certain human rights conferences, particularly with regard to the hazard posed by toxic waste. The World Conference on Human Rights declared in 1992 that 'dumping of toxic and dangerous substances and waste potentially constitutes a serious threat to the human rights to life and health of everyone' (quoted in Bothe, 1996). The United Nations Human Rights Commission similarly declared in April 1998 that the dumping of toxic waste 'had a humanitarian as well as an environmental angle' because of the threat posed to the right to life

(Capdevila, 1998). Moving beyond a focus on toxic waste, the Inter-American Commission on Human Rights has declared that, 'water is life' and stated that receiving water free from toxic pollution is a constituent component of the right to life (Fabra, 1996).

Domestic legal developments in several states have likewise recognized the threat posed by toxic pollution to the realization of the right to life. Rulings by judges in India have established that the right to life includes 'the right to live in a healthy environment, a pollution-free environment, and an environment in which ecological balance is protected by the state' (Anderson, 1996). The Supreme Court in India has further ruled that every individual has a fundamental right to the 'enjoyment of pollution free water and air' (Anderson, 1996). In the Tulua case, the Constitutional Court of Colombia stated that the right to a healthy environment is fundamental 'for the survival of the human species' and that there was 'an evident connection between the right to enjoy a healthy environment and other constitutional rights, such as the right to sanitation, to life, to work, and to the prevalence of the general interest' (quoted in Fabra, 1996). The Brazilian courts have similarly ruled that 'since the maintenance of an environmental quality is fundamental to human life, the legal protection of the environment is a realization of the right to life' (quoted in Fernandez, 1996). Anderson notes that zero pollution rights claims have strong historical precursors in the common law against public nuisance and in the Roman law that 'the use of one's property may not harm another', a precedent that has also been adopted in contemporary international law (Anderson, 1996). These cases reflect recognition from the courts that toxic pollution constitutes a possible causal violation of the right to life and suggests a role for law as a mechanism to codify, guarantee and implement the right to an environment free from toxic pollution. Herein lies the paradox of law, since, as argued in chapter four, the general efficacy of legal stipulations is a function of existent power relations. Enforcement of human rights that criminalize the production of toxic pollution would conflict with the interests of industry to pollute and would furthermore contradict the market allocation of resources that advocates an optimal, that is an efficient, level of toxic pollution. This contradiction severely circumscribes the ability of law to realize the human right to an environment free from toxic pollution.

With the notable exceptions of the cases listed above, domestic courts have consistently interpreted of the right to life in ways that exclude toxic pollution (Boyle and Anderson, 1996). Exemplifying this omission, the right to life provided in article two of the European Convention on Human Rights has been interpreted by the European Court in a limited sense of protection only against the arbitrary deprivation of life by the state (Hayward, 2000). Under such a circumscribed meaning of the right to life, the production of toxic pollution, along with other economic activities, is excused from constituting even a possible violation. Refuting the stated position of the courts on this matter, a wealth of epidemiological evidence demonstrates the process by which toxic pollutants violate the right to life. In Britain in the year 1998 for example, a governmental report attributed 24,000 deaths to the effects of ground level ozone, PM 10s and sulphur dioxide (Brown 1998a).

The general reluctance of the courts to interpret toxic pollution as a violation of the right to life is necessary to excuse polluting economic activities from constituting criminal offenses. Violations of the right to life caused by the routine exposure to toxic pollutants are accommodated and normalized as culturally acceptable by legal institutions. Violations of the right to life that result from the structural operations of the political economy are therefore accommodated by a legal system which is itself a central bloc of the capitalist architecture. Ownership of a car for example legitimizes use thereof, irrespective of the subsequent toxins emitted. As previously established, this argument is clearly untenable on liberal grounds. As Nozick articulates 'a person has the liberty to leave his knife wherever he wants, but not in someone else's back' (quoted in Davidson, 1995). Where use of private property causes harm for others, its use cannot be justified on liberal grounds, and for good reason.

The pressing issue of whether new legislation can institutionalize the universal human right to an environment free from toxic pollution is therefore ambiguous. As chapter four explained, it is the nature of the existing form of law that legislation cannot by itself resolve the structural causes of human rights violations. Yet it is also the case that, as a hegemonic instrument, law must maintain the veneer of impartiality rather than be overtly seen to operate in the interests of power. Therefore a scope exists for anti-systemic forces to subvert the function of law as an instrument of the powerful by working to enforce legally stipulated environmental human rights. Exemplifying this possibility, the environmental movement has had successes in the courts. For instance, in 1987 the Indian Supreme Court ordered the closure of certain limestone quarries on the grounds that the poisoning of local inhabitants caused by the mining amounted to a violation of the constitutional right to life (Agarwal and Narain, 1992). In this case a comprehensive interpretation of the right to life was implemented, prioritizing environmental human rights over commercial considerations and the corporate desire to pollute.

However, the extent to which law can be implemented on a widespread basis to combat systematic pollution is circumscribed by the structural constraints of power within which law operates. The Indian courts, for example, have certainly not subordinated general economic activity and social customs to the goal of eradicating toxic pollution.

Whereas legal recognition is necessary for the realization of the right to an environment free from toxic pollution, it is not by itself a sufficient condition. Legal recognition is a not a sufficient condition because of the ability of powerful social and economic interests to determine the efficacy of, rather than to be themselves defined by, legal stipulations. The opportunities available for the realization of the right to an environment free from toxic pollution in a capitalist legal system are non-existent. The realization of this human right would require phasing out anthropogenic sources of toxic pollution, addressing patterns of over-consumption and replacing dependency on fossil fuels with an investment in renewable forms of energy. This agenda of opposing economic rationality and capitalism links the requirements of basic human rights to the policies required to address pressing global environmental problems.

Pollution as Public Nuisance and Risk

Toxic pollution has been in part acknowledged under law as a 'public nuisance' and as 'risk' but not as 'harm'. Categorized as public nuisance, toxic pollution is legally recognized to threaten the legally codified human rights stipulation that:

> no one shall be subjected to arbitrary interference with his (sic) privacy, family, home or correspondence ... . Everyone has the right to the protection of the law against such interference or attacks (Universal Declaration article 12; ICCPR article 17).

Pollution has, for example, been acknowledged by the European Court on Human Rights to constitute a source of interference with individual privacy in cases when the individual has been arbitrarily exposed to disutility over which they have no influence or control (Roger, 1994; Bothe, 1996). In 1994, the Spanish government was for example ordered by the European Court to pay compensation of four million Pesetas to Gregoria Ostra who was found to have suffered a violation of her rights to a private and family life because of the pollution coming from a nearby tannery waste treatment plant (Roger, 1994). In this instance, pollution caused nausea, vomiting, allergic reactions, bronchitis and anorexic conditions within members of the complainant's family. The European Court ruled that:

> it is self evident that grave pollution of the environment can impair the well-being of the individual and so hinder the individual's use of his or her home and that his or her private and family life is also impaired, even when the health of the person concerned is not seriously endangered (quoted in Calliess, 1996, p. 31).

The right to privacy was also found by the European Court to have been violated in the cases of Arondelle v UK and Baggs v UK (Convention for the Protection of Human Rights and Fundamental Freedoms article 8). In these cases, home-owners complained that the noise pollution originating from the airports of Gatwick and Heathrow constituted a violation of the right to privacy (Rest, 1998). Recognition of pollution as a public nuisance that can violate privacy rights is therefore established in the law of the European Union (Rest, 1998).

Pollution has also been categorized by the courts as 'risk'. According to this classification, those individuals who suffer illnesses or indeed die from the effects of exposure to toxic pollutants have not been the victims of 'harm' as such, but have rather suffered the unfortunate consequences of exposure to environmental risks. Understanding both the political process of exposing individuals to such risks and the subsequent issues raised has generated much research within the discipline of political sociology in recent years (Adams, 1995; Beck, 1997). The well-rehearsed criticisms made by risk theorists in relation to political modernity are, however, somewhat misplaced in relation to toxic pollution. The crucial point is that although some (but not all) individuals exposed to carcinogenic and mutagenic pollutants may die as a result of that exposure, physiological harm is nonetheless incurred to the DNA of all individuals exposed to even low levels of these pollutants. Toxic pollution causes harm by definition, even if this harm does not manifest itself as a diagnosed disease in the exposed individuals. Deaths and diseases attributable to pollution are merely symptomatic of the harm incurred by the previous exposure to toxins. Harm is caused by the damaging of cellular material exposed to toxic pollution that may, or may not, subsequently influence or cause the onset of certain illnesses or indeed of death. As epidemiologists explain:

> many inhaled pollutants do not kill cells, but are responsible, directly or via their breakdown products, for mild, ongoing damage to DNA and other cellular structures. The combination of continuing cell division for repair and gradual DNA damage may eventually lead to the development of cancer (Lee and Manning, 1995).

By virtue of its capacity to damage DNA and cellular structures, toxic pollutants must be logically recognized for deleteriously affecting the health and well being of human and non-human animals alike. For a legal system to control toxic pollution as a 'public nuisance' and as 'environmental risk', rather than to prohibit its production as a 'harm' illustrates how legal concepts are selectively applied according to the imperative to accommodate and excuse the economic power relations of capitalism rather than to impartially implement a theory of justice.

Toxic Pollution as Harm

To recap the argument thus far, the harm principle is the main criterion which liberal theorists from both the Kantian and utilitarian traditions utilize to decide whether state intervention in the autonomy of individuals is justified or not. As Feinberg acknowledges 'no responsible theorist denies the validity of the harm principle, but the liberal would prefer to draw the line there, and deny validity to any other proposed ground for state intervention' (Feinberg, 1984, p.14). The existing legal definition of harm may recognize toxic pollution as a public nuisance and as risk but not as harm. This position is defended by Feinberg who argues that:

> the harm principle lends legitimacy to legislative efforts to solve the multidimensional problems of air and water pollution, but in its bare formulation without supplement, it offers no guide to policy (Feinberg, 1984, p. 232).

This section of the chapter examines this contention and argues that law has selectively applied the harm principle to unduly exempt dominant forms of production and exchange from consideration. This review illustrates the claims made in chapter four that the law exists to justify, legitimize and codify capitalism. From a review of the epidemiological evidence, it will be argued that toxic pollution harms people and the environment alike. The work of Feinberg will be focused upon to conduct this investigation since Feinberg provides a systematic and influential investigation into the nature of harm which incorporates some discussion of toxic pollution (Feinberg 1984; Feinberg 1988).

Feinberg asserts that one person harms another 'by invading, and thereby thwarting or setting back, his interest' (Feinberg, 1984, p. 34). Feinberg expands on this explanation to claim that:

A harms B when
1   A acts
2   in a manner which is defective or faulty in respect to the risks it creates to B, that is, with the intention of producing the consequences for B that follow, or similarly adverse ones, or with negligence or recklessness in respect to those consequences; and
3   A's acting in that manner is morally indefensible, that is, neither excusable nor justifiable; and
4   A's action is the cause of a setback to B's interests, which is also
5   a violation of B's right (Feinberg, 1984, pp. 105–106).

This definition of harm captures the current definition of harm in the legal system. It simultaneously demonstrates why the current notion of harm is fundamentally problematic from the perspective of ecological rationality. Concern for ecological well being is entirely absent under these provisions since the focus is instead on individual interests. Nonetheless, the following analysis concludes that toxic pollution necessarily constitutes harm according to the stated criteria.

It should be axiomatic that a toxic pollutant that is known to have a deleterious effect on health is by definition harmful and it takes a value system focusing almost exclusively on economic values and property rights to avoid this conclusion. Yet these economic rights are precisely the values that the capitalist legal system endorses and hence the ongoing rejection of toxic pollution as constituting harm. Feinberg's categorization of the harm principle given above will nonetheless be utilized in the following analysis since it does describe how harm is perceived under the existing legal system, which is the structure that those interested in social change must address. It should also be noted that any investigation of toxic pollution based on ecological values would in any event be disregarded as irrelevant by the existing legal system.

Identifiable Actors

Applying Feinberg's harm formula (as stated above) to toxic pollution, all individuals and corporations engaging in activities that emit toxic pollutants can be identified as subject 'A' since their activities generate harmful substances. It is these agents who act in such a manner as to expose others to toxic pollutants. Many toxic pollutants have a multitude of sources and this necessarily complicates the process of identifying and holding specific individuals responsible for the resultant harm. Yet, there is a clear distinction between a multitude of sources and no source for harmful pollutants. This is self-evident to the cyclist or rambler who encounters a car and can most precisely identify the exact source of the cocktail of pollutants which, from one breath to another, replaces the fresh air of a country lane.

Fault

Feinberg's second requisite for the application of the harm principle relates to fault. Under this proviso, A must act:

in a manner which is defective or faulty in respect to the risks it creates to B, that is, with the intention of producing the consequences for B that follow, or similarly adverse ones, or with negligence or recklessness in respect to those consequences (Feinberg, 1984, pp. 105–106).

In the case of the production of toxic pollutants, A's manner is faulty in respect to the risks it creates to B since such pollutants, by definition, damage the physical bodies of the exposed individuals. As Feinberg acknowledges in his formulation of fault, it is unnecessary for the harmful consequences of the act to be intended for that act to be categorized as harmful. According to the harm principle, any actions known to result in harm to others in society can be legitimately prohibited even where those consequences are an unintended by-product of the activity, rather than the motivation behind undertaking the course of action. It is for this reason that Feinberg incorporates negligence and recklessness in his definition of fault (Feinberg, 1984). For an act to be legitimately prohibited under the harm principle it must only be established that the act causes harm, irrespective of the intentions of the perpetrator of that harm. The only issue is therefore, whether or not toxic pollution is harmful, rather than the separate issue of the intentions of those who generate the pollution.

The routine use of certain pesticides in modern agriculture is one example of harm caused by toxins since many varieties are known to be poisonous to humans. For example, 90 per cent, by weight, of fungicides used in the US have a tumour forming capacity (Timberlake and Thomas, 1990). In the developing world where pesticide regulations are lax, the situation causes even more concern. A 1990 study estimated that 25 million agricultural workers in the developing world are, to a greater or lesser extent, physiological harmed each year by pesticides (Sachs, 1995). Moreover, some pesticides used as a matter of routine have a mutagenic effect. Such pesticides leave an insidious legacy since they cause mutation at the cellular level, and thereby pose a presently unknown threat to future generations (Johnston, 1997).

Another variety of toxins, heavy metals, accumulate in the bodies of animals and, after a threshold level is reached, can harm the individual through inhibiting enzyme activity (Simpkins, 1992). A notorious example was the release of mercury from the Chisso Corporation factory in Minimata, Japan, into a local bay in the 1950s. Forty-six members of the local community subsequently died as a result of consuming mercury-contaminated fish (Pickering and Owen, 1994). A number of Yanomami Indians have been similarly killed in the state of Brazil by poisoning from mercury released into their traditional lands by gold diggers (Sponzel, 1994).

Heavy industry in Eastern Europe operating under the totalitarian regimes of the post-war era left a legacy of soil, water and air pollution. Exposure to toxic pollutants has caused higher incidence of respiratory illnesses and childhood lead poisoning with many infants consequently exhibiting evidence of anemia and chromosome damage (Pearce, 1992b). The province of Katowice contains much of the heavy industry in Poland, and severe pollution has resulted from an almost complete absence of environmental regulations. The resident population of Katowice consequently suffers from 15 per cent more circulatory disease, 30 per cent more tumours and 47 per cent more respiratory disease than the average Pole (Timberlake and Thomas, 1990). In Hungary, one in every 17 deaths has been attributed by government estimates to air pollution (Timberlake and Thomas, 1990). In Bombay, the air is so heavily polluted that simply breathing in this Indian city has been reckoned to incur the same physiological harm as smoking ten cigarettes each day (Timberlake and Thomas, 1990).

The harm caused by toxic pollution is exemplified in the use of petrol and diesel powered cars as a favored mode of transport in modern society. The use of cars generates greenhouse gases and a cocktail of toxic pollutants. Cars produce over 900 million metric tons of carbon dioxide each year and are responsible for 23 per cent of all carbon dioxide emissions in OECD states (United Nations Development Programme, 1999). This figure excludes the carbon dioxide released from fuel extraction, processing, transport and associated road construction (Paterson, 1996b).

Vehicle emissions constitute the single most important categorized source of toxic air pollutants (Gould, 1989; Read and Read, 1991; Pickering and Owen, 1994). Specific pollutants harm the physiology of individuals by virtue of their capacity to damage cellular structures. Such harm can result in brain damage, cardiovascular diseases, respiratory problems or infections, bronchitis, lung cancer, a decline in lung function, emphysema, headaches, leukemia, damage to the immune system or damage to the nervous system or induce allergies (Dockery, Speizer, Strom *et al.*, 1989; Pope, Dockery, Spengler and Raizenne, 1991; Bates, 1992; Pope, Schwartz and Ransome, 1992; Pope and Kanner, 1993; Roemer, Hoek and Brunekreef, 1993; World Health, 1993; Hamer, 1994; Schwartz, 1994a; 1994b; Lee and Manning, 1995; Maclean's, 1995; Seaton, 1995; Seaton, McNee, Donaldson and Godden, 1995 and Paterson, 2000). A World Health Organization report into the health affects of exhaust pollutants emitted by cars in France, Austria and Switzerland found that toxic emissions are responsible for 21,000 deaths annually in the three states, significantly more deaths than are caused in traffic accidents (United Nations Development Programme, 1999). Furthermore, the report found that pollutants from car exhausts caused 300,000 extra cases of bronchitis in children and 15,000 additional hospital admissions for heart disease in the three states (United Nations Development Programme, 1999).

When the French Public Health Society conducted a study on the health effects of air pollution, 350 Parisians were estimated to die each year from heart problems caused by everyday pollution (Patel, 1994; Patel, 1996). The London smog of December 1952 lasted for five days and killed approximately 4,000 people. At the height of this episode, Londoners were dying at a faster rate than during the cholera epidemic in the previous century (Pearce, 1992c). Death rates rose by 10 per cent when a smog submerged London for four days in December 1991, indicating that this episode of pollution killed an additional 160 people (Bown, 1994c). During this incident, the number of deaths from respiratory and heart diseases were respectively 22 and 14 per cent higher than normal (Bown, 1994c).

Besides causing deaths through urban smog, vehicle exhaust fumes include a number of pollutants that can be individually isolated as causing physiological harm. Sulphur dioxide constitutes harm by virtue of its property to cause respiratory illness and to worsen a variety of health conditions (World Health, 1993; Lidstone, 1995). A 1998 government report on the effects of air pollution found that sulphur dioxide 'hastened the deaths' of 3,500 people in the UK each year (Bown, 1998a). It is instructive to note that although terrorists invariably hasten the deaths of their victims, the act is rarely described by the officials of states in such moderate and accepting terminology.

The existing epidemiological evidence suggests that nitrogen dioxide does not cause asthma, but that it can trigger asthma attacks in people genetically predisposed to the condition (Seaton, 1995). Being induced to have an asthma attack because of the release of nitrogen dioxide by a third party can be interpreted as a violation of rights to autonomy and security of the person. Specifically, a physical condition is created for the victim of an asthma attack that could even violate the right to life in the case of a serious episode. Keith Mason of the Center for Exploitation of Science and Technology has found that levels of nitrogen dioxide as low as two parts per billion are high enough to trigger an attack of asthma in people predisposed to the condition (Coghlan, 1993b). Nitrogen dioxide pollution also irritates the eyes and damages the lungs (Pearce, 1992c). Exposure to 400 parts per billion or more of nitrogen dioxide in inhaled air causes epithelial cell dysfunction in the lungs (Anto and Sunyer, 1995). During the episode of smog in London in December 1991, levels of nitrogen dioxide reached 423 ppb and death rates indeed increased, by 10 per cent according to an unpublished report for the Department of Health (Bown, 1994b). When in May 1995 levels of nitrogen oxides rose above levels regarded as safe by the European Community and the World Health Organization, asthma sufferers were warned to stay at home and 'hospital admissions for people with respiratory complaints soared' (*New Scientist*, 1995). In 1991 vehicles in Europe emitted 6.5 million tonnes of nitrogen oxides (Lidstone, 1995).

Research has highlighted particulates (PM10s) as a pollutant incurring the most serious harm in exhaust fumes. Each particulate is less than 10 micro-metres wide and carries damaging chemicals, such as acids, into the alveoli of the lungs. In the alveoli, PM10s inflame tissues, stimulating affected cells to produce the coagulants fibrinogen and factor 8 to levels that can strain the cardiovascular system (Hamer, 1994). Research has linked increasing levels of particulates with higher risks of heart and lung disease (Hamer, 1994). One epidemiologist concludes that:

> recent research provides convincing evidence for a link between mortality and PM10 ... higher levels of particulate correlate not only with more deaths, but also with more hospital admissions and more reports of symptoms from asthmatics' (Bown, 1994d, p. 13).

An incremental increase of 10 micrograms of PM10s per cubic meter causes a correlative and sustained rise in the death rate from heart attacks of 1 per cent, and from respiratory illnesses of 3.4 per cent (Pearce, 1994a; Hamer and MacKenzie, 1995). One group of epidemiologists in the United States has concluded that 'thousands of deaths every year are associated with particulate air pollution, even at levels well below that which the Environmental Protection Agency considers safe' (Greater Boston Physicians for Social Responsibility, 1998).

The only significant pollution in Provo, a town located in the Utah Valley, consists of PM10s emitted by a local steel mill. For this reason, Provo was selected for a major study into the health effects of PM10s. The results of this research found that for every increase of 100 micrograms per cubic meter of PM10 pollutants, there was a 16 per cent increase in the death rate, and no threshold level was observed (Montagu, 1989c). The lack of a threshold is noteworthy since it indicates that any amount of exposure to the pollutant, however small, causes a degree of physiological harm with the degree of harm increasing in line with higher levels of exposure. The study found that hospital admissions trebled when the PM10 level rose from normal levels to 150 micrograms per cubic meter (Lee and Manning, 1995).

A study in Athens linked high levels of PM10 pollution to a 5 per cent increase in deaths (*New Scientist*, 1996). This figure is consistent with research conducted by a World Health Organization (WHO) panel examining deaths from PM10s (Edwards, 1995). The WHO estimated that 'thousands' of Europeans who are exposed to airborne particles common in cities 'will suffer or die' (quoted in Edwards, 1995). A 1998 UK governmental report placed the number of annual deaths in Britain 'hastened' by PM10s at 8,100 with another 10,500 requiring hospital treatment as a result of exposure to the pollutant (Bown, 1994d). Bown observes that:

> there are no safe levels of PM10 .... On those few days of the year when concentrations of PM10 are high, there are peaks in mortality. But most of the deaths take place during the rest of the year, when PM10 levels are nearer average. For this reason, reducing only the peak levels of PM10 will have little effect on total mortality (Bown, 1994d).

The WHO has refused to set a safe limit for PM10 exposure since it has concluded that none exists (Edwards, 1995). Supporting evidence for this conclusion is provided by other epidemiological studies (Schwartz and Dockery, 1992). PM10s presently cause approximately 60,000 deaths per year in the US and 10,000 deaths in England and Wales (Weisskopf, 1991; Schwartz and Dockery, 1992; Bown, 1994d).

Another harmful pollutant, ground level ozone, is produced when sunlight reacts with vehicle exhaust fumes. Ground level ozone can worsen asthma conditions, increase susceptibility to binoviruses, impair the immune system and lung function, cause respiratory tract infections and coughing, difficulty in breathing, chest tightness, nausea and lung inflammations (Read, 1989; Read and Read, 1991; Pearce, 1992c; Hamer 1994). Ozone is a powerful oxidizing agent and consequently reacts with a number of biological molecules causing damage to the lungs (McDonnell, 1994). Vaughan and Cross point out that 'ozone weakens the body's immune system and attacks lung tissue: according to the US Center for Disease Control, ozone destroys lung tissue about as well as some chemical weapons do' (Vaughan and Cross, 1990). The 1998 UK government report on the effects of air pollution found that 12,500 people have their deaths 'hastened' by ground level ozone in Britain each year with the pollutant causing a further 9,900 to seek hospital treatment (Brown, 1998a).

Carbon monoxide produced by the combustion of petrol is 'highly toxic' since it combines with the hemoglobin of the blood more effectively than oxygen does (Fullick and Fullick, 1994). Half the urban populations in North America and Europe are routinely exposed to harmful levels of carbon monoxide (Timberlake and Thomas, 1990). In 1991 motor vehicles in Europe emitted 28 million tonnes of carbon monoxide, constituting 86 per cent of the total quantity of the pollutant found in urban areas (Vaughan and Cross, 1990; Read and Read, 1991).

1.3 butadiene is another toxic chemical found in exhaust fumes. It is a genotoxin, (a substance damaging to DNA), and is also classified by the US Environment Protection Agency as a 'probable human carcinogen' (Coghlan, 1993b). Hydrocarbons constitute yet another variety of exhaust pollutants. Hydrocarbons are 'both toxic and carcinogenic' at any level of exposure (Fullick and Fullick; 1994). Exhaust fumes from vehicles in Europe contained 5.5 million tonnes of hydrocarbons in 1990 (Read and Read, 1991).

Due to its effects of causing hyperactivity and impairing brain function in children, lead has been traditionally identified as the most damaging pollutant in petrol. However, in addition to the production of all the pollutants already reviewed above, unleaded petrol also emits a higher proportion of benzene than leaded petrol. Benzene is highly carcinogenic even at low levels, a fact which refutes the claim that unleaded petrol is in any sense a 'green' fuel (Read and Read, 1991; Williams, 1991; Pearce, 1992c). According to the definition of the Chemical Weapons Convention, chemical weapons are 'any chemical which, through its chemical action on life processes can cause death, temporary incapacitation or permanent harm to human or animals' (Kenyon, 2000). Applying this definition to the epidemiological evidence reviewed above, there appears to be a good *primâ facie* case for banning cars under the chemical weapons convention.

Episodes of high levels of air pollution are invariably characterized by higher concentrations of several pollutants, exacerbating the damaging health effects of exposure. Anto, for example, explains that the more complex mixtures of pollutants likely to be present in urban air induce larger inflammatory and functional changes than the inhalation of one form of pollutant alone (Read, 1989; Anto and Sunyer, 1995). Death rates from bronchitis, pneumonia and heart failure have, for example, been demonstrated to rise as the public is exposed to increased levels of sulphur dioxide in combination with smoke originating from the combustion of fossil fuels (Simpkins and William, 1992).

This detailed epidemiological evidence has been included here to establish that toxic pollution can harm health. This may seem axiomatic, even unnecessary, given the categorization of such pollution as toxic. Yet such a review demonstrates how the legal system downplays environmental considerations in applying the harm principle. That the originators of toxic pollution rarely intend to cause harm to others is largely irrelevant. As Feinberg acknowledges in his definition of fault, provided that the consequences of the activity performed by A are known to cause harm to B, the activity can be properly prohibited as negligence or recklessness. For individuals to decide to continue polluting regardless testifies to the characteristic tendency of individuals conditioned in modern society to subordinate considerations of the public good to those of private interest and personal convenience, exemplified in the popularity of car use as the preferred mode of transport.

Unintended harm is in no way excused from the provision of non-malfeasance (Machan, 1993). For example, manslaughter is a crime when death is unintentionally caused. Similarly, the bank robber is rarely motivated by the desire to deprive someone else of money; rather the harm to others occurs as a result of the desire of the thieves to enrich themselves irrespective of the implications for others. (Few bank robberies end with stolen cash being burnt or otherwise discarded). Few car drivers set out with the express intention of damaging the health of others, yet this inevitably occurs as a result of car use. In both bank robberies and car driving, the harm to others is known in advance and the action is conducted regardless, even though this was not the primary motivation in either case.

Moral Considerations

Feinberg includes as paragraph three in his formulation of the harm principle the provision that 'A's acting in that manner is morally indefensible, that is, neither excusable nor justifiable' (Feinberg, 1984). Defining his exceptions for moral considerations, Feinberg explains that 'I use the phrase "indefensible conduct" as the most generic term for actions and omissions that have no adequate justification of excuse' (Feinberg, 1984). Such a definition is not particularly precise since a detailed discussion of the standard of 'adequacy of justification' is entirely absent.

Since Feinberg is primarily concerned with law rather than ethics, it is perhaps to be expected that no theoretical defense of this ethical paradigm would be provided in his study. The provision may appear in any case to be uncontentious (morally justifiable actions cannot be simultaneously immoral). Yet in making moral judgments, it is necessary to have an internally coherent set of criteria with which to measure and evaluate ethical questions (chapter 1). The paradigm of morality assumed by Feinberg, indeed universalized to the exclusion of all other possibilities, is that of conventional morality, the dominant, 'common sense', view of right and wrong existing in modern society. Moral defensibility, excusability and justifiability are therefore defined in terms that presuppose the value basis of capitalism as opposed to any other contending ordering of values, such as that promoted by ecological ethics.

Upon the ethical criterion advanced by Feinberg, harmful actions based on 'normal' moral values, such as driving a car for personal convenience and comfort can be excused from the provisions of the harm principle. As such, paragraph three of Feinberg's definition of the harm principle becomes a self-legitimizing instrument for the legal system to excuse 'normal' social practices (such as car driving) as 'innocent' since they are accepted common practice, irrespective of the harm entailed.

The paradigm of conventional morality can be properly criticized since it falsely universalizes one particular system of ethics (which incorporates the values of economic rationality). As chapter one explained, social power works to construct dominant paradigms of ethics, epistemology and rationality by making certain actions appear not only 'right', but universally or naturally so. Paragraph three of the harm principle as defined by Feinberg is necessarily problematic for theorists who see the dominant moral standards of society as subject to ethical criticism, as opposed to the source of ethical criticism. The conservative ethical position advanced by Feinberg is particularly problematic from the particular perspective of ecological rationality since ecological ethics criticizes the predominance assigned to the goal of allocative efficiency in modern societies. Under the ethical paradigm given by Feinberg, toxic pollution is not only morally justified, but naturally so since it contributes to the efficient allocation of resources and contributes to the consumerist lifestyle which is assumed to be the ultimate social good.

Although the dominant ethical paradigm can usually dismiss challenges from external ethical codes by recourse to its own internal coherence, this possibility does not exist in Feinberg's project to excuse toxic pollution from constituting harm on the ground of moral considerations. Instead, three contradictions are exposed in Feinberg's argument; (i) methodological failing in investigating whether toxic pollution constitutes harm through engaging in economic analysis rather than reviewing the epidemiological evidence, (ii) the status of liberalism as a higher order theory is contravened, (iii) toxic pollution is omitted from the categories of 'substantial' and 'avoidable' harm for arbitrary reasons, rather than this criteria being universally and consistently applied to identify harm. These three contradictions will now be explained and investigated in turn.

Contradiction one: Methodological failings Feinberg asserts that toxic pollution cannot be classified as harm (and prohibited) since such an outcome contradicts the rules of allocative efficiency. A 'satisfactory solution' for Feinberg does not require a criminal prohibition of but rather 'an elaborate scheme of regulation, administered by a state agency empowered to grant, withhold and suspend licenses, following rules to promote fairness and efficiency' (Feinberg, 1984, p. 229). Regulating toxic pollution in such a way as to promote fairness and efficiency is in fact a thinly veiled argument for subordinating the harm principle to the logic of economic rationality since it does nothing to refute the epidemiological evidence that documents the harmful effects of toxins.

In order to organize society in such a way as to maximize levels of economic growth and efficiency the general population must be exposed to harmful levels of toxic pollution. In one revealing discussion, Feinberg interprets ethics in terms equating efficiency and justice claiming that:

> in the context of industrial polluting, wrongful must mean the unlawful as judged by a regulatory agency applying rules for allocating permits in accordance with specified requirements of fairness and efficiency. In these contexts, no prior standard of wrongfulness exists (Feinberg, 1984, p. 230).

This statement is methodologically insecure since 'fairness' and 'efficiency' is presented as the appropriate criteria through which to establish wrongful. Highlighting this criteria is a political choice that arbitrarily defines wrongful in terms that reflect economic rationality. Ecological rationality could in contrast identify wrongful through the criteria of 'fairness' and 'ecological integrity'. In conducting the investigation into harm, Feinberg is therefore exposed to the charge of using the wrong criterion (justice as efficiency) to establish harm. Contrary to Feinberg's assertion quoted above, the epidemiological evidence (some of which has been reviewed above) informs us when a pollutant causes physical harm to people and can therefore provide 'a prior standard' for judging wrongful. Acknowledging the validity of this standard would however require the elimination of toxic pollution, a possibility that is dismissed as 'utterly trivial and nearly vacuous' since it leads to an inefficient allocation of resources, a self-evidently irrational position (Feinberg, 1984, p. 227).

Contradiction two: Liberalism as a higher theory In defining harm in terms that prioritize a particular value (that of economic efficiency) over other values (such as physiological well being or ecological integrity), one version of the good, that of capitalism, is endorsed. Permitting the production of toxic (and therefore also harmful) pollution on the grounds that this produces the efficient allocation of resources is in no sense a neutral or impartial position. Rather, it is endorsing a vision of the good society in terms that subordinate ecological to economic values. The position advanced by Feinberg is a defence of allocative efficiency rather than of impartiality between competing values. This contradicts the stated defence of liberalism advanced by Feinberg since as established above, liberalism requires impartiality between different perspectives of the good (Feinberg, 1984). In one passage, Feinberg concedes that pollution can indeed contribute to harm but then asserts that:

> that can hardly be the sense of harm in any formulation of the harm principle that can serve as a guide to legislators, since it would provide a reason for banning indispensable innocent activities, like car driving and fossil-fuel-fired electricity-generating plants, across the board (Feinberg, 1984, p. 228).

In this passage, Feinberg delineates the possible remit of 'harm' not according to the epidemiological evidence (which would provide the wrong outcome). Instead, harm is defined in a selective manner to accommodate the desired activities of consumerism; car driving and fossil-fuel-fired electricity generating plants in this instance. At this point, the disjuncture between impartiality (the liberal position) and formulating laws in order to excuse existing social relations (the capitalist position) becomes most apparent. Harm is being explicitly defined in a way that accommodates the desired practices of accumulation and consumption that characterize capitalism and which require systematic environmental degradation. Such an endorsement contradicts the requirement for liberalism to be an impartial doctrine since it rules out the version of the good promoted by environmentalists that prioritize the protection of human health and ecological systems over the concern for macroeconomic statistics. Environmentalists have strongly disagreed with the assertion that driving cars is in any sense an innocent activity and rather see it as a preeminent social evil responsible for foul smelling and physically harmful fumes, for continual noise pollution, for alarms sounding all day and night, for the destruction of the countryside to make way for coagulated oil slicks, for the host of ecological disasters caused by the routine operations of the petrochemical industry, for climate change and for the inability of children to play or cycle safely on the streets any more. Aside from causing hundreds of thousands of deaths each year from pollution worldwide, cars have also been responsible for 17 million deaths in traffic accidents (Williams, 1991). Given that cars are responsible for far more deaths than are caused by terrorists each year, the claim that car driving is in any sense an innocent activity appears to rest solely on social norms, customs and practices created under conditions of capitalism rather than any considered position of impartiality.

In another passage, Feinberg again concedes that toxic pollution can constitute 'direct and serious' harm to citizens, but only 'rarely' since anti-pollution legislation defines harm and therefore prevents direct and serious harm to individuals. (Feinberg, 1984). Refuting this assertion, epidemiologists have demonstrated that legislation invariably accommodates levels of pollution that can cause harm, injury or death in the general population. Even in developed states with comparatively high standards of air quality, toxic pollution has been implicated in indiscriminately violating the right to life of the population in general, by an average of between one and two years according to the epidemiologist Douglas Dockery (*New Scientist*, 1994a). Levels of air pollutants below those limits set by environmental legislation in the US have been linked to higher rates of cancer, cardiopulmonary diseases and death (New Scientist, 1994a). Exposure to ground level ozone damages the biochemistry of the lungs 'at levels that are well below international limits for the maximum amount of ozone that should be present in clean air' (Read, 1989). Research published in *World Health* similarly concludes that 'even legally permissible levels of air pollution can lead to heart and lung disease' (*World Health*, 1993). Williams reports that in the 1990s, an estimated 2,500 Californians died each year as a result of cancers caused by exposure to toxic chemicals released by oil refining and petrochemicals (Williams, 1991). The absence of threshold levels for a wide range of toxic pollutants such as benzene, PM10s and hydrocarbons means that the only level of permissible emissions for this category that satisfies the conditions of the harm principle is zero. In allowing the anthropological production of toxic pollutants which lack safe exposure thresholds the law is subordinating the imperative of preventing physiological harm to the competing goals of economic growth and allocative efficiency. This is an overtly political decision that elevates economic values over ecological considerations and institutionalises the blatantly contradictory position that exposure to toxic pollution does not constitute harm. Legal institutions can be properly criticized for presenting (i) that which provides for economic efficiency and (ii) what is harmful, as mutually exclusive. In contrast to this expression of ideological dogma, the toxic pollution produced as a matter of routine in modern capitalist societies constitutes an ongoing and insidious source of harm.

Environmental laws that presently regulate toxic pollution are predicated upon the degree of harm (no other word is more appropriate here) that the general public may justifiably be exposed to (Montagu, 1989a). Under the leadership of William Reilly, the EPA of the US, for example, increased the permissible levels of benzene pollution from causing one death in a million to causing one death in 10,000 (Montagu, 1989a). The exposure of a constituency of one million individuals to a level of a toxic pollutant that, it is known, has a one in 10,000 chance of causing death, will logically result in the death of 100 individuals. The argument that no harm is caused because risk exposure is shared by all and that the identity of the victims of the pollution is not known in advance appears to evidence serious logical failings. By way of analogy, the terrorist who randomly exposes the public to risk of physical injury or death by planting a bomb in a busy shopping center can have little knowledge of the exact identity of the people who are subsequently killed when the bomb explodes. Although exact identity is not known in advance in either case, this in no way detracts from the very real harm subsequently caused. In both cases, it is known that a certain number of individuals are likely to die as a result of the act concerned. In the case of exposure to a bomb blast, injury is caused by foreign objects damaging bodily tissues and is mediated through an explosive device. In the case of exposure to toxins, injury is caused by foreign objects damaging the genetic integrity of cellular tissues and is mediated though a chemical pollutant.

Feinberg indeed acknowledges a similar analogy in his comparison of (i) a bomb placed in Grand Central Station, Manhattan and (ii) poison dropped in a city's water supply. Each case was conceded to constitute harm since, although injury is not necessarily caused to everyone in the city, a common danger was imposed on all resulting in 'actual injury to a large and indefinite number of persons, unidentifiable in advance' (Feinberg, 1984). In acknowledging the validity of an analogy between toxic pollution (in the form of poisoning of a water supply) and a bomb, Feinberg again, however unknowingly, acknowledges that toxic pollution can constitute harm.

Trying to understand the harm principle from legal analysis is flawed since the outcome will necessarily reflect the same power relations that construct the ideological component of legislation (chapter 4). This indicates that the environmental legislation presented by Feinberg as preventing harmful pollution are in fact based on the ideological premises of economic rationality that accommodates toxic pollution in the first place as a required condition to achieve allocative efficiency. Legislation has been constructed to codify social power relations. As such, law demonstrates contempt for an impartial implementation of the harm principle by applying the concept selectively to excuse the harm that is part and parcel of the capitalist economy.

Contradiction three: Selective application Feinberg claims that, 'clearly not every kind of act that causes harm to others can rightly be prohibited, but only those that cause avoidable and substantial harm' (Feinberg, 1984). This is arguably indeed the case. Nonetheless, the implementation of this principle by Feinberg constitutes the third contradiction in defining the harm principle to exclude toxic pollution. Feinberg asserts that pollution 'rarely [causes] clear and substantial harm to any specific person or group' (Feinberg, 1984).

The argument that the harm caused by pollutants is insignificant and does not constitute substantial or 'actual' harm is refuted by the epidemiological evidence which has been reviewed in some detail previously in this chapter. PM 10s alone cause between 300,000 and 700,000 deaths each year world wide (Sloep and Blowes, 1996). Most people would acknowledge that the estimated 3,000 deaths caused by the terrorist attacks in America on 11 September 2001 was substantial. Yet PM10s alone are responsible for 20 times as many deaths each and every year in the US as those killed on 11 September by terrorists flying jet planes into buildings (Weisskopf, 1991; Schwartz and Dockery, 1992; Bown, 1994d). The reason that toxic pollution is not elevated to the status that that terrorists have attained as a social evil is that legally permissible levels of toxic pollution are a product of, rather than a challenge to, the organisation of modern capitalist societies and have consequently been accepted as 'normal' or 'inevitable'. This double standard is employed for reasons of political expediency; to excuse the harm generated by the day to day operations of an ecologically disastrous economic system run to maximise efficiency and growth.

Toxic pollution is only seen as unavoidable and insubstantial from the perspective of economic rationality which restricts political possibilities to within the heavily circumscribed limits set by efficiency concerns. Processes responsible for the toxic pollution of the environment can be addressed by rejecting economic rationality in favor of adopting ecological rationality. The conservation of resources can be prioritized over the consumption of resources and fossil and nuclear fuels could be phased out and replaced by renewable forms of energy. Toxic pollution is only seen as unavoidable so long as society is based around the ecologically disastrous imperative to do whatever maximizes economic growth and efficiency concerns. This research has consistently argued that designing political policy around this focus is not even desirable let alone indispensable. Toxic pollution may be seen as unavoidable to politicians, economists, lawyers and citizens who are unwilling or unable to question the ideological basis of economic rationality but remains, nonetheless a matter of political choice rather than necessity. Furthermore, to those who see capitalism as a social evil to be overcome, the need to organize society around ecological rather than economic values becomes the most urgent social necessity.

This analysis demonstrates that toxic pollution cannot be excused from constituting harm on grounds of moral considerations since the ethical criteria must be selectively chosen and applied in order to reach such a conclusion. Such a project has consequently been found to suffer from serious methodological and epistemological failings.

Interests

The fourth stipulation of Feinberg's articulation of the harm principle requires that 'A's action is the cause of a setback to B's interests' (Feinberg, 1984). Toxic pollutants by definition harm the individuals who are exposed to them. All people have a very real interest in maintaining the best possible status of their health, a status that is deleteriously affected by exposure to legally permissible levels of toxic pollution (Dockery, Speizer, Strom *et al.*, 1989; Pope, Dockery, Spengler and Raizenne, 1991; Bates, 1992; Pope, Schwartz and Ransome, 1992; Pope and Kanner, 1993; Roemer, Hoek and Brunekreef, 1993; *World Health*, 1993; Hamer, 1994; Schwartz, 1994a; 1994b; Lee and Manning, 1995; Maclean's, 1995; Seaton, 1995; Seaton, McNee, Donaldson and Godden, 1995 and Paterson, 2000). Nagel identifies universal human interests when he points out that 'people don't want to be injured, robbed, or killed, and they don't want to get sick' (Nagel, 1994, p.66). Toxic pollution injures, kills and makes people sick and as such can be properly identified as a setback to three of the four universal interests identified by Nagel. Unless the universal human interests identified by Nagel can be demonstrated to be inaccurate, and there is very little evidence that such a conclusion can be reached, toxic pollution indeed constitutes a setback to the interests of subsequently exposed individuals.

Rights

The final condition that must be met for an action to be legitimately categorized as harm under Feinberg's formula is that it must be 'a violation of B's right'. This chapter has presented the case for the recognition of the human rights to an environment free from toxic pollution on the grounds that this is a prerequisite for existing legal rights to private life, autonomy (non-intervention), security of the person and the right to life to be realized. In one passage, Feinberg concedes a 'right to unpolluted air' as a 'moral right' (Feinberg, 1984, p. 110). Yet Feinberg then goes on to lament that this moral right cannot be realized because of the needs of the economy (Feinberg, 1984).

As the foregoing discussion has established, this position contradicts the liberal position and simply presents a case for sacrificing the harm principle at the alter of economic growth and efficiency. People presently lack legal rights to an environment free from toxic pollution since law exists to codify the economic values upon which capitalist society is predicated. In particular the legal system has been constructed to privilege processes of consumption and production over ecological concerns. As such this position is in no sense an impartial outcome and moreover contradicts fundamental tenets of liberal political philosophy.

People have a universal human right to an environment free from toxic pollution as a necessary component of the right to life. The foregoing analysis has therefore established that toxic pollution constitutes harm according to the formula presented by Feinberg for classifying harm. This analysis has however been largely superfluous. Toxic pollution is by definition harmful. If pollutants were not harmful, they would be classified as non-toxic rather than as toxic pollutants. The need to research and explain the links between toxic pollution and harm reflects the way in which law and conventional morality accommodates the needs of the economic system over and above the consistent and impartial implementation of the harm principle. This conclusion will be further vindicated by the future refusal of capitalist based law to recognize toxic pollution as harm, no matter how much epidemiological or ecological research is presented to the contrary.

Implications

For the harm and non-interference principles of liberalism to stand, it is necessary to phase out anthropogenic emissions of toxic pollution. Such a proposal already has political precedents. Ongoing international discussions are considering the elimination, rather than reduction, of a number of toxic pollutants such as dioxins (Reuters, 1999). Participants at the 2002 Earth Summit +10 conference in Johannesburg agreed to phase out selected toxic chemicals. However, delegates were careful not to eliminate those toxic chemicals that would significantly increase costs for industry or force changes to be made to polluting vehicle engines.

The Delaney clause in US federal law prohibited the use of carcinogenic pesticides that concentrate in processed foods. The clause explicitly stipulates a zero-risk policy and, against the vehement protestations of industry, emphasizes prevention rather than control of the toxins covered under its provisions (*Multinational Monitor*, 1994). Although such legislation remains exceptional in capitalist societies that have characteristically prioritized allocative efficiency over environmental protection, niche market firms have taken the initiative to phase out use of toxic pollutants. The Body Shop has released a policy statement stating that, 'processes should be designed to ensure zero toxic emissions for precautionary reasons' (quoted in Wheeler, 1993).

The elimination of toxic pollution would require phasing out usage of fossil fuels. Hydrogen fuel offers an alternative to power vehicles that can be readily produced by energy cells utilizing solar energy (Montagu, 1989b; Williams, 1989). Using such technology, alto voltaic cells can create power by electrochemically combining hydrogen from a fuel tank with oxygen from the air without the occurrence of combustion, so that the only by product is water vapor (McCarthy, 2000). Pollution free vehicles using hydrogen powered fuel cells have already been constructed (Williams, 1989). Several corporations have already developed vehicle engines to run on hydrogen (Montagu, 1989b; Radford, 1997a; 1997b). Daimler-Benz and Ford have developed prototypes of hydrogen powered cars, the latter corporation spending $1 billion developing a model that is due to go on general sale in 2004 (McCarthy, 2000). It is therefore possible to generate energy from sources that do not produce toxic pollution as a by-product. Continued dependency on fossil fuel continues because of the narrow focus on private economic costs promoted by economic rationality.

Contrary to the ideological protestations of proponents of capitalists, the human right to an environment free from toxic pollution can be realized in practice. The necessary sea change for such a realization is however, nothing short of monumental. Political decisions must be made according to ecological rationality rather than economic rationality. Concern for ecological well being must replace the concern for allocative efficiency as the central criterion for policy decisions (chapter one). Capitalism and implementing the human right to an environment free from toxic pollution are most certainly mutually exclusive goals. It has been argued here that those who want to see society based around a respect for the principles of non-malfeasance, justice as impartiality and respect for human rights can subsequently enlist the political philosophy of liberalism in the critique of the capitalist system.

Conclusion

The human right to an environment free from toxic pollution could conflict with the human right to economic development when this latter right is interpreted as endorsing a principal political focus on economic growth at the expense of environmental considerations. Such conflicts between human rights are, however, nothing new and established procedures exist to resolve such dilemmas (Hayward, 2000). The subsequent matter of implementation must be differentiated from establishing the validity of environmental human rights in the first place, which is the explicit purpose of this research. It has also been noted in this chapter that current patterns of economic organisation do more to redistribute resources from the poor to the rich than vice versa, a theme further developed in chapter 6.

By virtue of the deleterious effects of toxic pollution on health, the elimination of production and consumption process that create such pollutants is required to protect legally recognized human rights to privacy, to security of the person, to non-interference, to the highest attainable standards of health and to life. A universal human right to an environment free from toxic pollution can therefore be justifiably claimed as a mechanism to protect human health. Recognition of this right will help efforts aimed at environmental protection by giving a trumping status to political calls aimed at preventing toxic pollution of the eco-system.

The status of the right to an environment free from toxic pollution has been investigated in this chapter in terms of (i) political philosophy and (ii) legal political analysis. A juxtaposition of capitalism to liberalism on the subject of toxic pollution established a fundamental and inescapable contradiction between these two positions. Capitalism assumes a consumerist lifestyle for individuals and requires the organization of society in such a way as to maximize allocative efficiency. This political goal requires generating an optimal level of toxic pollution. These toxic pollutants by definition harm people and a substantial amount of epidemiological evidence has been incorporated in this chapter to verify this fact. The capitalist society is therefore predicated upon violating the harm principle and fundamental human rights, including the right to life, when this is required to achieve conditions of allocative efficiency. The relationship between capitalism and liberal political philosophy has consequently been found to be conflictual rather than complimentary in nature. Common confusion between liberalism and capitalism obfuscates this contradiction and serves the beneficiaries of capitalism since the economic system is ideologically supported by the veneer of a theory of justice.

Imperatives of private interest and economic rationality that characterize capitalist societies have normalized the harm caused by pollution as culturally acceptable. The courts, it has been argued, have accommodated this viewpoint by defining the harm principle in ways that exclude considerations of toxic pollution and by dismissing, denying, rejecting or ignoring the injury caused through exposure to toxic pollutants as a human rights issue. Whereas the most minor act of theft is categorized in legal terms as harm, the courts do not consider that harm is caused by car fumes, even when the carcinogenic substances found in these fumes damage cellular integrity and DNA. Law can be therefore seen to reify and legitimize the elevation of economic values over considerations of environmental protection. The argument that toxic pollution does not constitute harm lacks internal coherence. If a pollutant were not harmful to human health, it would be categorized as non-toxic. Yet the legal acceptance of toxic pollution stands since it provides the desired outcome, that the damage caused by the structural operations of capitalism is excused and accommodated. Law excuses toxic pollution from constituting harm to the extent that such pollution is required to ensure the desired attainment of allocative efficiency. Here, the veneer of impartiality is only maintained by refusing to accept the legitimacy of any demands to eradicate toxic pollution (for example that the demand is unrealistic since it does not express values of economic rationality). This self evidently biased position reveals the way through which the law employs double standards to serve power interests and why the interest based system of capitalism, rather than the liberal theory of justice, characterizes both modern society and law.

Notes

1   Response to research questionnaire received from Earth Rights International, 12 November 1998.
2   Response to research questionnaire received from Oregon Clearinghouse for Pollution Reduction, 10 December 1998.

Chapter 6

The Human Right to Natural Resources

> The poorest man hath as true a title and just a right to land as the richest man.
> – Gerard Winstanley

Introduction

This chapter examines and defends the environmental human right to ownership of natural resources. Ownership is 'the ideology of valid possession' (Sumner, 1979). The recognized system of ownership therefore legitimizes property rights (Sumner, 1979). For the purpose of this research, ownership rights to natural resources are defined as 'enforceable authority to undertake particular actions related to a specific domain' (Ostrom and Schlager, 1996). The claimed human right to natural resources is applicable to local environmental resources such as water, lakes, land, forests and sub soil resources. Ownership of industry, services or the global commons, such as the atmosphere and oceans lie outside of the focus in this chapter.

The chapter begins by establishing that ownership systems to natural resources are socially constructed. A choice therefore exists as to which system is to be adopted by a polity. Differentiating between six specific ownership systems will substantiate this claim. Two of these systems in particular; (i) private property rights and (ii) common property resources (CPRs) will be compared and contrasted from the perspective of basic human rights. The system of assigning rights to natural resources derived from the paradigm of economic rationality constructs property rights in terms that maximizes allocative efficiency and aggregate production. The focus on economic variables comes at the cost of dismissing claims of human rights to (i) cultural self-determination and (ii) freedom from hunger, as well as causing systematic environmental degradation. An alternative structuring of property rights based around CPRs is suggested to be more conducive to facilitating cultural diversity and the satisfaction of basic human needs, as will be exemplified through an analysis of global food provision. Juxtaposed to private property rights, CPRs are furthermore found to lessen the human impact on the environment.

Continuing the theme permeating previous chapters, the capitalist organization of the global economy is identified as the most important structural barrier for the recognition of the claimed environmental human right to natural resources. The characteristic ability of global markets to divert resources into supplying luxury goods for the opulent explains why essential resources are simultaneously denied to the impoverished.

By endorsing a subsistence based CPR economy, rather than the exchange based economy of capitalism, the environmental human right to natural resources links the human rights agenda to a less environmentally destructive economic system (*The*

Ecologist, 1993). Processes of environmental commodification and distanciation that characterize global capitalism will be examined as causing particular concern from the ecological perspective. Distanciation facilitates economic benefits to be acquired by an individual or institution in one location through a process that imposes the environmental and social costs on people living elsewhere in the world, thereby spatially separating the benefits of consumption from the environmental damage caused during the production process (Saurin, 1993).

Although the principle of CPRs is vindicated in this chapter as the ownership system most conducive to the realization of the claimed environmental human right to natural resources, this chapter does not address the practicalities of implementation. Such concerns relate, for example, to how specific resources can be equitably allocated between communities. These matters of implementation are best resolved in a case by case basis, taking all relevant local factors into account to ensure that all can meet basic needs (Costanza and Folke, 1996). Specifying a precise or universally applicable model for the implementation of this human right would also arbitrarily curtail, rather than facilitate cultural diversity (Hanna, Folke and Maler, 1996). Furthermore, discussion relating to the implementation of the claimed environmental human right is rather premature so long as the principle to the right remains unrecognized.

The Social Construction of Property Rights

Sagoff reminds us that far from being universal or unchangeable, the nature, meaning and extent of property rights to environmental resources is a constructed function of the legal and economic regimes that define them through utilizing a political ideology (Sagoff, 1995). The validity of this claim establishes the possibility to choose between alternative systems of resource ownership rights. Systems of rights to natural resources can be differentiated into the following six broad categories.

[i] Open Access Resources

An open access system of resource exploitation describes a situation that allows everyone unlimited access to environmental resources. This system has no mechanisms for limiting the ecological impact of human exploitation and has subsequently been correctly criticized for inexorably leading to overuse and environmental degradation (Vogler, 1995).

[ii] No Access

No access systems deny all humans access to a given spatial area. The only notable example of a no access system is the Antarctic Wilderness Area that, under international agreement, has been designated as an area from which anthropogenic activity is to remain entirely absent (Vogler, 1995). The no access model effectively reverses the benefits and drawbacks of the open access system. The model is of great benefit to biodiversity and habitat preservation but prevents humans from using environmental resources to provide even for their own needs. This model could be applied to designated areas that are of particular importance to biodiversity but is unattainable on a global scale given the needs of the human populace who are also living parts of the eco-system.

[iii] State Control

This system of environmental resource ownership places property rights under the control of the state and has been severely criticized from a number of positions. Neo-liberal economists characteristically decry the notorious allocative inefficiencies of such a centralized system. Further strengthening the state is also problematic for the realization of human rights, given the nature of the state as an instrument of power as discussed in chapter four. From the ecological perspective, state ownership of natural resources has often preempted environmental degradation as environmental concerns are subordinated to considerations of power and economic growth. This is exemplified through the granting of logging concessions to the corporations responsible for widespread deforestation in East Asian states (World Rainforest Movement and Forests Monitor Ltd., 1998). In cases where the state does not allow corporate control over resources but reserves this right for local inhabitants, nationalized resources invariably degenerate into open access systems as non-compliance with complex or inappropriate bureaucratic regulations becomes established as the norm (Berkes, 1996).

[iv] Public Goods Systems

Public goods relate to global environmental commons such as the atmosphere, climate and oceans which, by their global nature, lie outside the sovereign jurisdiction of any particular state (Vogler, 1995). Strictly speaking, public goods systems therefore describe the global nature of important environmental categories rather than conceptualizing property rights over environmental resources. The notion of public goods is nonetheless significant to discussions over resource rights since this highlights how resource decisions made at the local level can impact at the national, international and global levels, for example in the case of climate change or the over-exploitation of fish stocks (Vogler, 1995).

[v] Private Property Rights

Under the capitalist system of assigning resource rights, legal recognition of individual claims to environmental resources is a function of market (exchange) transactions. Land and environmental resources are treated as commodities, since they are demarcated and separated from the surrounding land. Land is therefore commodified by virtue of being bought and sold by individuals or corporations at a price specified by the market. Decisions relating to land use, as well as the resulting incomes, are thereafter seen as the private concern of the property holder. Under capitalist conditions, land-use decisions are invariably made according to commercial criteria and considerations of private gain. The landowner is legally empowered to exclude the rest of the community from utilizing privately owned land.

The private property system of environmental resource rights is therefore an expression of economic rationality. This position is predicated upon the normative belief that market conditions ought to define resource rights. This belief is derived from the ideology that the general good of society is achieved by maximizing (i) allocative efficiency and (ii) aggregate wealth.[1] Proponents of economic rationality characteristically universalize or normalize private property rights as the only legitimate system of resource ownership (Johnston, 1995).

Although most liberal political theorists defend individual property rights to land, not all conclude that ownership titles should be decided by the market (Kramer, 1997). From the broad range of positions advocated by different liberal theorists, radicals have allocated land rights on an egalitarian basis, irrespective of individual wealth. Beitz for example concludes on the grounds of equality of opportunity that, 'each inhabitant of the world has an equal basic entitlement to natural resources' (Beitz, 1981). Similarly Locke had previously stated a right for each individual to claim a part of nature, as long as they leave 'enough and as good' for others (Wood, 1984). Locke's designation of property rights was clearly influenced by his political agenda to justify the ownership of American lands by individuals, rather than the crown. Still, the fact remains that capitalist property rights over land can be criticized on radical liberal grounds since the latter utilizes the language of human rights to impose limits on the unlimited ownership of natural resources by the wealthy (Kramer, 1997). This claim articulates the concern that, when denied control over land, individuals are restricted in the potential to shape their lives. The requirements of freedom requires a basic entitlement to natural resources. Under this radical liberal interpretation, unfettered agrarian capitalism becomes a repressive social system denying the impoverished the means to provide for their own subsistence requirements.

The radical liberal critique of capitalism is nowhere better exemplified than through Thomas Paine. In *Agrarian Justice*, Paine claimed that the introduction of the system of private land ownership had deprived the community of the right to make free use of the earth. Paine demanded either respect for egalitarian ownership rights to land, or else a system of compensation for the loss of this right (Paine, 1987). Under the latter option, each owner of land should pay rent to a collective fund corresponding to the size of their holding and that the proceeds of this fund should be distributed amongst all members of the population equitably (Paine, 1987).

An example of the implementation of the radical liberal right to land is evident in the case of the distribution of land in America during the second half of the nineteenth century following Lincoln's Homestead Act. This legislation distributed free land titles to millions of acres that had been forcibly taken from the native Americans (Greider, 1997). The right of English people to allotments also reflects a right of individuals to land. A differentiation between capitalism and radical liberalism on the question of resource ownership has been noted here since it raises a degree of ambiguity relating to the defense of a market-based system of land rights from the perspective of liberal political theory.

[vi] Common Property Resources (CPR)

Australian Aborigines and indigenous North Americans had no concept of private land ownership until the first Europeans made land claims (Baird, 1987). Referring to indigenous culture in the Malaysian state of Sarawak, a native elder rejected private property rights to land by insisting that 'the land belongs to the countless numbers of people who are dead, the few who are living, and the multitude of those yet to be born' (quoted in World Rainforest Movement and Forests Monitor Ltd., 1998). In many non-capitalist cultures, land is perceived not as a commodity to be exploited for private profit, but rather as a spiritual phenomena, central to cultural practices and accessible for all members of the community who are duty bound to protect the land for other individuals. Resource rights in non-capitalist cultures are typically based upon a variant of the CPR system.

CPRs can be defined as systems within which long term use rights for environmental resources, such as land, timber, water and sub soil resources, are controlled by identifiable groups (Agarwal and Sunita, 1992). CPR systems are consequently characterized by a construction of resource management rules to meet communal needs based on collective choice arrangements (Clay, 1994; *The Ecologist*, 1995). CPRs are controlled by local community groups, rather than by individuals or states, and provide livelihoods for the people directly managing them, rather than commodities for global markets (Chatterjee and Finger, 1994). The decentralized and diverse nature of CPR systems prevents a more specific definition of this type of ownership regime, since the specific form taken is derived from local environmental conditions and cultural traditions.

To operate effectively, CPRs require clearly defined rules of resource access for communities, households and individuals, enforceable by a system of monitoring and graduated sanctions to prevent over usage at any of these levels (Costanza and Folke, 1996). Numerous studies have documented the various norms, monitoring systems and sanctions against rule breakers that have been implemented to protect resources. These studies relate for example to CPRs in Africa (du Bois, 1994); the forests in Törbel (Ostrom, 1990); three million hectares of agricultural land in the Hirano, Nagaike and Yamanoka regions of Japan (Ostrom, 1990), and the Cofyal forest run by the Yanesha Indians in the Peruvian Amazon (Sachs, 1995). The Huerta irrigation system of the Valencia region of Spain has allocated water between villages for up to 1,000 years and has various levels of monitoring to ensure the enforcement of the correct distribution of scarce water to each farmer. The success of this system is reflected in an infraction rate of only 0.008 per cent, despite the compelling incentive to cheat since 'stealing water during a dry season ... might on occasion save an entire season's crop from certain destruction' (Ostrom, 1990).

Research conducted by Ostrom supports the claim that CPRs can be effective in enforcing rules that restrict resource usage by individual members (Ostrom, 1990). Ostrom's study into the social and environmental effectiveness of CPRs concluded that violations of the usage rules in CPR systems was exceptional, even when opportunities to break the rules were plentiful and the sanctions relatively light (Ostrom, 1990). This result was achieved because of clearly defined boundaries of resource usage, collective (participatory) choice arrangements, monitoring systems, graduated sanctions, conflict resolution mechanisms and relative autonomy from state structures (Ostrom, 1990). The enforcement of rules in CPR systems is typically achieved by allowing a portion of the fines extracted from rule breakers to be kept by the individual who monitored and caught the infractor (Ostrom, 1990). In the same way that citizens generally pay the correct amount of taxes, Ostrom concludes that individuals in the commons generally adhere to the rules or adopt a strategy of quasi-voluntary compliance when they have confidence that the other members of the community will similarly adhere to the rules (Ostrom, 1990).

As well as requiring mechanisms to resolve disputes between individuals within a commons system, neighboring CPR systems must also have procedures for deciding conflicts. In the Philippines, for example, competing claims to water rights among different communities have customarily been decided by inter-village councils composed of elders from the relevant communities (*The Ecologist*, 1995). Dispute resolution mechanisms between communities have been credited with successfully extending the applicability of CPR systems beyond fixed resources such as land, forests and lakes and to migrating fish stocks and other non-exclusivist natural resources (Costanza and Folke, 1996).

Social Power as the Deciding Variable in Determining the System of Resource Rights

The political significance of deciding upon a system of ownership rights over environmental resources resides in the observation made by both Barry and Beitz that claims to natural resources stand logically prior to any claims to products which are subsequently produced from these resources (Goodin, 1985). Therefore, choosing a system of ownership rights to natural resources is a fundamental variable in questions of equity, of economic justice, of the distribution of power in society and of human rights. Identifying the criteria through which to establish ownership rights to natural resources therefore becomes a central question.

Goodin argues that unequal ownership of natural resources can be justified on the grounds that 'some people have done something to render those pre-existing resources useful to mankind, if only by discovering them' (Goodin, 1985). Yet Goodin presupposes here the very condition which is correctly problematized by Beitz and Barry, namely that of original ownership rights to natural resources. Whereas a petrochemical corporation for example locates and utilizes oil reserves in the Third World, this only occurs as a result of the legal and economic institutions that had previously been constructed to legitimize private property rights to natural resources (Wiwa, 1995). Constructing a legal basis to empower certain people and exclude others from making claims to natural resources is therefore in the first instance a social and political, rather than a jurisprudential or economic question, since a decision must be initially made as to whose claims to natural resources should be legitimized and protected.

The methodology that is employed here for understanding the legal institutionalization of one system of rights to natural resources over other possibilities is to focus on social power relations within which ownership rights are embedded (du Bois, 1994; Vogler, 1995; Taylor, 1998). Of the six categories of conceptualizing rights to environmental resources outlined above, this chapter now juxtaposes CPR to private property rights. Private property rights have been chosen for analysis since these represent the form of legal resource ownership rights in the capitalist global economy. CPRs have been chosen as the second system of resource ownership since this system offers a distinct and widespread alternative through which to compare and contrast the system of private property rights.

Private property rights institutionalize the power relations of capitalism by facilitating inequality in the allocation of environmental resources along the lines advocated by a focus on economic rationality. CPRs in contrast characteristically benefit the disempowered and marginalized since CPR systems tend to focus on self-reliance and on serving the basic needs of all members before resources are diverted into the production of luxury goods for profit, gain or income (Makhijani, 1992; *The Ecologist*, 1995).

Land Rights as Human Rights

A number of theorists have interpreted existing human rights texts as legitimizing the communal right to natural resources (Haas, 1970; Vincent, 1986; Crawford, 1992; Wisner, 1995). Endorsing this claim, it will now be argued that organizing rights to environmental resources according to the logic of economic rationality violates the human rights to self-determination and to be free from hunger. In particular, the global mining and cash crop economies exemplify how capitalism diverts resources to supply market demands at the expense of considerations of basic human rights.

The Right to Cultural Self-Determination

The stipulations of existing legal agreements on human rights assign environmental resource rights to groups rather than to individuals. Both the ICCPR and the ICESCR omit to even mention human rights to private property. Instead both covenants grant rights to natural resources to peoples, derived from the right to self-determination. The ICESCR, part 1, article 1 and the ICCPR part 1, article 1 stipulate the following in identical wording:

1 All peoples have the right of self-determination. By virtue of that right they freely determine their political status and freely pursue their economic, social and cultural development.
2 All peoples may, for their own ends, freely dispose of their natural wealth and resources without prejudice to any obligations arising out of international economic co-operation, based upon the principle of mutual benefit, and international law. In no case may a people be deprived of its own means of subsistence (Council of Europe, 1992, p. 18 and p. 32).

Of particular significance in this article is the derivation of a peoples distinct cultural development as an aspect of the right to self-determination.

Other articles in international human rights covenants that mention natural resource rights tend to reinforce this designation of group rights. ICCPR part 5, article 47 and ICESCR part 4, article 25 both state that; 'nothing in the present

Covenant shall be interpreted as impairing the inherent right of all peoples to enjoy and utilize fully and freely their natural wealth and resources'. The legal right of peoples to sovereignty over natural resources is further supported by General Assembly Resolution 1803, article 1, that declares a 'right of peoples and nations to permanent sovereignty over their natural resources'.[2] In all of these cases, rights to natural resources are linguistically stipulated as a group right. In no human rights text is it explicitly stated that ownership rights over natural resources are assigned to individuals or corporations.

Both the right to self-determination and the derived right to natural resources have been traditionally interpreted as an individual, rather than as a communal right in formal international human rights discussions (Evans, 1996). This interpretation facilitates iniquitous resource ownership benefiting corporate agribusiness at the expense of local communities, reflecting a political interpretation of human rights that accommodates the distribution of power in the capitalist political economy.

The systematic violation of the right to cultural self-determination remains a salient feature of organizing the global economy according to private property rights over natural resources. The supreme cultural importance of traditional lands to indigenous cultures is evident from the response of indigenous communities faced with separation from their lands. To facilitate commercial exploitation of sub soil resources on indigenous peoples lands, members of the Macuxi, Kaiowa and Guarani tribes in Brazil have, for example, been relocated to reserves in a demonstration of contempt for their rights to cultural identity (*The Ecologist*, 1993). Traditional lands are revered by these tribes 'as irreplaceable and even to be defended at all costs' (*The Ecologist*, 1993). Dramatically illustrating how commercial operations can violate cultural self-determination, members of the Guarani tribe have been committing mass suicide, 'as loss of their land leaves them with no reason to go on living' (*Brazil Network Newsletter*, 1996b).

The US based Occidental corporation is currently in a dispute with indigenous people in Colombia who have similarly threatened to commit mass suicide if oil exploration proceeds as planned on their traditional tribal lands. In 1992, Occidental signed a contract with the Colombian government to explore a 200,000 hectare area in eastern Colombia that is also home to 4,000 U'wa people (Luxner, 1997; Wright, 1997). Chief Cobaira of the U'wa tribe has stated that:

> any kind of tampering with our land goes against the core of our traditions, but our cries seem to be falling on deaf ears ... . If the white man starts making holes and sucking the veins of our most revered Mother Earth we will have no choice but to bring our lives to an end (quoted in Gamini, 1996, p. 13).

The culture of the U'wa is threatened by the privatization of their lands through (i) the pollution of their sacred lands that oil exploration entails, (ii) the increased violence that the oil project will inevitably bring, or (iii) by the tribe committing mass suicide in response to the project (Project International, 1997). This case exemplifies the centrality of traditional lands to the customs, culture and existence of tribal communities and the culturally destructive results of commodifying and privatizing rights to land. Indigenous communities characteristically have a spiritual relationship to their land, perceiving the environment as an intricate part of their cultural personality rather than as an exploitable commodity (Nettheim, 1992). Such a cultural interpretation of the land is incommensurate to that of the capitalist model. Floriano Carique, founder of Mapuche,[3] states that:

> Indigenous thought does not distinguish the environment from the self. Kume Moignen, or harmony, is central to our lives. We must live well with ourselves, with the community, our physical environment and with the cosmos (*Multinational Monitor*, 1995b).

Stockton similarly remarks that in Australia the aborigines commonly state that 'I am the land' (quoted in *The New Internationalist*, 1987). It is the cosmological aspect of their cultural beliefs that Aborigines view rights to land as originating with the design and creation of the world rather than with alienable legal title. Aborigines look at land as being a part of the wider whole and therefore also as a part of themselves, and that they are a part of the land (Hill, 1995). Demonstrating both the incommensurability of capitalism with aboriginal culture, and the subtle cultural imperialism evident in modern politics, Hill remarks that the focus on a cultural definition of land is a feature that white Australians fail to comprehend, regardless of their level of sympathy for Aboriginal land rights (Hill, 1995). The key conclusion to be drawn from these examples is to establish the relativism of the capitalist commodification of land. As we have seen, many indigenous cultures do not commodify land and suggest alternative land use systems that are not predicated upon short-term resource exploitation. Human rights to self-determination and to a traditional cultural heritage are ignored when the incommensurate values and ontological categories of capitalist conceptualizations of land use are imposed on non-capitalist cultures. Yet this is precisely the logic of global capitalism, of commodifying natural resources and allowing the market to decide subsequent usage, regardless of the non-economic purpose of land for distinct cultural traditions (*The Ecologist*, 1993).

The irrelevance demonstrated by the actions of commercial actors for environmental values and the cultural rights of non-capitalist societies is a structural feature of capitalism (Gill, 1995), as can be exemplified through the recent history of petrochemical MNCs. In 1996, Occidental received military assistance to force the Siona and Secoya peoples of the Ecuadorian Amazon to give up their land to enable oil exploration (Project Underground, 1997c). Survival International has charged Mobil with risking the lives of remote indigenous people in the Peruvian Amazon since Mobil workers introduced whooping cough and pneumonia to the communities whilst conducting oil explorations (*Multinational Monitor*, 1996).

Chevron and FINA have both demonstrated an interest to drill for oil and gas in the sacred Badger Two-Medecine land,[4] that is central to the cultural and religious practices of the Blackfeet Nation.[5] In 1987 the Human Rights Committee ruled that oil and gas exploration was threatening the culture of the indigenous Lake Lubicon Band in Canada in violation of article 27 of the ICCPR that guarantees the rights of minorities to culture, religion and language (Cameron and MacKenzie, 1996).

The same process of neglect for the cultural rights of indigenous communities is also evident in the case of certain hydroelectric projects. Fighting the James Bay hydroelectric project in northern Quebec in 1992 that affects an area containing 10,000 Cree and 6,000 Inuit, the Cree Vice-Grand Chief Diom Saganash asserted that tribal peoples are threatened by hydroelectric projects all over the world. He argued that:

> our basic human rights, right to a livelihood and right to survival are threatened by these projects being forced upon us. They are killing our ways of life (quoted in Park, 1992, p. 15).

Mining corporations have similarly pursued private commercial interests at the expense of the human right to cultural self-determination. *The Ecologist* states that 'indigenous people are regularly dispossessed of their lands to make way for mines without compensation or any share of the profits' (*The Ecologist*, 1993). The US mining giant Peabody has been reported to be strip-mining coal on sacred Dineh and Hopi lands in Arizona (*Inter Press Service*, 1997). In 1985, mining corporations operating in Australia campaigned against political recognition of aboriginal land rights because of a concern over potential rising costs and denial of access to resources in the event of land being ceded to aboriginal communities (*The New Internationalist*, 1987). In 1992, US based Golden Star Resources began mining gold reserves in the interior of Suriname.[6] The firm's operations led to the forced eviction of thousands of indigenous people. In September 1995, conflict at mining sites exploded as police shot at Maroon people trying to access their traditional forests (Colchester, 1995). In all these cases, corporations benefit from the enforcement of private property rights to natural resources at the expense of indigenous communities losing control over their cultural lands.

Cultural rights to self-determination are routinely subordinated to accommodating mining operations when this contributes to economic growth. The same pattern is also evident in the case of logging operations. McMillan Bloedell and Interfor have been criticized for over-exploiting the temperate rain forests of the Nuu-Chah-Nulth and Nuxalk indigenous peoples of British Colombia, Canada (*Inter Press Service*, 1997). Mitsubishi's operations have polluted the lands of the Lubicon Cree of Alberta, Canada (*Inter Press Service*, 1997). Logging by Russian, Japanese, South Korean, and US MNCs has destroyed the resource base of the Udege indigenous people of Siberia and caused soil erosion and siltation of river systems upon which the indigenous community depended for its subsistence (Sachs, 1995; Worldwatch Institute, 1995). These cases exemplify how corporations violate the right to cultural self-determination and how the trend is legitimized through the system of private property rights to natural resources. For the right to cultural self-determination to mean anything other than subordination to the global capitalist economy, the resource base required for the subsistence and independence of non-capitalist cultures must first be secured (Hitchcock, 1997). Property and ownership rights to natural resources are required since there can be no cultural self-determination where non-capitalist communities suffer invasions of their lands at the behest of global markets. The granting of access or usufruct rather than ownership rights to natural resources would be insufficient conditions for the realization of the right to self-determination since ultimate ownership of lands would not be controlled by the communities themselves. The ability and readiness of corporations to disregard considerations of cultural diversity in favor of the search for profits means that non-capitalist societies require the conditions for independence and self sufficiency, of which the ownership of traditional lands is the most important prerequisite.

For the reasons given in chapter five in the case of the right to an environment free from toxic pollution, the legal recognition of the right to environmental resources is an insufficient requirement for the realization of this right. It is unlikely in the extreme that new laws by themselves will protect the cultural diversity of non-capitalist cultures from corporate interests, given that the efficacy of law depends on power relations in the political economy as explained in chapter four. For the human right to environmental resources to be realized, anti-systemic forces have to organize and campaign to challenge the power relations that presently legitimize the cultural imperialism of global capitalism. Recent political activism by indigenous communities in Latin America exemplifies how human rights claims to natural resources can garner popular support around an organic challenge to the global market system.

The Committee for the Defense of Human Rights in Honduras (CODEH) has campaigned for the rights to ownership of tribal lands on the grounds that this is 'inextricably linked' to human rights of free expression of tribal identity and lifestyle (Phillips, 1997). Claims to land rights from indigenous peoples were affirmed at the Legal Commission of the International NGO Conference on Indigenous Peoples and the Land.[7] Stressing the importance of land to cultural traditions of indigenous nations, the declaration produced at this venue stated an 'inseparable connection between land rights of Indigenous Peoples and the right of self-determination' (Nettheim, 1992). The 1986 Quito Declaration,[8] similarly challenged the capitalist political economy by demanding 'an end to assimilationist policies' and 'juridical recognition of territorial rights based on prior ownership including rights to the resources of the sub-soil and recognition of systems of self government' (Smith, 1992). Rights to natural resources are therefore claimed in this declaration as a means for achieving cultural and political independence from the forces of the capitalist economy (Smith, 1992).

Coinciding with the day that NAFTA took effect,[9] the Zapatista Army of National Liberation (EZLN) launched an armed revolt against the Mexican government. Based in the Chiapas region, the rebellion was composed largely by Mayans who challenged the loss of indigenous lands, or ejidos.[10] The right to ejidos, guaranteed under article 27 of the 1917 Mexican constitution, was abolished in 1992 as a part of pro-market reforms undertaken by President Carlos Salinas de Gortari (Stea, Elguea and Bustillo, 1997). A significant feature of the Zapatista uprising was the way in which the movement rejected the pro-market structural adjustments of the Salinas government and instead demanded land rights as a means of securing political and economic independence from the market (Pi-Sunyer and Thomas, 1997). The uprising was also characterized by indigenous opposition to the environmental degradation of the forests in Chiapas, especially in the Lacandon Biosphere Reserve, where the introduction of monoculture cash crops had degraded the ecological biodiversity of this region (Stea, Elguea and Bustillo, 1997). The Zapatista uprising therefore exemplifies a campaign for cultural independence and environmental protection based around demands for land rights.

The conclusion of this discussion is that private property rights to natural resources are unable to secure human rights to cultural self-determination since land use patterns are instead determined by market forces. Placing rights to natural resources in the hands of local communities would empower local groups with the means to achieve independence from the tyranny of the market. The foregoing analysis argued that such empowerment is a prerequisite for the human right to cultural self-determination to be prioritized over considerations of profit that are institutionalized in the capitalist system.

The Right to be Free From Hunger

The claimed human right to ownership of environmental resources is necessary to realize the right to be free from hunger as stipulated in the ICESCR.[11] Hunger is a necessary consequence of adopting a market based system of natural resource ownership rights and is largely avoidable through assigning rights over environmental resources to local communities.

Capitalist property rights to land ownership are excellent at supplying market demands but at the necessary expense of causing hunger for hundreds of millions of people who lack the funds to access the market mechanism (Goodman and Redclift, 1991). This situation presently applies to 1.3 billion people, approximately one fifth of the world's population (Flavin, 1997). Subsequently, 40,000 children die daily from the combination of malnutrition and poor sanitation (Galtung, 1994). More than 800 million people suffered from chronic under-nourishment during the period 1980–90 (Chanrasekhar, 1997).

These statistics result from individuals and groups lacking the sufficient land to provide for their own subsistence requirements. Refuting the claim that hunger results from a lack of overall land availability, the evidence demonstrates that hunger is the principal result of commodifying land and thereby redirecting use to serve market demands. This process is exemplified in the case of those living in the Dande Valley of northern Zimbabwe, who were deprived of access to wildlife, forests and fish after their traditional lands were sold off as by the state to raise revenue. The land is now used for cash crops and hunting by paying tourists. Traditional hunting practiced by the indigenous population has been criminalized as poaching and a formally self-sufficient community has become dependent for survival on food from NGOs and from the Zimbabwean state (Tandon, 1993).

The trend towards cash crop production exemplifies how environmental resources are skewed away from providing for basic needs and towards serving luxury markets when land rights are privatized. That starvation is a function of food entitlement rather than of overall availability explains why only sectors of the population who lack income starve and why, 'there has probably never been a famine in which every group has suffered' (Sen, 1983). The net weight of food exported from Ireland during the 1845–50 famine exceeded the weight of foods imported during the same period (Metress, 1996). Similarly, more food was exported from famine areas than was imported in the cases of the 1973 Ethiopian famine and of the 1974 Bangladeshi famine (Sen, 1983). Despite the threat of famine, Sudan sold 400,000 tons of sorghum to the EC in 1989 (*Third World Resurgence* editors, 1994). Further evidence for this trend is provided by Goodman and Redclift who conclude that the food crisis in developing states is caused primarily by a regressive distribution of income (Goodman and Redclift, 1991).

Therefore, hunger is a consequence of land use being diverted through the market mechanism to prioritize the fancies of opulent consumers who are disproportionately located in Western states (Smith, 1981).

The privatization of communal lands in Mexico has changed the use of agricultural lands from serving communal needs to serving luxury markets. Land has been diverted into producing luxury goods such as strawberries and feed grains for animals, foods that are priced beyond the means of most Mexicans (Goodman and Redclift, 1991). Honduras has the lowest level of per-person daily calorific consumption in the Western hemisphere. Governmental incentives for cash crops have ensured rapid expansion in this sector of the Honduran economy since 1965, whilst the availability of basic foods such as maize, beans and sorghum for the domestic population has consistently declined (Phillips, 1997).

This evidence refutes the contention that hunger is a consequence of overall scarcity, a theory typically advanced by corporate agribusiness. Monsanto's Chief Executive Officer (CEO), Robert Shapiro, writes for example in the introduction to the company's 1996 Environmental Review that the use of genetically engineered crops 'will help immensely in closing the gap between hungry people and adequate food supplies' (quoted in Bruno, 1997). In contrast to this claim, the evidence reviewed above suggests that hunger is a function of skewed production patterns in favor of luxury markets under conditions of capitalism. For example, 5 million hectares of land around the world are used to grow tobacco, illustrating how capitalism determines land use to serve frivolous market fads rather than in response to human needs (Brown, 1997). This conclusion is further supported by the fact that during the Ethiopian famine of 1983–4, while thousands died of hunger, fields bloomed with carnations destined for European markets (Sachs, 1995).

Mass starvation continues because under conditions of capitalism, those without the necessary money to buy food have no legally recognizable claim to food. In 1980 the world cereal harvest measured 1,556 million tons. Only 0.002 per cent of this would have been required to adequately feed the 15 million children who died that year from hunger and hunger related illnesses (George, 1984). The UNESCO summarizes that 'the overall availability of food in the world is not a problem. There is enough food to offer everyone in the world around 2,500 calories a day – 200 calories more than the basic minimum' (UNESCO, 1995).

Current patterns of starvation are a constructed function of the global market economy, of commodifying land in the hands of private individuals and corporations who thereafter use the land for cash crops to maximize profits. This fact is made most evident through analysis of the global meat industry. Rifkin observes that:

> 145 million tons of grain were fed to livestock in 1979. Of that, only 21 million tons were available to human beings, after the energy conversion, in the form of meat, poultry and eggs. The rest, 124 million tons of grain and soybeans became inaccessible to human consumption .... If world-wide agricultural production were shifted from livestock feed to grains for direct human consumption, more than a billion people on the planet could be fed (Rifkin, 1992, p. 13).

Energy conversion refers to the 90 per cent of calorific energy that is lost to humans when plants are fed to non-human animals that are subsequently consumed by humans (Regan, 1984). The Artist Hunger Network highlights the inverted logic of the argument of raising cattle to provide protein for humans in pointing out that 'it takes 10 pounds of protein in the form of grain to create 1 pound of protein in the form of flesh to be eaten'.[12] Sagoff reminds us that 'the world already produces enough cereals and oilseeds to feed 10 billion people a vegetarian diet adequate in protein and calories' (Sagoff, 1997).

The criticism that the right to be free from hunger is unattainable, meaning that it can be neither expected nor delivered due to an aggregate lack of resources, must therefore be recognized as an untenable claim. It has been argued here that hunger is a product not of an aggregate lack of resource, but rather a product of relying upon the market mechanism to decide between competing claims to resources. In 1998 the UNDP estimated that an additional $13 billion would have been required to achieve basic health and nutrition for all (Thomas, 1999). This compares with global military spending in the same year of $780 billion (Thomas, 1999). Violations of the right to be free from hunger are tolerated, normalized and reproduced by political choices designed to serve powerful groups benefiting from the capitalist political economy and can be effectively redressed by changing political priorities to focus on satisfying basic human needs.

One effective way through which the prioritization of basic needs can be institutionalized is by implementing a communal right to the ownership of natural resources. The dynamics of this process can be summarized as following from the tendency of community controlled lands to be used to provide for the basic needs of all members and to therefore cultivate food rather than cash crops. Food security theorists have convincingly demonstrated that hunger is most effectively avoided through ensuring that communities have the environmental resources required to meet their own subsistence needs (George, 1984). Through an analysis of the implementation of land reforms in Mexico, Bolivia and Kenya, Rehman concluded that distributing the ownership of natural resources to local communities, 'realizes equitable growth in the agricultural sector whilst arresting the growth of rural poverty' (Rehman, 1993). Further evidence in support of this claim is provided by the International Labor Organization (ILO) which found that, 'redistribution of land rights is the most direct and effective method of improving food entitlements of the poor' (quoted in Tomasevski, 1993). The communal right to natural resources would compliment and help realize the right to be free from hunger since local communities are thereby empowered with both the resources and opportunities to provide for their own subsistence requirements.

Land Rights as a Function of Environmental Criteria

A pressing resource issue from the perspective of environmental politics is of how to construct human activity to ensure that the impact of human societies upon natural habitats is minimized. In the case of rights to environmental resources, CPR systems have been identified by a number of theorists as being advantageous from the perspective of environmental protection. It is important to state that this does nothing to validate claims to environmental resources made using the discourse of human rights, but environmental considerations nonetheless offer another set of criteria to inform political decisions relating to the design of resource rights.

Private Property Land Rights Cause Environmental Degradation

Exemplified by Garret Hardin, many neo-liberal economists maintain that CPR systems are, in environmental terms, inherently disaster prone (Hardin, 1968). Predicting the actions of each individual within a CPR system, Hardin concluded that over-exploitation would result from all members seeking to maximize their personal income from the common resource, leading inexorably to environmental degradation. Applying his theory to the case of a number of herdsmen sharing a single grazing field, Hardin argued that:

> the rational herdsman concludes that the only sensible course for him to pursue is to add another animal to his herd. And another ... . Each man is locked into a system that compels him to increase his herd without limit, thereby leading to overuse and environmental degradation (Hardin, 1968, p. 1244).

As Vogler points out, the assumptions of this 'tragedy of the commons' scenario are, however, a product of capitalist theory, making the claim at best questionable when applied to diverse societies that are sustained by value systems typified by communitarian norms (Vogler, 1995). In particular, Hardin assumes that all individuals will make choices characterizing the logic of economic rationality. Yet these values are often absent from non-capitalist societies. Hanna and Jentoft have for example demonstrated that people naturally act collectively when there are positive incentives in their specific cultures to do so (Hanna and Jentoft, 1996). Human nature is largely defined by the structural incentives of the societies in which people have been conditioned. Hardin's research is therefore vulnerable to the charge of falsely universalizing the individualistic and materialistic values of economic rationality. Moreover, environmental degradation often occurs when natural resources are privatized because the anti-social assumption of individualism of the Hardin model becomes a self-fulfilling prophecy. Citing cases of fisheries in Norway and Canada, Hanna and Jentoft demonstrate that it is the removal of the individual interest from the collective interest that causes overuse of resources:

> Traditional resource management practices of many local subsistence exchange economies have been weakened or destroyed through interactions with external markets that have undermined the moral authority for resource management (Hanna and Jentoft, 1996, p. 48).

Thus, in extending the market mechanism in an attempt to prevent the tragedy of the commons, environmental damage is exacerbated rather than alleviated (Hanna and Jentoft, 1996). As *The Ecologist* editors point out, the tragedy of the commons is therefore more accurately described as a 'tragedy of enclosure', where traditional communal controls on resource use are destroyed by the wider structural incentives of profit concerns operating in a capitalist economy (*The Ecologist*, 1993).

In failing to differentiate between CPR and open access systems, Hardin also fails to appreciate how CPRs institutionalize community controls to prevent patterns of over-exploitation. Typifying confusion on this issue, Demsetz interpreted overhunting and the subsequent eradication of many fur-bearing animals in eastern Canada as being due to a lack of property rights (Gowdy, 1999). In fact, as Gowdy demonstrates, it was the introduction of the capitalist economy that caused the collapse in numbers of favored species as profit concerns replaced traditional customs in determining hunting patterns (Gowdy, 1999). Traditional customs that had previously prevented overuse related to environmental awareness, religious restrictions and a fear of reprisal from the spirit world. Indeed, indigenous cultures are typified by a characteristic underuse of resources, compared to the ecological potential (Gowdy, 1999). That native American hunters drove large numbers of bison off cliffs has been presented as evidence that indigenous cultures are unable to maintain ecological sustainability. Yet it was only with the arrival of the Europeans that numbers of bison in North America were decimated from 40 million to 500 animals (Gowdy, 1999).

Organizing land use according to economic criterion is mutually exclusive to the organization of use according to ecological principles. The capitalist system of natural resource rights leads inexorably to environmental degradation because the economically efficient use of resources requires the usage of pesticides, monocultures, cash crops, deforestation and habitat destruction. Monocultures are crops that are grown in isolation from other species to maximize yields, typically in combination with the use of pesticides and insecticides. From the ecological perspective, such an approach creates de facto deserts, devoid of any notable biodiversity, except for the single species of cultivated crop. Cash cropping also entails environmental damage since large numbers of landless or land-poor peasants deprived of the land turned over to cash crop production are forced onto steep hillsides, rain forests, and other environmentally sensitive or agriculturally marginal areas (Thomas, 1996). The clearing of land for cash crops in the Brazilian Amazon resulted in the destruction of 40,000 square miles of rain forest between 1966 and 1983 (Rifkin, 1992; Monbiot, 1996). Jose Lutzenberger, former Brazilian Minister of the Environment, testified that the iniquitous ownership of land in the state was creating land shortages and pushing peasants into the Amazonian rain forest (Human Rights Watch and the Natural Resources Defense Council, 1992).

Private property rights systems of land ownership also tend to cause environmental damage because of the feature of distanciation. Distanciation separates areas of environmental degradation caused in the manufacturing of a product from the place where the good is finally consumed. That is to say, distanciation 'increases the distance between those making the decision and experiencing the consequences' of environmental policies relating to land use (Johnston, 1995). The inevitable result is less environmental protection since the individuals making decisions are spatially and consequentially removed from the environmental impact of their decisions. By way of an example, the British based corporation Rio Tinto Zinc plans to mine ilmenite and titanium dioxide in 4,000 hectares of pristine Madagascan rainforest for use in toothpaste (Nuttall, 1995). Eventual consumers will almost certainly be unaware that the production of their toothpaste involved the destruction of rain forests and will neither suffer, nor pay for that environmental damage, since they will most likely live as far from the site of destruction as the employees who proposed the mining operation. In an increasingly deregulated global economic system, the possibilities available for guaranteeing meaningful environmental protection become increasingly circumscribed.

CPR Protection of the Environment

Communal ownership systems to natural resources are more environmentally benign than the market model because subsistence and long term environmental sustainability typically replace the profit motive in determining resource use. The decentralized nature of CPR systems as well as the pool of common knowledge about the local environment built into CPRs over the generations allow commons based systems to effectively respond to natural disturbances and reduce the chances of large scale ecological collapse (Costanza and Folke, 1996).

The right to ownership of natural resources could be implemented to minimize economic activity that degrades the environment over the long term. A decentralized economic system cannot eradicate the conflict between human interests and environmental protection, but evidence suggests that the CPR systems can help minimize the environmental effects of human activities. George Monbiot succinctly explains the predisposition of CPRs to conserve resources when he asserted that:

> I had seen environmental destruction following land alienation. When traditional landholders are dispossessed and either private businesses, large proprietors or state bureaucracies take over, habitats are destroyed. I came to see that rural communities are often constrained to look after their land well, as it is the only thing they have, and they need to protect a diversity of resources in order to meet their diverse needs (Monbiot, 1996).

Examples of the ways in which CPRs are conducive to environmental protection can be illustrated through specific cases. One such study describes how a 1988 National Forest Policy in India granted usufruct resource rights to local communities and subsequently reversed a policy of deforestation (Pye-Smith and Feyerabend, 1995). The Communal Areas Management Program for Indigenous Resources (CAMPFIRE) in Zimbabwe uses customary practices of group ownership to sustain the natural wildlife resource base, allocating resource usage rights around the criterion of ecological sustainability (Zimbabwe Trust, 1990; Derman, 1995).

Another example of an ecologically beneficial CPR system is that of forest management practiced by the Sherpas of Nepal. Traditionally, the 'shingo naua', or forest guards, have prevented deforestation by controlling which trees could be felled and by punishing transgressors (McNeely, 1991). The extractive reserves established by the rubber tappers of the Brazilian Amazon also exemplify an ecologically sustainable CPR. These reserves are co-operatives of rubber tappers and indigenous communities based around an economic system that preserves the forest eco-system whilst harvesting renewable forest products such as rubber, fish and nuts (Mendes, 1989; World Rainforest Movement and Forests Monitor Ltd, 1998). This system has protected biodiversity and the eco-system from quick profit uses and deforestation and is now practiced in 10 per cent of the land area in the

Brazilian province of Acre (McNeely, 1991). Refuting the assumptions underlying Hardin's critique of the commons, successful exclusion under CPR systems is the rule rather than the exception (Berkes, 1996). There was, for example, no widespread tragedy of the commons in England before the enclosure movement since rules such as 'stinting' limited the number of animals each owner could graze on the commons (Berkes, 1996). Because of the fusing of individual and public interests in CPR systems, members adhere to norms and social values since these are (i) identified with self interest, (ii) enforceable through sanctions and (iii) individuals are politically involved and ethically committed to the group (Hanna and Jentoft, 1996).

Resource Rights and Global Capitalism

CPR systems of resource use are a necessary, rather than a sufficient, condition for environmental protection (*The Ecologist*, 1995). The institutionalization of CPRs alone will be unlikely to prevent ongoing environmental degradation whilst global capitalism remains in place. Implementing CPRs without structural changes to global capitalism can be expected to change only the agents of environmental destruction. Chapters one and four detailed how the capitalist political economy structurally determines patterns of environmental degradation. When placed within a capitalist structure, traditional taboos on resource overuse in CPRs are broken down and, as numerous examples testify, individuals typically become over exploiters to gain short term profits (McNeely, 1991; Bodley, 1997).

The director of indigenous governance programs of the University of Victoria points out that there is no basis for rationalizing processes of environmental degradation within North American indigenous cultures and traditions.[13] When such degradation has occurred on indigenous lands, this has invariably been as a result of the structural commercial incentives operating in the global economy rather than because of the indigenous culture. In particular, the commodification of nature combined with market incentives dictate that it is more profitable for the present owners of resources to exploit, and thereby gain revenue from mineral and forest reserves, rather than to conserve them.

Exemplifying the limitations placed by global capitalism upon the possibilities for CPRs to protect the environment, the Kayapo Indians of the Brazilian Amazon negotiated contracts with loggers and miners for large-scale extraction of mahogany and gold on their lands after a successful and high profile land rights campaign led the Brazilian government to cede to the indigenous group a 65,000 square-kilometer reserve (Sachs, 1995). Several Kayapo chiefs have since used the income from the sale of the contracts to buy satellite dishes, cars and private jets, whilst most tribal members continue to suffer endemic poverty (Sachs, 1995). Transferring resource rights to communities in the absence of structural changes to the global economy will therefore dictate that these groups will most likely replace individuals, states or corporations as the agents of environmental degradation. An inquiry into alternative structural arrangements more conducive than capitalism to long term environmental protection lies largely outside the scope of this research, but the reader can be directed to the works of Herman Daly for some useful analysis (Daly, 1994; Daly and Cobb, 1995).

Conclusions

Private property rights legitimize ownership of natural resource in the global capitalist economy. This system of ownership commodifies land and grants legal title to individuals or corporations who purchase the land. Under this system, land rights are therefore a function of private wealth. An alternative system of ownership rights provided by CPRs has been discussed in this chapter. CPR systems suggest an alternative to the choice between market and state that have both proved so disastrous for the environment in the past. CPR systems politicize the ownership of natural resources and thereby facilitate the use of land according to socially agreed criteria (Ostrom, 1990).

The conclusions of this chapter are threefold. Firstly, recognition of the human right to ownership of natural resources was argued to be required for the realization of human rights to (i) cultural self-determination and (ii) freedom from hunger. Secondly, the implementation of this right is required on a communal, rather than an individual, basis. Formal, politically motivated interpretations of international law notwithstanding, neither the ICCPR nor the ICESCR stipulate rights for individuals to own natural resources. Resource rights are instead reserved in both covenants for peoples, indicating a focus on basic needs and self-determination rather than global capital.

Although CPRs have historically prioritized social and environmental over economic criteria in determining patterns of resource usage, this feature has been largely corrupted by the expansion of global capitalism. The third conclusion of this chapter is therefore to reject the possibility of achieving ecological sustainability in the global capitalist economy. It has been argued that the characteristic ability of capitalism to provide a multitude of goods for the rich alongside insufficient goods for the impoverished makes the structure incapable of providing for universal basic needs. Exemplified through cash crops, the consumption of luxury consumer goods necessarily deprives the impoverished of entitlement to resources that are instead diverted by the market mechanism to satisfying frivolous desires of the opulent. Future generations will inherit a world impoverished through climate change, biodiversity impoverishment and resource depletion as a result of current economic decisions predicated upon the use of the environment as advocated by the logic of economic rationality. The human rights and environmental discourses have therefore separately and in tandem problematized the capitalist economic system.

Notes

1   See chapters 1 and 5 for a detailed discussion of the role and significance of these concepts.
2   See 'Permanent Sovereignty Over Natural Resources', General Assembly Resolution 1803 (XVII), United Nations GAOR Supp. (Number 17) at 15, UN Doc A/5217 (1962); http://www.umn.edu/humanrts/ instree/c2psnr.htm.
3   Peoples Organization, Chile.
4   An area south of Glacier National Park in Montana, USA.

5   Response to research questionnaire received from Darrell Geist, president, Cold Mountain, Cold Rivers, 28 October 1998 and from Jamie Lennox, membership coordinator, Alliance for the Wild Rockies, 10 June 1998.
6   North East Latin America.
7   Held at Geneva in 1981.
8   A declaration from the indigenous people of Latin America.
9   1 January 1994.
10 The Zapatistas are composed primarily of the Tzotzil, Tzeltal, Chol, Tojolabal, Mam and Zoque Mayans.
11 Article 11 (para 2) stipulates 'the States Parties to the present Covenant, recognizing the fundamental right of everyone to be free from hunger, shall take, individually and through international co-operation, the measures, including specific programmes, which are needed ... taking into account the problems of both food-importing and food-exporting countries, to ensure an equitable distribution of world food supplies in relation to need'.
12 Response to research questionnaire received from Artist Hunger Network, 31 October 1998.
13 Interview with Dr Taiaiake Alfred at the University of Southampton, 29 April 1999.

Conclusion

Environmental Human Rights in Theory and Application

This research has argued that universal environmental human rights to (i) an environment free from toxic pollution and to (ii) natural resources, are required for existing legally stipulated human rights to be realized. The central theme in this research has identified the power relations of capitalism as the barrier to the realization of the two claimed environmental human rights. The market mechanism is problematic from the perspective of both human rights and environmental protection since it disproportionately serves powerful social groups irrespective of any broader principle of justice.

Chapter 1 argued that economic rationality determines 'normal' political choices made in the capitalist political economy. Environmental protection is only deemed appropriate by the logic of economic rationality when such action leads to the efficient allocation of resources, utility maximization and economic growth, upon which criteria 'rational' political decisions are to be made (Pearce and Turner, 1990). Chapter 1 demonstrated how environmental degradation and resource depletion are the inevitable consequences of accepting the political terms of reference advocated by economic rationality. For example, forests, biodiversity, wilderness habitats, non-human life and biological systems are all devoid of inherent value according to economic rationality. From this viewpoint, deforestation can become an appropriate and rational option since timber can be sold as a commodity on the market irrespective of the broader ecological function of the forest (Gowdy, 1999).

Environmental degradation is further inherent to the logic of economic rationality since the concept of discounting legitimizes, and indeed advocates as rational, policies that produce severe environmental damage in the distant future when such choices satisfy conditions of allocative efficiency in the present. Endorsing consumerism, unlimited economic growth, distanciation and global free trade illustrates how economic rationality advocates environmental damage as the inescapable consequence of the epistemological focus on macroeconomic variables.

Ecological rationality was introduced as an alternative conceptualization of political terms of reference to critique economic rationality from the perspective of environmental politics. Expressing ecological rationality in a protest against corporate plans to drill oil on their traditional lands, the U'wa nation declared that:

> we are left with no alternative other than to continue fighting on the side of the sky and earth and spirits or else disappear when the irrationality of the invader violates the most sacred of our laws ... . Our words should be a warning that reunites us again as one family in order to ensure our future in harmony with the whole universe, or they will be one more

voice that prophesises the destruction of life because of the absurd disposition of the white man (Cobaria *et al.*, 1998).

Ecological rationality rejects allocative efficiency as the decision-making criterion of the political economy and instead advocates the integrity and well being of life as the central organizing principle (Leopold, 1949). Both ecological and economic variants of rationality are internally consistent. This research has stated the case for ecological rationality. Economic rationality has been charged with advocating policies that harm life, the wider environment and people.

The epistemological dominance of a particular form of rationality has been argued to be a function of social power (Carroll, 1989). This research has highlighted in particular the interests of global plutocrats who, through a manifestation of power as normalization, validate those forms of rationality conducive to their self-interest (Foucault, 1994). The position of the powerful is justified as objective, neutral and even as beneficial to all.

Chapter 2 examined the nature of structural power in world politics. This topic was included to understand the possibilities and constraints on the realization of specific human rights and in particular, how power relations of capitalism prevent the realization of the two claimed environmental human rights. An investigation into the nature of power held by agents and structures revealed a limited capacity for individuals to reform political structures. Marginal policies and questions of implementation can be affected by the lobbying efforts of environmental groups but the fundamental value premises and political goals of governments remain insulted from the consultation process. Such insulation occurs because power operates in part through conditioning how individuals think and act as well by more overtly controlling the issues and agenda discussed in formal political channels (Attias, 1996). For example, many environmental critics of global capitalism assume the dominant political terms of reference given by economic rationality. Demands for environmental protection are made on grounds of efficiency since advocacy of the inherent value of nature appears judgmental or even embarrassing in a political culture where a discourse of economic rationality is dominant (Sagoff, 1997). The way in which values become prioritized in society is therefore a significant manifestation of structural power since this process establishes the criteria that must be used by all parties to make persuasive arguments in policy making circles.

Further investigation of structural power highlighted the feature of co-option as the most important mechanism by which challenges to capitalism are diffused and negated. Politicians offering symbolic gestures of environmental protection divide opposition to capitalism from environmental groups. Less radical groups are co-opted with the offer of concessions and become eager participants in the negotiating process, thereby legitimizing formal politics with the veneer of impartiality and inclusivity. More radical groups rejecting the concessions as window dressing and instead insisting upon fundamental change appear as isolated extremists and are marginalized in the formal political process (Taylor, 1998). A policy of co-option therefore promotes the appearance of participatory and open governance whilst simultaneously diffusing opposition to capitalism and retaining tight control over policy outcomes.

The application of this framework to analysis of the environmental and human rights movements demonstrated how the radical potential of these forces to initiate value changes in society have been eviscerated by a policy of co-option. The conclusion of this examination was to suggest a limited effectiveness for NGOs who adopt a co-operative strategy with formal political institutions in an effort to mitigate the environmental degradation and human rights violations caused by capitalism. To institutionalize respect for environmental protection and human rights, a fundamental change in values is instead required that rejects economic rationality and the hegemonic politics of capitalism. A role for environmental human rights in initiating such a process of political change was suggested, since these rights insist on values of environmental protection and the human security of all people over the possessive individualism of capitalism. A challenge to capitalism based around a radical conception of environmental human rights is therefore less susceptible to co-option when the claim articulates ecological rationality and explicitly rejects the values, discourse and political terms of reference of economic rationality. Until the dominance of economic rationality is challenged in society, capitalism (and the associated environmental degradation) will be justified since capitalism realizes the values and political objectives of economic rationality. Through an examination of structural power, environmental human rights were therefore suggested to function both (i) as a goal for institutionalizing environmental values and (ii) as a campaigning instrument for a counter hegemonic bloc to realize systemic change.

Chapter 3 examined the demands for environmental human rights made by the human rights and environmental movements. This investigation was based on a questionnaire circulated to NGOs. The results revealed three findings; (i) a consensus endorsing environmental human rights, (ii) that campaigns are being conducted both for the formal recognition of environmental human rights and by demanding environmental protection through claims to human rights regardless of their legal status and (iii) advocacy of environmental human rights was based on the holistic assumptions characterizing ecological rationality. With only three exceptions, all of the NGOs responding to the questionnaire who stated a preference replied that they recognized environmental human rights. Campaigns demanding environmental human rights are being conducted both within formal political channels and as protests against the capitalist institutional structure. In line with the arguments made in chapter two, the ability of NGOs to realize environmental human rights within the capitalist structure has been of limited success, restricted to gaining symbolic concessions at the margins of policy making.

The use of environmental human rights as an instrument of political protest was exemplified in two case studies relating to campaigns in Irian Jaya and Nigeria. These two campaigns were based not on demands for financial aid or greater access to global markets but rather on a fundamental rejection of the allocation of resources by the capitalist system. The efficient allocation of local resources by the global market was opposed through demands for communal rights to environmental resources that were made on the grounds of cultural autonomy and environmental protection. These campaigns illustrate the tactical use of environmental human rights as an instrument of praxis through which to challenge the value basis of capitalism. Exemplifying the central theme of this research, both of these protest campaigns have failed to achieve the environmental human rights that they demanded because of the defense by commercial actors of their self-interest. Existent power relations institutionalized under capitalism through the designation of property rights, and expressed through economic rationality, have prevented the success of protest campaigns for environmental human rights. However, environmental human rights campaigns have generated significant international exposure, for example the hanging of Ken Saro-Wiwa in Nigeria led to the suspension of that state from the Commonwealth (Black, Bowcott and Vidal, 1995). The importance of these campaigns lies therefore not in their ability to reform capitalist structures, but rather in rejecting the legitimacy of capitalism and the associated system of values that is a necessary starting point for the long term realization of the claimed environmental human rights.

A significant finding of the survey established that a considerable number of NGOs justified environmental human rights through the values characterizing ecological rationality. The most popular reason given by NGOs for recognizing environmental human rights was a perceived interconnectedness between all elements of the environment, including human societies. Under the epistemological assumptions of ecological rationality, the interests of people and nature are one and the same, rather than in inherent conflict. By identifying human interests and rights with the long-term health and protection of the wider eco-system, ecological rationality redefines the purpose of human society as ensuring the health and well being of the entire eco-system. From the perspective of ecological rationality, consumer society and the pursuit of profit becomes the cause of environmental degradation and harm, rather than human societies *per se*.

The formal political response to social demands for environmental human rights was examined in chapter four through analysis of the current legal status of environmental rights in both domestic and international law. An evident trend towards the legal recognition of environmental human rights was noted. However, this modality contrasts the systematic violation of these same rights in actual practice. The apparent contradiction between legal stipulations and the social reality was explained by identifying law as an instrument of hegemonic power rather than as an impartial rule based instrument. Whereas a methodological investigation of environmental human rights based on legal analysis presupposes that considerations of jurisprudence and legislation determine social relations, the evaluation conducted in chapter four argued that the converse is the case. The social power relations of capitalism broadly determine the capabilities and efficacy of legal stipulations. This modality explains the design and implementation of both domestic and international law. Chapter four analyzed the nature of the power held by MNCs and international finance capital to argue that policy and law making is increasingly restricted to the corporate agenda of deregulation and market freedom.

State sovereignty was problematized from the perspective of human rights since the power of global capital induces individual states to adopt policies that accommodate the corporate interest. State sovereignty is furthermore problematic for the realization of human rights and environmental protection since the state has historically facilitated or indeed actively engaged in violations of these considerations as a consequence of focusing on the consolidation of political power and economic growth.

Overt political rejection of environmental protection as a human right is, however, becoming increasingly untenable given social campaigns highlighting the many evident connections. Academic research has further detailed the linkages between environmental degradation and human rights violations (Shelton, 1991; Johnston, 1994; Rest, 1994; Rogers, 1994; Deimann and Dyssli, 1995; Sachs, 1995; Johnston, 1997; Rest, 1998; Hayward, 2000). Therefore, states are increasingly recognizing environmental human rights in domestic and international legislation (Boyle and Anderson, 1996). However, the formal recognition of environmental human rights was not found to necessarily lead to the realization of those rights. Domestic and international categories of environmental rights have been characteristically formulated in vague, indeed vacuous terms and have had little impact on social practice, eviscerating the potential of environmental human rights as a challenge to capitalist power relations. The formal recognition of environmental human rights can instead be understood in terms of hegemony, whereby states seek to enhance credibility and legitimacy by institutionalizing in formal rights the environmental concerns raised by environmental NGOs and citizens, whilst prioritizing corporate interests by neglecting the implementation of the stipulated rights. The most blatant acts of environmental degradation perpetrated by unscrupulous corporations have been visibly addressed through human rights legislation in domestic courts, whilst the environmental damage built into the everyday working of the economy continues unaffected by the symbolic changes enacted. The centrality of power relations in determining the efficacy of law is epitomized in the construction and implementation of a sanctions regime that enforces adherence to stipulations. Compliance with trade laws is ensured by the WTO through a relatively sophisticated and precise system of sanctions. The lack of any similar organization or of an enforcement mechanism to implement global environmental regimes or human rights legislation points to the role of law as a hegemonic instrument.

The hegemonic role of law is further revealed by the way in which legal terms and concepts have been defined and implemented in accordance with the values of economic rationality. Chapter 5 examined the application of the legal principle of harm in the context of the claimed environmental human right to an environment free from toxic pollution. Toxic pollution is by definition harmful. If a pollutant were not harmful, it would be categorized as non-toxic. The damage incurred on human physiology by the plethora of toxic pollutants released into the atmosphere by modern economies becomes manifest though a range of symptoms ranging from asthma attacks and allergies to cancer and death (Dockery, Speizer, Strom *et al.*, 1989; Pope, Dockery, Spengler and Raizenne, 1991; Bates, 1992; Pope, Schwartz and Ransome, 1992; Pope and Kanner, 1993; Roemer, Hoek and Brunekreef, 1993; World Health, 1993; Hamer, 1994; Schwartz, 1994a; 1994b; Lee and Manning, 1995; Maclean's, 1995; Seaton, 1995; Seaton, McNee, Donaldson and Godden, 1995 and Paterson, 2000). According to a definition of harm that incorporates considerations of health and ecological well-being, it follows that the production of toxic pollution should be legally prohibited under the stipulations of the harm principle. The law rejects this logic because of desired focus on economic values that codifies and legitimizes capitalism. The subsequent argument that toxic pollution does not constitute harm was criticized as being selectively decided in order to protect the power relations of capitalism. Being injured or deprived of life by the actions of others in society appears to be the most blatant example of harm. Indeed, denying this fact quite literally adds insult to injury. The categorization of infractions of property laws as harm whilst simultaneously denying that exposure to toxic pollution constitutes harm exemplifies how the legal concept of harm has been defined in terms that support existent modes of consumption, production and exchange at the expense of environmental and health considerations.

Chapter 5 examined the various loopholes and double standards employed by law to avoid reaching the undesired conclusion that toxic pollution constitutes harm. Typically, the harm caused by toxic pollution is downplayed, rejected, disputed, denied or else considered unfortunate but necessary. Refuting these denials, the epidemiological evidence makes clear that toxic pollutants routinely emitted in vehicle exhaust fumes are responsible for many times the number of deaths than are caused by terrorists each year. The argument that anyone 'needs' a private jet is perhaps beyond the sophistry skills of even the most adamant proponent of materialistic values. Given the political will, toxic pollutants could be phased out. Such a policy also becomes the rational choice when ecological rather than economic criterion is applied in the decision-making process.

Law was subsequently found to reflect the values not of liberalism, but rather the values of capitalism. Capitalism is based on the pursuit of economic self-interest within the legally stipulated boundaries that prevent social disintegration, irrespective of any broader principle of justice. The political theory of liberalism is commonly assumed to provide a philosophical justification of the capitalist political economy. Such a claim was found untenable since the two positions of liberalism and capitalism can be clearly differentiated on the grounds of harm. Under the liberal concept of non-malfeasance, toxic pollution should be prohibited for arbitrarily contravening the rights of individuals not to be harmed by the actions of others. In contrast, an optimal level of toxic pollution (and therefore also of harm) is advocated from the capitalist perspective as a means of achieving allocative efficiency and economic growth and is furthermore enthusiastically generated by industry and individuals seeking to minimize private costs. Law has accommodated this private interest and political view of the good by facilitating the toxic pollution of the environment within legally specified boundaries. In so doing, law has contradicted the two central pillars of liberalism which insist on the basis of (i) impartiality and (ii) the harm principle, that one version of the good cannot be implemented by some members of society at the expense of harming others.

In addition to being derived from the principle of non-malfeasance, the claimed environmental human right to an environment free from toxic pollution was found necessary for existing human rights to be realized. The systematic violations of human rights to (i) life, (ii) security of the person and to (iii) the highest attainable standards of health, are caused by the harmful effects of toxic pollution (ICCPR articles 3, 12; ICCPR articles 6, 9).

Control over natural resources was examined from a human rights perspective in chapter six and the principle of communal ownership rights to natural resources was subsequently claimed as a second environmental human right. CPRs were suggested as a method to realize this claimed right. The right to natural resources was derived from existing legally recognized human rights to (i) freedom from hunger, and (ii) cultural self-determination (ICCPR article 1; ICESCR articles 1, 11). Both of these human rights will continue to be violated in the absence of impoverished communities controlling the natural resources that they require to provide for their own subsistence needs.

Supporting the central theme of this research, the global capitalist economy was identified as the structural barrier to the realization of the claimed human right to natural resources. The characteristic ability of capitalism to provide a multitude of luxury goods for the opulent, alongside insufficient goods for the impoverished, makes the system fundamentally problematic for the universal satisfaction of basic human needs. The diversion of resources to serve the wealthy under conditions of capitalism was exemplified through the global cash crop economy. Under market conditions, needs provide no legitimization of access to resources and 20 per cent of the world's population subsequently fail to meet their sustenance requirements in the market due to poverty. The argument that starvation continues because of an overall lack of resources was rejected as an untenable claim since iniquitous land ownership, rather than overall availability, was found to determine hunger for the impoverished in a market based economy.

The economic values of capitalism praised by the opulent for providing freedom and independence becomes an oppressive mechanism for institutionalizing the starvation and squalor of the impoverished. It is for this reason that Chomsky observes that:

> it's becoming more difficult to tell the difference between economists and Nazi doctors [since] half a million children in Africa die every year simply from debt service ... . It's estimated that about eleven million children die every year from easily curable diseases, most of which could be overcome by treatments that cost a couple of cents. But the economists tell us that to do this would be interference with the market system (Chomsky, 1997b).

Here, Chomsky characteristically highlights the structural oppression in the market mechanism that justifies mass suffering and the denial of basic resources to the impoverished when this outcome is conducive to allocative efficiency.

The production of meat for human consumption exemplifies the waste of resources to serve market desires at the expense of basic needs. Feeding crops to farm animals that are then consumed by humans results in the loss of 90 per cent of the calorific intake of food (Rifkin, 1992). Yet demand for meat in luxury markets determines that the market allocates crops to rearing farm animals, crops that could otherwise by used to feed people or else to return farmland to wilderness areas and thereby enhance biodiversity. Overall resources exist to satisfy the basic needs of all people (UNESCO, 1995). It is as an inescapable consequence of adopting allocative efficiency as its central point of reference that capitalism ensures continuing hunger and suffering for the impoverished.

This research has argued that the increasingly desperate plight of impoverished communities around the world can be significantly improved through equitably redistributing the means to provide for subsistence requirements. Land reforms expressed in the human right to ownership of natural resources were suggested to allow presently dispossessed communities to meet their needs in a self-reliant manner. Furthermore, land rights are being claimed, especially by indigenous groups. Such demands are characteristically based on claims for cultural self-determination and independence from the market mechanism, rather than calls for financial aid or further inclusion into the capitalist system. Land rights claims are therefore anti-systemic since they reject the values of economic rationality in favor of cultural autonomy and a subsistence-based economy. CPR systems that characterize non-capitalist economies focus typically on providing for basic human needs whilst prioritizing resource conservation and ecological integrity over the production of luxury goods (Ostrom, 1990). The human right to natural resources expressed through the CPR system can therefore be expected to promote environmental protection and cultural diversity by rejecting the consumerist values that are mistakenly universalized by economic rationality.

Both of the environmental human rights claimed in this research could be expected to benefit the environment. Toxic pollution harms not only people, but also organisms in the wider ecosystem and any policies to reduce the amounts of toxic pollution entering the environment can only be beneficial from the perspective of ecological well-being. The environmental human right to natural resources can also be expected to protect the environment since market forces and the application of economic rationality necessarily result in environmental degradation (chapter 1). Small-scale subsistence based economies offer an alternative model to global free trade, allocative efficiency and the associated environmental degradation.

Suggestions for Further Research

This research raises a number of questions that could be investigated by future research projects. The research questionnaire demonstrated a high degree of recognition and endorsement of environmental human rights amongst advocacy NGOs. The realization of environmental human rights is, in part, dependent upon the success of NGOs to effectuate this positive endorsement of the concept. As such, a future research project could conduct a similar questionnaire of NGOs to establish whether demands for environmental human rights are growing in resonance, the extent to which use of the concept features in specific campaigns and the effectiveness of such demands. The key variable in this study would be to establish the extent to which NGOs can promote anti-systemic values in society in order to encourage environmental awareness.

The main difficulty in conducting such a project would relate in the first instance to the problem of measuring changes in abstract values that are not easily reducible to empirical measurements. In addition to this problem, the causes of any changes in social values would have to be clearly established. Such changes could result from (i) the effects of critical academic discourse, (ii) a growth in the number of high profile environmental catastrophes or (iii) from advancements in scientific knowledge clarifying the nature and extent of environmental threats, in addition to the campaigning activities of NGOs. Most likely, value change would result from a combination of these factors, complicating empirical investigation into the process of value change in society. A future survey of NGOs could also investigate readiness to co-operate with formal political channels. Such a project could identify the extent to which NGOs are being co-opted into hegemonic politics or are rejecting the validity of formal politics through engaging in protest campaigns.

This research has investigated the existence of environmental human rights using criteria of existing human rights legislation, although where appropriate, reference has been made to rationality and epistemological paradigms. The two environmental human rights claimed in this research are rights that are required for existing human rights stipulations to be realized. A more extensive list of environmental human rights could be arrived at from an inquiry predicated upon environmental ethics. Another research project could therefore examine the existence of environmental human rights in political philosophy. Looking at questions relating to the basis of human rights from the position of environmental politics can provide an innovative and distinctive approach to the topic of human rights. For example, chapter six argued that the environmental human right to natural resources is necessary for the protection of cultural diversity, inverting the enduring lament that universal human rights necessarily curtails cultural diversity. Furthermore, this research has suggested that basic human rights provide reasons not for continued environmental degradation in the furtherance of human interests, but rather for the protection of the Earth's organic heritage from the destructive tendencies of the capitalist political economy.

Bibliography

Abbey, E. (1998), 'Edward Abbey', http://www.envirolink.org/elib/enviroethics/ abbeyindex.html.

Achterhuis, H. (1994) in W. Zweers and J. Boersema (ed.), *Ecology, Technology and Culture: Essays in Environmental Philosophy*, White Horse Press, Cambridge.

Adams, J. (1995), *Risk*, UCL Press, London.

Adams, P. (1991), *Odious Debt*, Earthscan, London.

Against Nature, Channel 4 Documentary, 30 November, 1997.

Agar, N. (2001), *Life's Intrinsic Value,* Columbia University Press, New York.

Agarwal, A. and Narain, S. (1992), *Towards a Green World*, Centre for Science and Environment, New Delhi.

Albert, B. (1994), in B.R. Johnston (ed.), *Who Pays the Price?* Island Press, Washington DC.

Alder, J. (1993), in Interdisciplinary Research Network on the Environment and Society, *Perspectives on the Environment*, Avebury, Brookfield, Vermont.

Alonso, S. (1998), 'Burma's Pain – Mitsubishi's Profit', *International Rivers Network*, http://www.ran.org/ran/ran_campaigns/mitsubishi/mit_burma.html.

Amiya, K. et. al. (1982), *The Political Economy of Underdevelopment*, Cambridge University Press, Cambridge.

Amnesty International (1998), *Amnesty*, Issue 88, March/April.

Anderson, M.R. (1996) in A.E. Boyle and M.R. Anderson (eds), *Human Rights Approaches to Environmental Protection*, Clarendon Press, Oxford.

Anderson, S. and Cavanagh, J. (1996), 'Corporate Empires', *Multinational Monitor*, Vol. 17 (12), December, http://www.essential.org/monitor/hyper/mm1296.08. html.

Annan, K. (1999), 'A Compact for the New Century: Address to the World Economic Forum in Davos, Switzerland', 31 January, http:www.corpwatch.org/ trac/undp/ annan.html.

Anti-Consumerist Campaign (1999), 'Champagne and Poverty', http://www. enviroweb.org/enviroissues/enough/enough03.html.

Anto, J. and Sunyer, J. (1995), 'Nitrogen Dioxide and Allergic Asthma: Starting to Clarify an Obscure Association', *Lancet*, 18 February, p. 402.

Aragon, L.V. (1997) in B.R. Johnston (ed.), *Human Rights and the Environment at the End of the Millennium*, Alta Mira, Walnut Creek.

Arruda, M. (1995), 'Building Strategies on the International Financial Institutions', 25 October, http://www.hartford-hwp.com/archives/25/012.html.

Arthur, C. (1996), 'Greenhouse Effect Worse Than Forecast', *The Independent*, 21 May, p. 9.

Ashley, R. (1996) in S. Smith, K. Booth and M. Zalewski (eds), *International Theory: Positivism and Beyond*, Cambridge University Press, Cambridge, pp. 240–253.

Attias, B. (1996), 'Intellectuals and Power: A Conservation Between Michel Foucault and Gilles Deleuze', 18 June, http://www.csun.edu/~hfspc002/foucB3.html.

Augelli, E. and Murphy, C. (1988), *America's Quest for Supremacy and the Third World*, Pinter Publishers, London.

Australian Greenhouse Office (2002), 'A Message from Marrakesh', 29 January, http://www.greenhouse.gov.au/international/marrakesh.html.

Axelrod, R. (1990), *The Evolution of Co-operation*, Penguin, Harmondsworth.

Bacon, D. (1999), 'Oil Rules Nigeria', *Labor News*, http://www.hartfordhwp.com/archives/34a/024.html.

Bailey, S. (1996), 'The IMF's Contract on the World', *Workers World*, 4 January, http://www.hartford-hwp.com/archives/25/014.html.

Baird, V. (1987), 'Land Rights and Wrongs', *The New Internationalist*, No 177, November, pp. 4–6.

Bakunin, M. (1996), 'The Capitalist System', http://www.dis.org/daver/anarchism/bakunin/capstate.html.

Baldwin, D.A. (1989), *Paradoxes of Power*, Basil Blackwell, Oxford.

Banuri, T. and Marglin, F.A. (1993) in T. Banuri and F.A. Marglin (eds), *Who Will Save the Forests? Knowledge, Power and Environmental Destruction*, Zed Books, London.

Barber, M. and Ryder, G. (1993) in M. Barber and G. Ryder (eds), *Damning the Three Gorges: What Dam Builders Don't Want You To Know*, Earthscan, London.

Barbic, S. (1996), 'Brazil's Genocide Decree', *Multinational Monitor*, Vol. 17(3), March, http://www.essential.org/monitor/hyper/mm0396.03.html.

Barkun, M. (1968), *Law Without Sanctions: Order in Primitive Societies and the World Community*, Yale University Press, New Haven and London.

Barry, B. (1995), *Justice as Impartiality*, Clarendon Press, Oxford.

Barry, J. (1993) in Interdisciplinary Research Network on the Environment and Society (eds), *Perspectives on the Environment*, Avebury, Brookfield, Vermont.

Bartlett, R.V. (1986), 'Ecological Rationality: Reason and Environmental Policy', *Environmental Ethics*, Vol. 8, pp. 221–39.

Bartley, T. and Bergessen, A. (1997), 'World-System Studies of the Environment', *Journal of World-Systems Research*, Vol. 3(3), pp. 369–80, http://csf.colorado.edu/wsystems/jwsr.html.

Basque Institute of Public Administration (1999), 'Experts' Seminar on the Right to the Environment', Euskalduna Concert and Congress Hall, Bilbao, 10–13 February, http://www.bizkaia.net/bizkaia/English.council?Environment/Seminar/in_semi. html.

Basque Institute of Public Administration (1999), 'The Right to the Environment: Declaration of Bizkaia on the Right to the Environment', Euskalduna Concert and Congress Hall, Bilbao, 10–13 February, http://www.bizkaia.net/Bizkaia/English/ Foral_Council/Environment/in_dia.html.

Bast, J.L. (1998), 'The Battle Within the Environmental Movement', *The Heartland Institute*, http://www.heartland.org/battle.html.

Bast, J.L., Hill, P.J. and Rue, R.C. (1999), 'Eco-Sanity: A Common-Sense Guide to Environmentalism', *The Heartland Institute*, http://www.heartland.org/eco-sanexecsumm.html.

Bates, C. and Fankhauser, S. (1995), 'Price of a Life', *New Scientist*, Vol. 147, 23 September, p. 51.

Bates, D.J. (1992), 'Health Indices of the Adverse Effects of Air Pollution: The Question of Coherence', *Environmental Research*, Vol. 59, pp. 336–49.

Bauer, J. (1995), 'International Human Rights and Asian Commitment', *Human Rights Dialogue*, Vol. 3, http://www.cceia.org/dialog3.html.

Bauer, J. (1998), *Human Rights Dialogue*, http://www.cceia.org/dialog10.html.

Baxter, B. (2000), 'Ecological Justice as Impartiality', *Environmental Politics*, Vol. 9(3), pp. 43–64.

Beck, U. (1997) in M. Jacobs (ed.), *Greening the Millennium?* Blackwell, Oxford.

Begg, D., Fischer, S. and Dornbusch, R. (1987), *Economics*, McGraw-Hill, London.

Beiner, R. (1992), *What's the Matter with Liberalism?*, University of California Press, Berkley.

Beitz, C. (1981), 'Economic Rights and Distributive Justice in Developing Societies', *World Politics*, Vol. 33(3), pp. 321–46.

Beitz, C. (1985), in C. Beitz (ed.), *International Ethics*, Princeton University Press, Princeton.

Bell, M. and Walker, M.J.C. (1992), *Late Quaternary Environmental Change: Physical and Human Perspectives*, John Wiley and Sons, New York.

Bello, W. (1996), 'The Geopolitics of APEC' (Interview), *Multinational Monitor*, Vol. 17(11), http://www.essential.org/monitor/hyper/mm 1196.07.html.

Bello, W. (1998), 'Testimony Before Banking Oversight Subcommittee, Banking and Financial Services Committee', *US House of Representatives*, 21 April, http://www.igc. org/dgap/walden.html.

Bello, W. and Collins, J. (1987), 'Cory's Cop-out', *The New Internationalist*, No 177, pp. 18–9.

Bello, W., Cunningham, S. and Rau, B. (1995), 'Creating a Wasteland: The Impact of Structural Adjustment on the South, 1980–1994', *Food First*, http://tdg.uoguelph.ca/~kwakely/polstudies/readings/imf.wasteland.html.

Bellona (1998), 'Nikitin Trial: The Most Important Trial in Russian Legal History', http://www.bellona.no/e/russia/nikitin/overview.html.

Benenson, B. (1995), 'A Mature Green America Spawns Grass Roots Anti-Regulatory Rebellion', *Congressional Quarterly Weekly Report*, Vol. 53(24), 17 June, pp. 1694–7.

Benton, T. (1997) in M. Jacobs (ed.), *Greening the Millennium?*, Blackwell, Oxford.

Bergesen, A. and Parisi, L. (1997), 'Discovering the Environment', *Journal of World-Systems Research*, Vol. 3(3), pp. 364–8.

Bergman, B.J. (1995), 'Standing up for the Planet', *Sierra*, Vol. 80(3), May/June, p. 79.

Berkes, F. (1996) in S. Hanna, C. Folke and K. Maler (eds), *Rights to Nature: Ecological, Economic, Cultural and Political Principles of Institutions for the Environment*, Island Press, Washington DC, p. 87.

Berlan, J. and Lewontin, R.C. (1999), 'Analysis Special: Genetically Modified Foods', *The Guardian*, 22 February, p. 14.

Bhagwati, J. (1995) in K. Conca, M. Alberty and G. Dabelko (eds), *Green Planet Blues: Environmental Politics from Stockholm to Rio*, Westview Press, Boulder.

Binyon, M. (1997), 'Human Rights Central to Labour Policy', *The Times*, 15 February, p. 19.

Black, I. (1998), 'Analysis: Human Rights – Robin Cook's Tour of the Global Badlands', *The Guardian*, 22 April, p. 13.

Black, I. Bowcott, O. and Vidal, J. (1995), 'Nigeria Defies World with Writer's Judicial Murder', *The Guardian*, 11 November, p. 1.

Blackstone, W. (1974) in W.T. Blackstone (ed.), *Philosophy and Environmental Crisis*, University of Georgia Press, Athens.

Blamires, D. (1998), 'Green Attack for Quarry Support', *The Independent*, 22 June, p. 7.

Blaug, M. (1968), *Economic Theory in Retrospect*, Heinemann, London.

Bodley, S. (1997) in B.R. Johnston (ed.), *Human Rights and the Environment at the End of the Millennium*, Alta Mira, Walnut Creek.

Bojo, J. Maler, K. and Unemo, L. (1990), *Environment and Development: An Economic Approach*, Kluwer Academic Publishers, Dordrecht.

Bond, P. and Mayekiso, M. (1996), 'Toward the Integration of Urban Social Movements at the World Scale', *Journal of World-Systems Research*, Vol. 2(2), http://csf.colorado.edu/jwsr.html.

Bookchin, M. (1995), *From Urbanisation to Cities: Toward a New Politics of Citizenship*, Cassell, London.

Bookchin, M. (1995), *Social Anarchism or Lifestyle Anarchism?*, AK Press, Edinburgh.

Borge, T. (1992), 'The Reality of Latin America', *Race and Class*, Vol. 33(3), January–March .

Bostick, B. (1995), 'NAFTA's First Year of Pollution, Poverty and Corruption', *People's Weekly World*, 4 February, http://www.hartfordhwp.com/archives/40/008.html.

Boswell, T. (1995), 'Hegemony and Bifurcation Points in World History', *Journal of World-Systems Research*, Vol. 1(1), http://csf.colorado.edu/wsystems/jwsr.html.

Boswell, T. (1996), 'Nationalism and World Governance: Comment on Warren Wagar's Praxis', *Journal of World-Systems Research*, Vol. 2(2), http://csf.colorado. edu/wsystems/jwsr.html.

Bothe, M. (1996) in M. Bothe (Chair and Project Co-ordinator), *The Right to a Healthy Environment in the European Union* (Report of a Working Group Established by the European Environmental Law Association).

Bown, W. (1994a), 'Forum: How Green Were Our Hopes for Diesel?', *New Scientist*, Vol. 142(1928), 4 June, pp. 47–8.

Bown, W. (1994b), 'Comment: Smog Alert', *New Scientist*, Vol. 142(1931), 25 June, p. 3.

Bown, W. (1994c), 'Deaths Linked to London Smog', *New Scientist*, Vol. 142(1931), 25 June, p. 4.

Bown, W. (1994d), 'Dying From Too Much Dust: Calculations Based on Unpublished Government Data Suggest that Fine Particles in Exhaust Fumes Are Killing 10,000 People a Year in England and Wales', *New Scientist*, Vol. 141 (1916), 12 March, pp. 12–13.

Boyle, A.E. (1996) in A.E. Boyle and M.R. Anderson (eds), *Human Rights Approaches to Environmental Protection*, Clarendon Press, Oxford.

Brazier, C. (1998), 'State of the World Report', *The New Internationalist*, Issue 287, http://www.oneworld.org/ni/issue287/keynote.html.

Brazil Network (1996a), *Brazil Network Newsletter*, March/April.

Brazil Network (1996b), *Brazil Network Newsletter*, May/June.

Brazil Network (1997), *Brazil Network Newsletter*, January/February.

Brennan, A. (1995) in A. Brennan (ed.), *The Ethics of the Environment*, Dartmouth, London.

Brenton, T. (1994), *The Greening of Machiavelli: The Evolution of International Environmental Politics*, Earthscan, London.

Brick, P. and McGreggor Cawley, R. (1996), *A Wolf in the Garden: The Land Rights Movement and the New Environmental Debate*, Rowman and Littlefield, Lanham, Maryland, http://www.cdfe.org/ideology.html.

Broderick, J. (1998), 'Clinton's Foreign Policy Agenda', *Politics Review*, Vol. 8(2), November, pp. 16–9.

Broecker, W.S. and Denton, G.H. (1990), 'What Drives Glacial Cycles?', *Scientific American*, Vol. 262(1), pp. 42–50.

Brouillet, C. (1995), 'The Debt: Crisis or Opportunity?', 22 January, http://www.hartford-hwp.com/archives/25/009.html.

Brown, A. and McCully, P. (1997), 'Uniting to Block the Dams', *Multinational Monitor*, Vol. 18(5), May, http://www.essential.org/monitor/hyper/mm0597.04.html.

Brown, C. (1992), *International Relations Theory*, Harvester Wheatsheaf, New York.

Brown, C. (1994), *Political Restructuring in Europe: Ethical Perspectives*, Routledge, London.

Brown, D.E. (1991), *Human Universals*, McGraw-Hill, New York.

Brown, G. and Short, C. (1999), 'Levelling Mountain of Misery', *The Guardian*, 22 February, p. 19.

Brown, L. *et al.* (1997), *State of the World 1997*, WW Norton and Company, New York.

Brown, L. *et al.* (1999), *State of the World 1998*, Earthscan, London.

Brown, P. (1997), 'How US Put a Damper on the Climate Change Debate', *The Guardian*, 23 October, p. 3.

Brown, P. (1998a), 'Alarm at Killer Traffic Fumes', *The Guardian*, 14 January, p. 2.

Brown, P. (1998b), 'Britain Leads the Way in Greenhouse Gas Emissions Deal', *The Guardian*, 18 June, p. 12.

Brown, P. (1998c), 'Nordic States Demand Ban on Sellafield', *The Guardian*, 18 June, p. 9.

Brown, P. (1998d), 'Aid Focus Shifting from Country to Shanty Towns', *The Guardian*, 24 June, p. 14.

Brown, P. (1998e), 'Road Accidents Set to be World's Biggest Killer', *The Guardian*, 24 June, p. 14.

Brown, P. (1998f), 'Climate Talks Near Collapse', *The Guardian*, 11 November, p. 2.

Brown, P. (1999), 'G7 Insists Chernobyl Must Stay Nuclear', *The Guardian*, 22 February, p. 12.

Brown, P. (2002a), 'Oil Giant Bids to Replace Climate Expert', *The Guardian*, 5 April, http://www.guardian.co.uk/Archive/Article/o,4273,4387939,00.html.

Brown, P. (2002b), 'US Dashes Hopes for Climate Change', *The Guardian*, 14 May, http://www.guardian.co.uk.

Brown, T. (1997), 'Ideological Hegemony and Global Governance', *Journal of World-Systems Research*, Vol. 3(2), pp. 250–58.

Brummer, A. (1998), 'Analysis: The IMF – Hey, Big Spender', *The Guardian*, 21 January, p. 15.

Brummer, A. (1998), 'Relief the World Can Count On', *The Guardian*, 13 May, http:// reports.guardian.co.uk/debt/analysis/19980512–02.html.

Brummer, A. (1998), 'Premier Pours Oil on Ethics Blaze', *The Guardian*, 15 May, p. 19.

Bruno, K. (1995), 'Rejecting Toxic Technology', *Multinational Monitor*, January/February, http://www.essential.org/monitor/hyper/mm0195.html.

Bruno, K. (1997), 'Corporate Watch Gives Winter Greenwash Award to Monsanto', *The Corporate Planet*, http://www.corpwatch.org/trac/greenwash/monsanto.html.

Buffett, S. (1998), 'Environment and Development: Macroeconomic Issues', http://gurukul.ucc.american.edu/ted/papers/doc1.htm.

Buncombe, A. Lloyd-Smith, J. and Abrams, F. (2000), 'Fuel For Thought: Where Do We Go From Here?', *The Independent*, 16 September, p. 3.

Bunting, M. (1998), 'Justice in a Global Village', *The Guardian* (debt supplement), 15 May, p. 3.

Burch, K. (1995), 'Invigorating World System Theory as Critical Theory: Exploring Philosophical Foundations and Postpositivist Contributions', *Journal of World-Systems Research*, Vol. 1(18), http://csf.colorado.edu/wsystems/ jwsr.html.

Burson Marsteller (1998), 'Communications Programme for Europabio', *Corporate Watch*, http://www.corpwatch.org/trac/feature/planet/eu_ bm.html.

Bush, J. (1995), 'Thinking Big Makes Little Sense For the World's Poor', *The Times*, 10 March, p. 27.

Byrne, K. (1997), *Environmental Science*, Thomas Nelson and Sons Ltd., London.

Callaghan, J. (1997), 'Time to Stop the Third World Treadmill', *The Times*, 18 September, p. 22.

Calliess, C. (1996) in M. Bothe (Chair and Project Co-ordinator), *The Right to a Healthy Environment in the European Union* (Report of a Working Group Established by the European Environmental Law Association).

Cameron and MacKenzie (1996) in A.E. Boyle and M.R. Anderson (eds), *Human Rights Approaches to Environmental Protection*, Clarendon Press, Oxford.

Campbell, T. (1983), *The Left and Rights: A Conceptual Analysis of the Idea of Socialist Rights*, Routledge, London.

Capdevila, G. (1998), 'Dumping of Toxic Waste Affects Human Rights', *Inter Press Service*, April, http://www.oneworld.org/ips2/apr98/16_44_044.html.

Carlton, J. (1991) in J. Davis (ed.), *The Earth First! Reader*, Gibbs Smith, Layton, UT pp. 105–17.

Carr, E.H. (1939), *The Twenty Years' Crisis*, Macmillan, London.

Carrell, S. and Lean, G. (2001), 'Sea Breezes to Power Britain', *Independent*, 1 April, p. 13.

Carroll, D. (1989), *Paraesthetics: Foucault, Lyotard, Derrida*, Routledge, London.

Carty, B. (1991), 'Guatemala's Killing Fields', *The New Internationalist*, No. 226, December, pp. 2–3.

Castleman, B. and Lemen, R. (1998), 'Corporate Junk Science: Corporate Influence at International Science Organizations', *Multinational Monitor*, Vol. 19(1,2), January/February, http://www.essential.org/monitor/mm1998/mm9801.07.html.

Centre for Economic and Social Rights (1997), http://www.cesr.org/.html.

Chambers (1990), *Chambers English Dictionary*, W and R Chambers, Edinburgh.

Chandler, G. (1999), 'Do the Right Thing', *Green Futures*, March/April, pp. 22–3.

Chanrasekhar, C.P. (1997), 'The Right to Food', *Third World Resurgence*, No. 79, March, pp. 35–6.

Charlesworth, K. (1998), 'Going Green', *T Magazine*, September, pp. 18–20.

Chase-Dunn, C. and Hall, T.D. (1997) 'Ecological Degradation and the Evolution of World-Systems', *Journal of World-Systems Research*, Vol. 3(3), pp. 403–31.

Chatterjee, P. (1991), 'North and South Divided on Environmental Charter', *New Scientist*, Vol. 131(1785), 7 September, p. 21.

Chatterjee, P. (1992), 'Earth Summit Delegates Accused of Hypocrisy', *New Scientist*, Vol. 133(1812), 14 March, p. 12.

Chatterjee, P. (1994), 'Slush Funds, Corrupt Consultants and Bidding for Bank Business', *Multinational Monitor*, July/August, http://www.essential.org/monitor/hyper/mm0894.html.

Chatterjee, P. (1996), 'The Mining Menace of Freeport-McMoran', *Multinational Monitor*, Vol. 17(4), April, http://www.essential.org/monitor/hyper/mm0496.05.html.

Chatterjee, P. (1997a), 'Peru's New Conquistadors', *Covert Action Quarterly*, No 60, Spring, http://caq.com/caq60/CAQ60peru.html.

Chatterjee, P. (1997b), 'Conquering Peru: Newmont's Yamacocha Mine Recalls the Days of Pizarro', *Multinational Monitor*, Vol. 18(4), April, http://www.essential.org/monitor/hyper/mm0497.04.html.

Chatterjee, P. (1997c), 'Peru Goes Beneath the Shell', *Multinational Monitor*, Vol. 18(5), May, http://www.essential.org/monitor/hyper/mm0597.12.html.

Chatterjee, P. and Finger, M. (1994), *The Earth Brokers: Power, Politics and World Development*, Routledge, London and New York.

Cheng, D. (1979), *Elementary Particle Physics*, Addison-Wesley, Reading, MA.

Chew, S.C. (1997), 'For Nature: Deep Greening World Systems Analysis for the 21st Century', *Journal of World-Systems Research*, Vol. 3(3), http://csf.colorado.edu/wsystems/jwsr.html.

Chimni, B.S. (1999), 'Marxism and International Law: A Contemporary Analysis', *Economic and Political Weekly*, Vol. 34(6), 6 February, pp. 337–49.

Cho, G. (1995), *Trade, Aid and Global Interdependence*, Routledge, London.

Chomsky, N. (1986), *Knowledge of Language: Its Nature, Origins and Use*, Praeger, New York.

Chomsky, N. (1987), *On Power and Ideology: The Managua Lectures*, South End Press, Boston.

Chomsky, N. (1988), *The Culture of Terrorism*, Pluto Press, London.

Chomsky, N. (1992a), *Chronicles of Dissent*, AK Press, Edinburgh.

Chomsky, N. (1992b), *Deterring Democracy*, Verso, Reading.

Chomsky, N. (1993a), *Rethinking Camelot*, Verso, London.

Chomsky, N. (1993b), *What Uncle Sam Really Wants*, http://www.worldmedia.com/archive/sam/sam-3–5.html.

Chomsky, N. (1993c), *Year 501: The Conquest Continues*, Verso, London.

Chomsky, N. (1993d), 'The Clinton Vision', *Z Magazine*, December 1993, http://www.worldmedia.com/archives/articles/z9312–clinton-vision.html.

Chomsky, N. (1994), *Keeping the Rabble in Line*, AK Press, Edinburgh.

Chomsky, N. (1995), 'Letter From Noam Chomsky', *Covert Action Quarterly*, No 54, Fall, http://caq.com/CAQ54chmky.html.

Chomsky, N. (1996a), *Powers and Prospects: Reflections on Human Nature and the Social Order*, Pluto Press, London.

Chomsky, N. (1996b), 'Notes on Anarchism', http://www.worldmedia.com/archive/other/notes-on-anarchism.html.

Chomsky, N. (1997a), 'Market Democracy in a Neo-liberal Order: Doctrines and Reality', *Davie Lecture* (University of Cape Town), May, http://www.lol.shareworld.com/Zmag/chomskydavie.htm.

Chomsky, N. (1997b), 'Dead Children and Debt Service', *Secrets, Lies and Democracy* http://www.worldmedia.com/archive/sld/sld-2–08.html.

Chomsky, N. (1998a), 'Interview: Just Intuition', *Third Way*, Vol. 20(2), January, pp. 16–9.

Chomsky, N. (1998b), 'Debt: The People Always Pay', *The Guardian* (debt supplement), 15 May, p. 7.

Chomsky, N. (1999), 'Judge the US by Deeds, Not Words', *New Statesman*, 9 April, pp. 11–3.

Churchill, R.R. (1996) in A.E. Boyle and M.R. Anderson (eds), *Human Rights Approaches to Environmental Protection*, Clarendon Press, Oxford.

Clay, J.W. (1994) in B.R. Johnston (ed.), *Who Pays the Price?*, Island Press, Washington DC.

Clearinghouse on Environmental Advocacy and Research (1993), 'The Wise Use Movement: Strategic Analysis and Fifty State Review', March, http://www.ewg.org/pub/home/ clear/by_clear/Fifty.html.

Clearinghouse on Environmental Advocacy and Research (1995), 'Wise Use Launches a Stealth Anti-Endangered Species Act Campaign', 4 October, http://www.ewg.org/pub/home/clear/players/ 10_4_95.html.

Clearinghouse on Environmental Advocacy and Research (1996), 'Clearing the Air with Burson-Marsteller', 12 July, http://www.ewg.org/pub/home/clear/players/7_12_96.html.

Clearinghouse on Environmental Advocacy and Research (1997), 'Industry anti-Clean Air Campaign Alert', 17 January, http://www.ewg.org/pub/home/clear/players/1_1_797.html.

Clearinghouse on Environmental Advocacy and Research (1998), 'Industry Deploys New Anti-Environmental Strategy', http://www.ewg.org/pub/home/clear/by_ clear/air_attack.html.

Clement, B. (2000), 'Tax on Lorries Fails to Cover Cost of Road Damage', *The Independent*, 23 September, p. 10.

Cobaria, R.A. (1997), 'Open Letter from the U'wa People to the National Government and People of Colombia', February, http://www.nativeweb.org/ saiic/actions/urgent8.html.

Cobaria, R. *et al.* (1998), 'Communique from the U'wa People', *Earth Island Journal*, 10 August, http://www.earthisland.org/eijournal/fall98/wn_fall98uwa. html.

Coburn, C. (1997), 'Third World Debt – The Silent Killer', *Houston Catholic Worker Newspaper*, http://www.cjd.org/paper/third1.html.

Cockcroft, C. (2000), 'Hunting Ozone', *The Guardian*, 27 January, Science p. 2.

Coghlan, A. (1993a), 'The Green Empire', *New Scientist*, Vol. 140, No, 1893, 2 October, pp. 48–50.

Coghlan, A. (1993b), 'Britain's Green Vision Stuck in Traffic Jam', *New Scientist*, Vol. 140(1902), 4 December, p. 6.

Colchester, M. (1987), 'Paradise Promised', *The New Internationalist*, No 177, November, pp. 24–5.

Colchester, M. (1995), 'Asia Logs Surniname', *Multinational Monitor*, Vol. 16(11), November, http://www.essential.org/monitor/hyper/mm1195.05.html.

Coleman, J.L. (1988), *Markets, Morals and the Law*, Cambridge University Press, Cambridge.

Collins, H. (1982), *Marxism and Law*, Oxford University Press, Oxford.

Commission on Human Rights (1996), 'Human Rights and the Environment', E/ CN.4/1997/18, 9 December, http://www.unhchr.ch/HTML/menu4/chrrep/1897. html.

Conca, K., Alberty, M. and Dabelko, G.D. (1995) in K. Conca, M. Alberty and G.D. Dabelko (eds), *Green Planet Blues: Environmental Politics from Stockholm to Rio*, Westview Press, Boulder.

Connor, S. (1998), 'Toxic Waste Spreads to Deep Ocean', *The Independent*, 2 July, p. 12.

Convention Concerning Occupational Safety and Health Convention and the Working Environment (1983), ILO No 155, 1331 UNTS 279, 11 August, http:// www.umn.edu/humanrts/instree/n6ccoshwe.htm.

Cornwell, R. (1998), 'Made in Britain: The Tanks on Jakarta's Streets', *The Independent*, 21 May, p. 14.

Corporate Europe Observatory (1997), *Europe Inc: Dangerous Liaisons Between EU Institutions and Industry*, Corporate Europe Observatory, Amsterdam.

Corporate Europe Observatory (1998), 'The Weather Gods: How Industry Blocks Progress at Kyoto Climate Summit', *The Corporate Planet*, http:// www.corpwatch.org/trac/feature/planet/gods/html.

Corporate Europe Observatory (1999), 'Summary of Europe Inc', http://www. corpwatch.org/trac/feature/planet/eu_ceo.html.

Corporate Watch (1997), 'Thirteenth Anniversary Fact Sheet on the Union Carbide Disaster in Bhopal', *The Corporate Planet*, http://www.corwatch.org/trac/feature/ india/profiles/bhopal/bhopal13facts.html.

Corporate Watch (1998a), 'Methyl Bromide Working Group', http:// www.corpwatch. org/trac/feature/bromide/mbwg.html.

Corporate Watch (1998b), 'Greenwash Award of the Month', *The Corporate Planet*, http://www.corpwatch.org/trac/greenwash/wbcsd.html.

Corporate Watch (1998c), 'Greenwash Award of the Month', *The Corporate Planet*, http://www.corpwatch.org/trac/greenwash/ford.html.

Corporate Watch (1998d), 'Greenwash Award of the Month: Chevron', *The Corporate Planet*, http://www.corpwatch.org/trac/greenwash/chevron.html.

Corporate Watch (1998e), 'The Global Shell Game', *The Corporate Planet*, http:// www. corpwatch.org/trac/gallery/shell/index.html.

Corporate Watch (1998f), 'Surfing the Pipeline: Chevron and the Environmental Impact of Oil', *The Corporate Planet*, http://corpwatch.org/trac/gallery/chevron/kutubu.html.

Corporate Watch (1998g), 'USA: The Ethyl Corporation has Filed a $251 Million Lawsuit Against the Canadian Government', *The Corporate Planet*, http://www.corpwatch.org/trac/corner/worldnews/other/other44.html.

Corporate Watch (1999a), 'Deadly Partners', *The Corporate Planet*, http://www.corpwatch.org/trac/feature/planet/gods/html.

Corporate Watch (1999b), 'Big Oil's Secret Plan to Block the Global Warming Treaty', 25 February, http://www.corpwatch.org/trac/feature/climate/culprits/bigoil.html.

Corriveau, S. (1995) in S. Deimann, and B. Dyssli (eds), *Environmental Rights*, Cameron May, London.

Cosananund, J. (1995), 'Authoritarian Culture and the Struggle for Human Rights in Thailand', *Human Rights Dialogue*, Vol. 3, December, http://www.cceia.org/dialog3.html.

Costanza, R. and Folke, C. (1996) in S. Hanna, C. Folke and K.G. Maler (eds), *Rights to Nature: Ecological, Economic, Cultural and Political Principles of Institutions for the Environment*, Island Press, Washington DC.

Council of Europe (1992), *Human Rights in International Law*, Council of Europe Press, Brussels.

Cowe, R. (1998), 'Oil Company Inflames Burma Boycott Row', *The Guardian*, 15 May, p. 21.

Cox, R.W. (1981), 'Social Forces, States and World Orders: Beyond International Relations Theory', *Millennium*, Vol. 10(2), pp. 126–55.

Cox, R.W. (1983), 'Gramsci, Hegemony and International Relations: An Essay in Method', *Millennium*, Vol. 12(2), pp. 162–75.

Cox, R.W. (1987), *Production, Power and World Order: Social Forces in the Making of History*, Columbia University Press, New York.

Cox, R. (1994), 'The Crisis in World Order and the Challenge to International Organization', *Cooperation and Conflict*, Vol. 29(2), pp. 99–112.

Cox, R.W. with Sinclair, T.J. (1996), *Approaches to World Order*, Cambridge University Press, Cambridge.

Coyle, D. (1997), 'Oxfam Report Attacks the West's Unbending and Self-Serving Approach to Third World Debt', *The Independent*, 18 April, p. 1.

Coyle, D. (1998a), 'The Big, Bad Multinationals Are Really the Good Guys of Global Investment', *The Independent*, 22 January, p. 24.

Coyle, D. (1998b), 'Is Capitalism Heading for Breakdown?', *The Independent*, 2 December, p. 19.

Cranston M. (1967) in D.D. Raphael (ed.), *Political Theory and the Rights of Man*, Macmillan, Basingstoke.

Crawford, J. (1992) in J. Crawford (ed.), *The Rights of People*, Clarendon Press, Oxford.

Crawford, M. (1991), 'Green Futures on Wall Street', *New Scientist*, Vol. 129(1750), 5 January, pp. 38–40.

Curtis, C. (1992), 'Standing in the Way of Progress: US Obstruction of the Earth Summit', *Greenpeace International*, http://www.greenpeace.org/home/gopher/ campaigns/politics/1992/usunced.html.

Cutler, C. (2001), 'Critical Reflections on the Westphalian Assumptions of International Law and Organisation: A Crisis of Legitimacy', *Review of International Studies*, Vol. 27(2), pp. 133–50.

D'Amato, A. (1990), 'What Obligation Does our Generation Owe to the Next? An Approach to Global Environmental Responsibility', *American Journal of International Law*, Vol. 84(1), pp. 190–98.

Daly, H. (1995) in J. Kirkby, P. O'Keefe and L. Timberlake (eds), *The Earthscan Reader in Sustainable Development*, Earthscan, London.

Daly, H. and Cobb, J. (1994), *For the Common Good*, Beacon Press, Boston.

Davidson, M.D. (1995), 'Basic Rights and the Environment', *Milieu*, May, http:// www.xs4all.nl/~mdd/discus2.html.

Davis, J. (1991) in J. Davis (ed.), *The Earth First! Reader*, Gibbs Smith. Layton, UT.

de Toqueville, A. (1979), *Democracy in America*, Penguin, Harmondsworth.

Deane, P. (1978), *The Evolution of Economic Ideas*, Cambridge University Press, Cambridge.

Declaration of Bizkaia on the Right to the Environment, Bilbao, 12 February, 1999.

Deimann, S. and Dyssli, B. (1995) in S. Deimann and B. Dyssli (eds), *Environmental Rights*, Cameron May, London.

Dejevsky, M. (1997), 'Clinton Pulls out the Stops to Turn the US Green', *The Independent*, 3 October, p. 16.

Derman, B. (1995), 'Environmental NGO's, Dispossession and the State: The Ideology and Praxis of African Nature and Development', *Human Ecology*, Vol. 23(2), pp. 199–215.

Desgagne, R. (1995), 'Integrating Environmental Values into the European Convention on Human Rights', *American Journal of International Law*, Vol. 85(2), April, pp. 263–94.

Development Group for Alternative Politics, The (1997), 'Structural Adjustment and the Spreading Crisis in Latin America', http://www.igc.org/dgap/crisis.html.

Development Group for Alternative Politics, The (1998), 'On the Wrong Track: A Summary Assessment of IMF Interventions in Selected Countries', January, http://www.igc.org/dgap/wrong.html.

Devlin, J.F. and Yap N.T. (1993) in C. Thomas (ed.), *Rio: Unravelling the Consequences*, Frank Cass, Ilford.

Dicken, P. (1999), *Global Shift: Transforming the World Economy*, Sage, London.

Dockery, D.W. *et al.* (1989), 'Effects of Inhaled Particles on Respiratory Health of Children', *American Review of Respiratory Disease*, Vol. 139, pp. 587–94.

Doherty, B. and de Geus, M. (1996) in B. Doherty and M. de Geus (eds), *Democracy and Green Political Thought*, Routledge, London.

Donnelly, J. (1989), *Universal Human Rights in Theory and Practice*, Cornell University Press, New York.

Donnelly, J. (1993), *International Human Rights*, Westview Press, Boulder, CO.

Douglas-Scott (1996) in A.E. Boyle and M.R. Anderson (eds), *Human Rights Approaches to Environmental Protection*, Clarendon Press, Oxford.

Dow Jones Newswires (1998), 'UN Envoy Urges Probe of Damage Caused by Oil Companies in Nigeria', 30 November, received via email from *The Sierra Club*.

Downstream (1997), Fall, http://www.geocities.com/Rainforest/8073/down. html.

Doyle, M. (1996), 'Busting Banana Unions in Belize', *Multinational Monitor*, Vol. 17(9), September, http://www.essential.org/monitor/hyper/mm0996.08.html.

Draft Declaration of Principles on Human Rights and the Environment (1994), http://www.umn.edu/humanrts/instree/1994–dec.html.

Draft Declaration on the Rights of Indigenous Peoples, E/CN.4/SUB.2/1994/2/ Add.1 (1994), http://www.umn.edu/humanrts/instree/declra.htm.

Drengson, A.R. (1980), 'Shifting Paradigms: From the Technocratic to the Person-Planetary', *Environmental Ethics*, Vol. 2(3), pp. 221–40.

Drexler, J. (1997), 'Texaco Sale of Burma Gas Project a Big Victory for Burma's Democracy Movement', *Sierra Club*, 25 September, http://www.sierraclub.org/ human-rights/Texaco.html.

Dryzek, J.S. (1990), *Discursive Democracy: Politics, Policy and Political Science*, Cambridge University Press, Cambridge.

Dryzek, J.S. (1992), 'Ecology and Discursive Democracy: Beyond Liberal Capitalism and the Administrative State', *Capitalism, Nature, Socialism*, Vol. 3(2), pp. 18–42.

du Bois, F. (1994), 'Water Rights and the Limits of Environmental Law', *Journal of International Law*, Vol. 6(1), pp. 73–84.

du Bois, F. (1996), in A. Boyle and M. Anderson (eds), *Human Rights Approaches to Environmental Protection*, Clarendon Press, Oxford.

Dunaway, W.A. and Clelland, D.A. (1995), 'Book Review', *Journal of World-Systems Research*, Vol. 1(5), http://csf.colorado.edu/jwsr.html.

Dunn, J. (1995), in J. Dunn (ed.), *Contemporary Crisis of the Nation State?* Blackwell, Oxford.

Duval-Smith, A. (1998), 'Zambia Sells Off its Red Gold for Scrap', *The Guardian*, 14 May, p. 6.

Dworkin, G. (1994) in G. Dworkin (ed.), *Morality, Harm and the Law*, Westview Press, Boulder.

Dyer, H.C. (1992), 'Environmental Ethics and International Relations', British International Studies Association conference paper, Swansea, 14–16 December.

Dynes, M. (1996), 'Ogoni Activists in Plea to West over Nigeria Frame-up', *The Times*, 15 May, p. 15.

Eckersley, R. (1996) in B. Doherty and M. de Geus (eds), *Democracy and Green Political Thought*, Routledge, London.

Eckstein, G. and Gitlin, M. (1998), 'Human Rights and Environmentalism: Forging Common Ground', *Human Rights Brief*, http://www.wcl.american.edu/pub/humright/development/brief/i23/envt-hr.html.

The Ecologist (1993), *Whose Common Future? Reclaiming the Commons*, Earthscan, London.

The Ecologist (1995) in J. Kirkby, P. O'Keefe and L. Timberlake (eds), *The Earthscan Reader in Sustainable Development*, Earthscan, London.

Economic Working Group (1998), 'MAI: Democracy for Sale?', http://www.igc.org/ econwg/MAI/index.html.

Eden, S. (1993) in Interdisciplinary Research Network on the Environment and Society (eds), *Perspectives on the Environment*, Avebury, Brookfield.

Edwards, R. (1995), 'Industry Denies Dangers of Particle Pollution', *New Scientist*, Vol. 148(2002), 4 November, p. 5.

Edwards, T. (2000), *Contradictions of Consumption: Concepts, Practices and Politics in Consumer Society*, Open University Press, Buckingham.

Elliott, L. (1998a), 'Fury at G8's Debt Failure', *The Guardian*, 18 May, pp. 1–2.

Elliott, L. (1998b), 'Analysis: World Trade', *The Guardian*, 20 May, p. 17.

Elliott, L. and Brummer, A. (1998), 'One Size Does not Fit All', *The Guardian*, 3 July, p. 17.

Elliott, L. and Denny, C. (1998), 'A Question of Political Will', *The Guardian*, 14 May, p. 6.

Ellwood, W. (1991), 'Hidden History: Columbus and the Colonial Legacy', *The New Internationalist*, No. 226, December, pp. 4–7.

Evans, T. (1996), *US Hegemony and the Project of Universal Human Rights*, Macmillan, Basingstoke.

Evans, T. (2000), 'Citizenship and Human Rights in the Age of Globalization', *Alternatives*, Vol. 25, pp. 415–38.

Evans, T. and Hancock, J. (1998), 'Doing Something Without Doing Anything: International Human Rights Law and the Challenge of Globalisation', *The International Journal of Human Rights*, Vol. 2(3), pp. 1–21.

Eyal Press (1998), 'Doing Business with Indonesia's Dictator', *The Christian Science Monitor*, http://plweb.csmonitor.com/plweb-turbo.html.

Fabra, A. (1996) in A.E. Boyle and M.R. Anderson (eds), *Human Rights Approaches to Environmental Protection*, Clarendon Press, Oxford.

Fadope, C.M. (1996), 'Production vs. Reproduction', *Multinational Monitor*, Vol. 17(10), October, http://www.essential.org/monitor/hyper/mm1096.03.html.

Feinberg, J. (1984), *Harm to Others*, Oxford University Press, Oxford.

Feinberg, J. (1988), *Harmless Wrongdoing: The Moral Limits of the Criminal Law*, Vol. 4, Oxford University Press, Oxford.

Felix, D. (1998), 'In Focus: IMF Bailouts and Global Financial Flows', *US Foreign Policy In Focus*, Vol. 3(5), April, http://www.foreignpolicy-infocus.org/ briefs.org/briefs/vol3/v3n5fimf.html.

Fernandez (1996) in A.E. Boyle and M.R. Anderson (eds), *Human Rights Approaches to Environmental Protection*, Clarendon Press, Oxford.

Finch, J. (1998), 'Human Rights Force Way On To Agenda', *The Guardian*, 13 May, p. 23.

Flavin C. (1997) in L. Brown *et al.*, *State of the World 1997*, WW Norton and Company, New York.

Forcese, C. (1997), *Commerce with Conscience?*, International Centre for Human Rights and Democratic Development, Montreal.

Ford, K. (1997), 'The Life and Ideas of Thomas Paine', *Politics Review*, Vol. 7(1), September, pp. 27–9.

Ford, P. (1998), 'A Pact to Guide Global Investing Promises Jobs – But at What Cost?', *The Christian Science Monitor*, 25 February, http://www.csmonitor.com/durable/1998/02/25/intl/intl.6.html.

Forest Futures (1999), 'Should a US Giant Control BC Forests?', *Times Colonist*, 7 September, p. A16.

Forsythe, D.P. (2000), *Human Rights in International Relations*, Cambridge University Press, Cambridge.

Fortin, M. (1998), 'He Who Pays His Debts', *Africana Plus*, http://www.dania.com/~magma/pover2a.html.

Foucault, M. (1994a), *Ethics: Subjectivity and the Truth*, The New Press, New York.

Foucault, M. (1994b) in M. Kelly (ed.), *Critique and Power: Recasting the Foucault/Habermas Debate*, MIT Press, Cambridge, MA.

Franck, T.M. (1992), *Political Questions/Judicial Answers*, Princeton University Press, Princeton.

Fraser, C.G. (1996), 'NAFTAs Environmental Problems', *Earth Times News Service*, 22 January, http://www.hartford-hwp.com/archives/40/022.html.

Free Burma Digest (1997), 'USA: Legal Victory over Unocal, Total and Yadana Cas Pipeline Project', 4 December, http://www.corpwatch.org/trac/corner/worldnews/ other/other38.html.

Freeden, M. (1991), *Rights*, Open University Press, Milton Keynes.

Freeden, M. (1994), 'The Philosophical Foundations of Human Rights', *Human Rights Quarterly*, Vol. 16(3), pp. 491–514.

Freeman, A. (1996), 'Clearcutting Democracy', *Multinational Monitor*, Vol. 17(5), May, http://www.essential.org/monitor/hyper/mm0596.03.html.

Freeman, A. (1994), 'Post-NAFTA Labour Abuses', *Multinational Monitor*, Vol. 15(7,8), July/August, http://www.essential.org/monitor/hyper/mm0894.html.

Freyfoygle, E.T. (1994), 'Owning the Wolf', *Dissent*, Vol. 41(4), pp. 481–7.

Friedman, H. (1992), 'Distance and Durability: Shaky Foundations of the World Food Economy', *Third World Quarterly*, Vol. 13(2), pp. 371–84.

Friends of the Earth (1993), 'Citizen's Charter or Polluter's Charter?', *Earth Matters*, Issue 20, Winter, p. 6.

Friends of the Earth (1995), 'Getting the Facts on the IFC: Private Sector Lending of the World Bank', 19 October, http://www.hartford-hwp.com/archives/25/013.html.

Friends of the Earth (1996), 'Economic Deal Spells Doom for Madagascar Forests', 10 October, http://www.foe.co.uk/pubsinfo/infoteam/pressrel/1996/19960910182500.html.

Friends of the Earth (1998a), 'Leaked Letter Tips US Hand at Climate Talks', 12 November, http://www.foe.co.uk/pubsinfo/infoteam/pressrel/1998/1998111 214282 2.html.

Friends of the Earth (1998b), 'Shell Environment Report Condemned as Greenwash', http://www.foe.co.uk/pubsinfo/infoteam/pressrel/1997/1997050 6170500.html.

Frynas, J.G. (1998), 'Political Instability and Business: Focus on Shell in Nigeria', *Third World Quarterly*, Vol. 19(3), pp. 457–78.

Fukuyama, F. (1992), *The End of History and the Last Man*, Penguin, London.

Fullick, A.and Fullick, P. (1994), *Chemistry*, Heinemann, Oxford.

Galbraith, J.K. (1984), *The Anatomy of Power*, Hamish Hamilton, London.

Galbraith, J.K. (1992), *The Culture of Contentment*, Penguin, London.

Gallie, W.B. (1956) in A.A. Kassman (ed.), *Proceedings of the Aristotelian Society*, University of Oklahoma Press, Norman, OK, pp. 167–98.

Galtung, J. (1994), *Human Rights in Another Key*, Polity Press, Cambridge.

Galtung, J. (1995), 'Peace and Conflict Research in the Age of the Cholera: Ten Pointers to the Future of Peace Studies', *Peace and Conflict Studies*, Vol. 2(1), June, pp. 5–17.

Gamini, G. (1996), 'Andes Tribe Makes Suicide Threat to Halt Oil Drilling', *The Times*, 4 October, p. 13.

Gauer, A. (1983) in A. Gauer (ed.), *South – South Strategy*, Third World Foundation, Penang.

Gauslaa, J. (1996), 'The Nikitin Case', *Bellona*, 18 October, http://www.bellona.no/ e/ russia/nikitin/juridic/wp96–6/index.html.

Gedicks, A. (1997), 'The Wise Use Movement and People for Wisconsin', *Downstream*, Fall/Winter, http://www.geocities.com/Rainforest/8073/down1. html.

George, S. (1984), *Ill Fares the Land*, Institute for Policy Studies, Washington DC.

Gibbon, P. (1993) in G. Sorenson (ed.), *Political Conditionality*, Frank Cass, London.

Giddens, A. (1981), *A Contemporary Critique of Historical Materialism Vol. 1: Power, Property and the State*, Macmillan, London.

Gill, S. (1990), *American Hegemony and the Trilateral Commission*, Cambridge University Press, Cambridge.

Gill, S. (1995), 'Globalisation, Market Civilisation and Disciplinary Neo-liberalism', *Millennium*, Vol. 24(3), pp. 399–424.

Gills, B.J.R. and Wilson, R. (1993), *Low Intensity Democracy*, Pluto Press, London.

Gills, B.K. (1995), 'Whither Democracy? Globalisation and the New Hellenism', paper presented at the British International Studies Association Conference, Southampton, 20 December.

Gittings, J. (1999), 'US and China Trade Rights Charges', *The Guardian*, 2 March, p. 11.

Glazewski J. (1996) in A.E. Boyle and M.R Anderson (eds), *Human Rights Approaches to Environmental Protection*, Clarendon, Oxford.

Gleeson, B. and Low N. (1999) in B. Gleeson and N. Low (eds), *Government for the Environment*, Macmillan, London.

Goldfrank, W.L. (1996), 'Praxis, Shmaxis: Commentary on Wagar', *Journal of World-Systems Research*, Vol. 2(2), http://csf.colorado.edu/wsystems/jwsr.html.

Goldsmith, J. (1994), 'The New Utopia: GATT and Global Free Trade', testimony before the Senate Commerce Committee, 5 October, http://www.hartford-hwp.com/archives/25a/004.html.

Goldsmith, Z. (1998), 'Legalized, Random Genocide', *The Ecologist*, January/February, http://www.gn.apc.org/ecologist/janfeb/editorial-janfeb.html.

Goodin, R.E. (1985), *Protecting the Vulnerable*, University of Chicago Press, Chicago.

Goodman, D. and Redclift, M. (1991), *Food, Ecology and Culture*, Routledge, London.

Gormley, W. (1976), *Human Rights and the Environment*, Sijthoff, Leyden.

Gorz, A. (1973), 'Ecology, Politics', *Le Sanvage*, The Institute of Social Disengineering, Oxford.

Gorz, A. (1988), *Critique of Economic Reason*, Verso, London.

Gosling, P. (1998), 'Investment Pact Sparks Turf War', *The Independent*, 11 February, p. 19.

Gould, R. (1989), 'The Exhausting Options of Modern Vehicles', *New Scientist*, Vol. 122(1664), 13 May, pp. 42–7.

Gow, D. (1999), 'Green Tax Imperils Steel Jobs', *The Guardian*, 25 March, p. 23.

Gowdy, J. (1999), *Coevolutionary Economics: The Economy, Society and the Environment*, Kluwer, Boston.

Grant, W. (1996), 'Making Economic Policy in a Global Economy', *Politics Review*, Vol. 6(1), September, pp. 23–6.

Gray, J. (1983), *Mill on Liberty: A Defence*, Routledge, London.

Gray, J. (1989), *Liberalism*, Routledge, London.

Gray, J. (1998), 'Globalisation – The Dark Side', *The New Statesman*, 13 March, pp. 32–4.

Gray, J. (1999), 'The Myth of Progress', *New Statesman*, 9 April, pp. 27–8.

Gray, K. (1995) in J. Kirkby, P. O'Keefe and L. Timberlake (ed.), *The Earthscan Reader in Sustainable Development*, Earthscan, London.

Gray, M. (1999), 'Nikitin Treason Trial Goes to Round 2', *National Post*, 7 June, p. A11.

Greater Boston Physicians for Social Responsibility (1998), 'Health Effects of Air Pollution', http://www.igc.apc.org/psr/airpol.html.

Green, P. (1990), *The Enemy Without*, Open University Press, Milton Keynes.

Green, T. (1998), 'Ecology, Ethics, Power', *Adbusters*, http://www.adbusters/Articles/ green.html.

Greenpeace (1998a), *Campaign Report*, Spring.

Greenpeace (1998b), http://www.greenpeace.org/

Greenpeace (1998c), 'Shell in Nigeria'; http://www.web.apc.org/~embargo/shell.htm.

Greenpeace (1999), 'The Decline of Corporate Accountability', http://www.greenpeace.org/~comms/97/summit/account.html.

Greenpeace (2001), 'Conferences', http://www.greenpeace.org/~climate/politics/reports/conferences.html.

Greider, W. (1997), *One World, Ready or Not: The Manic Logic of Global Capitalism*, Simon and Schuster, New York.

Griesgrober, J.M. and Gunter, B.G. (1996) in J.M. Griesgrober and B.G. Gunter (eds), *The World's Monetary System: Toward Stability and Sustainability in the Twenty-First Century*, Pluto Press, London.

Grossman, Z. (1995), 'Linking the Native Movement for Sovereignty and the Environmental Movement', http://conbio.rice.edu/nae/docs/grossman.html, reprinted in *Z Magazine*, Vol. 8(11), November, pp. 42–50.

Gvora, E. (1999), 'Microcredit: Turning Points for the Poorest', *Times Colonist*, 22 June, p. A12.

Haas, E.B. (1970), *The Web of Interdependence*, Prentice Hall, Englewood Cliffs, NJ.

Habermas, J. (1994) in K. Michael (ed.), *Critique and Power: Recasting the Foucault/Habermas Debate*, MIT Press, Cambridge, MA.

Hadfield, B. (1995) in B. Hadfield (ed.), *Judicial Review: A Thematic Approach*, Gill and Macmillan, Dublin.

Hall, K. (1996), 'NAFTA Affects Health and Safety', *NAFTA Inter-American Trade Monitor*, 13 December, http://www.hartford-hwp.com/archives/40/028.html.

Hall, T.D. (1995), 'Book Review', *Journal of World-Systems Research*, Vol. 1(3), http://csf.colorado.edu/jwsr.html.

Hamer, M. (1994), 'Drivers Can Damage Your Health', *New Scientist*, Vol. 143(1938), 13 August, p. 8.

Hamer, M. and MacKenzie, D. (1995), 'Brussels Blocks Britain's Clean Air Plan', *New Scientist*, Vol. 148(2004), 18 November, p. 6.

Hamill, J. (1997), 'New Labour, New Ethics, New Foreign Policy?', *Politics Review*, Vol. 7(2), pp. 29–33.

Hanbury-Tenison, R. (1990), 'No Surrender in Sarawak', *New Scientist*, Vol. 128(1745), 1 December, pp. 28–9.

Hanlon, J. (1996), 'Strangling Mozambique: International Monetary Fund Stabilization in the World's Poorest Country', *Multinational Monitor*, Vol. 17(7,8), July/August, http://www.essentialorg/monitor/hyper/mm0796.06.html.

Hanna, S. and Jentoft, S. (1996) in S. Hanna, C. Folke and K.G. Maler (eds), *Rights to Nature: Ecological, Economic, Cultural and Political Principles of Institutions for the Environment*, Island Press, Washington DC.

Hanna, S., Folke, C. and Maler, K.G. (1996) in S. Hanna, C. Folke, and K.G. Maler (eds), *Rights to Nature: Ecological, Economic, Cultural and Political Principles of Institutions for the Environment*, Island Press, Washington DC.

Haq, F. (1997), 'Earth Summit + 5: A Betrayal of Rio', *Third World Resurgence*, No 83, pp. 8–9.

Harcombe, M.J. (1998), 'Letter to the Editor', *The Times*, 27 November, p. 25.

Hardin, G. (1968), 'The Tragedy of the Commons', *Science*, Vol. 162, pp. 1243–8.

Harding, A. (1996) in A.E. Boyle and M.R. Anderson (eds), *Human Rights Approaches to Environmental Protection*, Clarendon Press, Oxford.

Hargrove, E.C. (1989), *Foundations of Environmental Ethics*, Prentice Hall, New York.

Harris, I. (1992), 'The Life and Ideas of John Locke', *Politics Review*, Vol. 1(3), February, pp. 5–8.

Harrison, L. (1993) in L. Harrison (ed.), *Environmental Auditing Handbook*, McGraw Hill, New York.

Harrison, M. (1998), 'What Shell Said About Itself', *The Independent*, 22 April, p. 19.

Harrison, P. (1980), *Inside the Third World*, Harvester Press, London.

Hart H.L.A. (1984) in J. Waldron (ed.), *Theories of Rights*, Oxford University Press, Oxford.

Hayward, T. (1997), 'Anthropocentrism: A Misunderstood Problem,' *Environmental Values*, Vol. 6, pp. 49–63.

Hayward, T. (2000), 'Constitutional Environmental Rights: A Case for Political Analysis', *Political Studies*, Vol. 48(3), pp. 558–73.

Healy, B. (1997), 'Development Threat to Amazon Indians Rainforest', *Green Left Weekly*, http://www3.silas.unsw.edu.au/~greenlft/1997/292/292p21b.htm.

Heinberg, R. (1994), 'Our Global Future', *Museletter*, No 26, February, http://www.igc.org/museletter/MUSE26.html.

Heinberg, R. (1994), 'Native Wisdom in the Modern World', *Museletter*, No 29, May, http://www.igc.org/museletter/MUSE29.html.

Heinberg, R. (1994), 'A Different Kind of Progress', *Museletter*, No 33, September, http://www.igc.org/museletter/MUSE33.html.

Held, D. (1996), 'Rethinking Democracy: The Cosmopolitan Model', *Politics Review*, Vol. 5(3), February, pp. 7–9.

Hellinger, S. (1996), 'Mexico's House of Cards', *Out of Washington*, Issue 2, 4 April, http://www.igc.org/dgap/oow2.html.

Herrmann, P. (1995), 'Human Environmental Crisis and the Transnational Corporation: The Question of Culpability', *Human Ecology*, Vol. 23(2), June, pp. 285–9.

Hewitt, T., Johnson, H. and Wield, D. (1994) in T. Hewitt, H. Johnson and D. Wield (eds), *Industrialisation and Development*, Oxford University Press in association with the Open University, Oxford.

Hill, R.P. (1995), 'Blackfellas and Whitefellas: Aboriginal Land Rights, The Mabo Decision and the Meaning of Land', *Human Rights Quarterly*, Vol. 17(2), pp. 303–22.

Hindess, B. (1996), *Discourses of Power*, Blackwell, Oxford.

Hitchcock, R.K. (1995), 'Centralisation, Resource Depletion and Coercive Conservation Among the Tyua of the Northeast Kalahari', *Human Ecology*, Vol. 23(2), pp. 169–98.

Hitchcock, R.K. (1997) in B.R. Johnston (ed.), *Human Rights and the Environment at the End of the Millennium*, Alta Mira, Walnut Creek.

Hoare, Q. and Nowell Smith, G. (1971), *Antonio Gramsci: Selections from Prison Notebooks*, Lawrence and Wishart, London.

Hobart, M. (1993) in M. Hobart (ed.), *Anthropological Critique of Development: The Growth of Ignorance*, Routledge, London.

Hobsbawm, E. (1994), *Age of Extremes: The Short Twentieth Century*, Michael Joseph, London.

Hoffman, J. (1988), 'The Life and Ideas of Antonio Gramsci', *Social Studies Review*, January, pp. 93–7.

Hoffman, J. (1996), 'Concept: Sovereignty', *Politics Review*, Vol. 6(2), November, pp. 10–11.

Hoffman, J. (1998), *Sovereignty*, Open University Press, Buckingham.

Hollist, W.L. and LaMond Tullis, F. (1987) in W.L. Hollist, and F. LaMond Tullis (eds), *Pursuing Food Security*, Lynne Rienner Boulder, London.

Honda (1998), Advertisement, *Radio Times*, 24 October, pp. 86–7.

Hope Mason, J. (1994), 'The Life and Ideas of Jean-Jacques Rousseau', *Politics Review*, Vol. 3(5), February, pp. 2–4.

Horkheimer, M. and Adorno, T.W. (1972), *Dialectic of Enlightenment*, Herder and Herder, New York.

Howitt, R. (1997), 'The Other Side of the Table: Corporate Culture and Negotiating with Resource Companies', Regional Agreements Paper No 3, *Land, Rights, Laws: Issues of Native Title*, August.

Hoy, D.C. (1986) in D.C. Hoy (ed.), *Foucault: A Critical Reader*, Blackwell, Oxford.

Human Rights Watch and the Natural Resources Defense Council (1992), *Defending the Earth: Abuses of Human Rights and the Environment*, Natural Resources Defense Council, Washington DC.

Hunt, L. (1998), 'Send in the Clouds', *New Scientist*, 30 May, pp. 28–33.

Hunter, M. (1996), 'EPZs in Ghana: A Dismal Story', *Multinational Monitor*, Vol. 17(7,8), July/August, http://www.essentialorg/monitor/hyper/mm0796.05.html.

Hutchings, K. (1999), *International Political Theory*, Sage, London.

Imhof, A. (1996), 'The Big, Ugly Australian Goes to Ok Tedi', *Multinational Monitor*, Vol. 17(3), March, http://www.essential.org/monitor/hyper/mm0396.05.html.

Ingram, A. (1994), *A Political Theory of Rights*, Clarendon Press, Oxford.

Ingram, D. and Ingram J. (1992) in D. Ingram and J. Ingram (eds), *Critical Theory*, Paragon House, New York.

Instituto del Tercer Mundo (1995), *The World: A Third World Guide 1995/1996*, Instituto del Tercer Mundo, London.

Inter Press Service (1997), 'G-7 Environment: Indigenous Tribunal to Try Sumiteers', 19 June, http://www.oneworld.org/ips2/.

Interdisciplinary Research Network on the Environment and Society (1993), *Perspectives on the Environment*, Avebury, Brookfield, Vermont.

International Peoples' Tribunal on Human Rights and the Environment (1998), 'Statement of the International Peoples' Tribunal on Human Rights and the Environment: Sustainable Development in the Context of Globalization', *Alternatives*, Vol. 23(1), pp. 109–46.

Jackson, S. (1998), 'US Trade Group to Attack Sanctions Laws in Court', *Agence-France Presse*, 17 March, received via email from *The Sierra Club*.

Jacobs, M. (1997), in M. Jacobs (ed.), *Greening the Millennium?* Blackwell, Oxford.

Jaising, I. and Sathyamala, C. (1995) in J. Kirkby, P. O'Keefe and L. Timberlake (eds), *The Earthscan Reader in Sustainable Development*, Earthscan, London.

Jochnick, C. (1995), 'Amazon Oil Offensive', *Multinational Monitor*, Vol. 16(1,2), January/February, http://www.essential.org/monitor/hyper/mm0195.html.

Johnston, B.R. (1994) in B.R. Johnston (ed.), *Who Pays the Price?*, Island Press, Washington DC.

Johnston, B.R. (1995), 'Human Rights and the Environment', *Human Ecology*, Vol. 23(2), pp. 111–23.

Johnston, B.R. (1997) in B.R. Johnston (ed.), *Human Rights and the Environment at the End of the Millennium*, Alta Mira, Walnut Creek.

Johnston, B.R. and Button (1994) in B.R. Johnston (ed.), *Who Pays the Price?*, Island Press, Washington DC.

Johnston B.R. and Byrne M.A. (1994) in B.R. Johnston (ed.), *Who Pays the Price?*, Island Press, Washington DC.

Jones, K. (1994), 'Waterborne Diseases', *New Scientist*, Vol. 143(1933), 9 July, pp. 1–4.

Jones, P. (1994), *Rights*, MacMillan, Basingstoke.

Kamen, A. (1997), 'Lost in the Ozone', *Washington Post*, 3 February, p. 4.

Kandela, P. (1994), 'Dialogue Between Health and Human Rights Groups', *Lancet*, Vol. 344(8928), 8 October, pp. 1011–12.

Kane, M.J. (1993), 'Promoting Political Rights to Protect the Environment', *Yale Journal of International Law*, Vol. 18(1), pp. 389–411.

Karacs, I. Dejevsky M. and Schoon, N. (1997), 'America Reveals her Policy on Global Warming: Too Little, Too Late', *The Independent*, 23 October, p. 1.

Kausikan, B. (1993), 'Asia's Different Standard', *Foreign Policy*, Vol. 92(3), pp. 24–41.

Kelly, M. (1994) in M. Kelly (ed.), *Critique and Power: Recasting the Foucault/ Habermas Debate*, MIT Press, Cambridge, MA.

Kennedy, D. (1996), 'Ok Tedi All Over Again: Placer and the Porgera Gold Mine', *Multinational Monitor*, Vol. 17(3), March, http://www.essential.org/monitor/ hyper/mm0396.07.html.

Kenny, M. (1996), 'Debate: Re-evaluating Rio – Introduction', *New Political Economy*, Vol. 1(3), pp. 399–400.

Kenwood, M. (1989), 'Science Stays Up the Pole: After Five Years of Battering, Science Remains Healthy, At Least in the Eyes of the Public', *New Scientist*, Vol. 123(1682), 16 September, p. 57.

Kenyon, I. (2000), 'Chemical Weapons in the Twentieth Century', *The Chemical and Biological Weapons Conventions Bulletin*, Vol. 48, p. 1.

Keohane, R. and Nye, J. (1977), *Power and Interdependence: World Politics in Transition*, Addison-Wesley Educational Publishers Inc, Boston.

Kernohan, A. (1998), *Liberalism, Equality and Cultural Oppression*, Cambridge University Press, Cambridge.

Kettle, M. (1998), 'Blair Puts Debt Relief on Agenda', *The Guardian*, 15 May, p. 1.

Kettle, M. Brown, P. and Traynor, I. (1997), 'US Rips up Green Treaty', *The Guardian*, 23 October, p. 1.

Kimerling, J. (1991), *Amazon Crude*, Natural Resources Defence Council, Washington DC.

King, P. (1967), *Fear of Power*, Frank Cass, London.

Kirkby, J., O'Keefe, P. and Timberlake, L. (1995) in J. Kirkby, P. O'Keefe and L. Timberlake (eds), *The Earthscan Reader in Sustainable Development*, Earthscan, London.

Knight, D. (1997a), 'Multinationals Undermine Environment', *Inter Press Service*, 14 October, http://www.oneworld.org/ips2/oct/multinationals.html.

Knight, D. (1997b), 'Police Take Hard Line With Activists', *Inter Press Service*, 14 November, http://www.oneworld.org/ips2/nov/activists.html.

Knight, D. (1998), 'Indonesians Sue US Mining Giant', *Inter Press Service*, March, http://www.oneworld.org/ips2/mar98/16_02_057.html.

Kontnik, L. (1980), 'Comment. Increment Allocation Under Prevention of Significant Deterioration: How to Decide Who is Allowed to Pollute', *Northwestern Law Review*, Vol. 74, pp. 936–69.

Korten, D. (1995), *When Corporations Rule the World*, Earthscan, London.

Korten, D. (1997), 'The Financial Casino and Corporate Rule', *Corporate Watch*, http://www.corpwatch.org/trac/feature/planet/casino_rule.html.

Korten, D. (1998), 'Taming the Giants', http://www.geocities.com/~combusem/korten.html.

Kramer, M. (1997), *John Locke and the Origin of Private Property*, University of Cambridge Press, Cambridge.

Kravis, M.J. (1999), 'Tide of Protectionism Faces Trade Talks', *National Post*, 4 June, p. C7.

Kudrik, I. (1998), 'The Socio-Ecological Union Appeals to Yeltsin: Stop Criminal Prosecution of Environmentalists', *Bellona*, 20 April, http://www.bellona.no/e/russia/nikitin/news/980420.html.

Kuhn, T. (1962), *The Structure of Scientific Revolutions*, University of Chicago Press, Chicago.

Kuhonta, E. (1995), 'The Language of Human Rights in East Asia', *Human Rights Dialogue*, Vol. 2, September, http://www.cceia.org/dialog2.html.

Laferriere, E. (1996), 'Emancipating International Relations Theory: An Ecological Perspective', *Millennium*, Vol. 25(1), pp. 53–76.

Lake, D.A. (1993), 'Leadership, Hegemony and the International Economy: Naked Emperor or Tattooed Monarch with Potential?', *International Studies Quarterly*, Vol. 37.

Langer, A. (1997), 'Protect Environment Through Law, Not By Creating New Rights', *Defenders of Property Rights Florida Project*, http://www.willjohnston.com/articles/10_16_97pebl.html.

Lapp, D. (1994), 'The Demanding Side of Utility Conservation', *Multinational Monitor*, September, http://www.essential.org/monitor/hyper/mm0994.html.

Lasne, K. (1998), 'Voodoo at the Summit', *Adbusters*, http://www.adbusters.org/adbusters/Articles/voodoo.html.

Lawrence, R. (1995), 'Water, Waste, Sour Gas', *The People's Voice*, January, http://www.hartford-hwp.com/archives/41/019.html.

Lee, J. and Manning, L. (1995), 'Environmental Lung Disease', *New Scientist*, Vol. 147(1995), 16 September, pp. 4–5.

Lentner, H. (2000) in H. Goverde, P. Cerny, M. Haugaard and H. Lentner (eds), *Power in Contemporary Politics*, Sage, London.

Leon, M. (1973), *Particle Physics: An Introduction*, Academic Press, New York.

Leonard, A. (1994), 'Dumping Pepsi's Plastic', *Multinational Monitor*, September, http://www.essential.org/monitor/hyper/mm0994.html.

Leonard, A. and Rispens, J. (1996), 'Exposing the Recycling Hoax: Bharat Zinc and the Politics of the International Waste Trade', *Multinational Monitor*, Vol. 17(1, 2), January/February, http://www.essential.org/monitor/hyper/mm0196.09. html.

Leopold, A. (1949), *A Sand County Almanac*, Oxford University Press, Oxford.

Lewin, R. (1996), 'All for One: One for All', *New Scientist*, Vol. 152(2060), 14 December, pp. 28–33.

Lidstone, J. (1995) in J. Lidstone (ed.), *Global Issues of Our Time*, Cambridge University Press, Cambridge.

Linklater, A. (1990), *Men and Citizens in the Theory of International Relations*, 2nd edition, Macmillan, London.

Linton, B. (1998), 'Letter: Bad Debts', *The Independent*, 7 January, p. 18.

Lisco, A.E. (1991), 'The Pain of Mother Earth', *The New Internationalist*, No. 226, December, pp. 16–7.

Little, R. and Smith, M. (1991) in R. Little, and M. Smith (eds), *Perspectives on World Politics*, Second Edition, Routledge, London.

Litvinoff, M. (1990), *The Earthscan Action Handbook for People and Planet*, Earthscan, London.

Ljunggren, D. (1998), 'Interview: Amnesty Rights Group to Target Oil Firms', *Reuters*, 13 May, received via email from *The Sierra Club*.

Lloyd Parry, R. (1997a), 'Kyoto Gets off to an Icy Start', *The Independent*, 2 December, p. 11.

Lloyd Parry, R. (1997b), 'Greenhouse Optimist Takes the Stage with Lunatic Fringe', *The Independent*, 10 December, p. 8.

Lohman, L. (1995) in Conca, K. Alberty M. and Dabelko, G.D. (eds), *Green Planet Blues: Environmental Politics from Stockholm to Rio*, Westview Press, Boulder.

Lomborg, B. (2001), 'Why Kyoto will not stop this', *The Guardian*, 17 August, http://www.gurdian.co.uk/g2/story/0,3604,538027,00.html.

Long, D. (1977), *Bentham on Liberty*, University of Toronto Press, Toronto.

Lukes, S. (1974), *Power: A Radical View*, Macmillan, London.

Lukes, S. (1986) in S. Lukes (ed.), *Power*, Blackwell, Oxford.

Luxner, L. (1997), 'Business Bats for Colombia', *Multinational Monitor*, Vol. 18(5), May, http://www.essential.org/monitor/hyper/mm0597.12.html.

Lye, J. (1999), 'Foucault, The Discourse on Language: A Summary', 11 June, http://www.brocku.ca/english/courses/4F70/discourse.html.

Lynch, T. (1995), 'Polluting Our Principles: Environmental Prosecutions and the Bill of Rights', *Policy Analysis*, CATO Institute, No 223, 20 April.

Lyotard, J.F. (1993), *Political Writings*, UCL Press, London.

McCarthy, M. (1998), 'US Pledges Will Wreck Kyoto Deal', *The Independent*, 11 November, p. 2.

McCarthy, M. (2000), 'The $1bn Ford is Spending to Rid Your Car of Petrol', *The Independent*, 16 September, p. 4.

McCarthy, M. and Nash, E. (1998), 'Poisons Ruin Wildlife Paradise', *The Independent*, 29 April, p. 1,12.

McChesney, A. (1995), 'Environment and Human Rights', *Canadian Human Rights Foundation Newsletter*, Vol. 10(2), http://www.web.net/~chrfrene/news4.html.

McCormack, G. (1997), 'Village Versus State', *The Ecologist*, November/December, http://www.gn.apc.org/ecologist/novdec/villages.html.

McDonnell, W. (Interview) (1994), 'The Effects of Ozone on Human Health', *Environmental Review Newsletter*, Vol. 1(1), January, http://www.igc.org/envreview/mcdonnel.htm.

McGowan, L. (1997), 'Democracy Undermined, Economic Justice Denied: Structural Adjustment and the AID Juggernaut in Haiti', January, http://www.igc.org/dgap/ haiti97.html.

McGrory, M. (1997), 'Human Rights, Presidential Wrongs', *The Washington Post*, 18 May, p. C1.

McLellan, D. (1977), *Karl Marx: Selected Writings*, Oxford University Press, Oxford.

McNeely, J.A. (1991), 'Common Property Resource Management or Government Ownership?', *International Relations*, Vol. 10(3), May, pp. 211–26.

McRae, H. (1998), 'How to Cope with the Cheapest Energy Ever – Make it Expensive', *The Independent*, 25 February, p. 19.

McSpotlight (1997), 'Texaco in the McSpotlight', http://www.mcspotlight.org/beyond/ companies/texaco.html.

McSpotlight (1998), 'British Petroleum in the McSpotlight', http://www.mcspotlight. org/beyond/companies/bp.html.

Machan, T.R. (1984) in T. Regan (ed.), *Earthbound*, Temple University Press, Philadelphia, pp. 74–106.

Machan, T.R. (1993), 'Individual Rights, the Common Good and the Environment', *International Journal of Social Economics*, Vol. 20(9), pp. 54–65.

MacKenzie, D. (1990), 'Review: Children Measure the Planet's Health', *New Scientist*, Vol. 126(1722), 23 June, p. 68.

MacKenzie, D. (1994), 'Will Tomorrow's Children Starve?', *New Scientist*, Vol. 143(1941), 3 September, pp. 24–9.

Maclean's (1995), 'Wheezing and Worrying', *Maclean's*, Vol. 108, Issue 24, 12 June, p. 3.

MacNeill, J., Winsemius, P. and Yakushiji, T. (1991), *Beyond Interdependence*, Oxford University Press, New York and Oxford.

Maddox, B. (1997), 'Americans Lose Faith in Federal Politics', *The Times*, 30 August, p. 15.

Majot, J. (1994), 'Brave New World Bank: 50 Years is Enough', *TEX*, Vol. 1(4), December, http://www.ups.edu/polgov/oneil/calss/brave.htm.

Makhijani, A. (1992), *From Global Capitalism to Economic Justice*, Apex Press, New York and London.

Malhotra, K. (1997), 'Celebration of Miracle Turns Into Damage Control by IMF', 3 October, http://www.igc.org/dgap/saprin/thai2.html.

Marshall, A. (1998), 'Defence Cuts to Help Human Rights', *The Independent*, 27 February, p. 1.

Marshall, G. (1998), *Oxford Dictionary of Sociology*, Oxford University Press, Oxford.

Maughan, R. (1993), 'What's Old and What's New About the Wise Use Movement', 23 April, http://www-personal.ksu.edu/~jwkplan/ruralsem/wiseuse.html.

Mayer, A.E. (1995), *Islam and Human Rights: Tradition and Politics*, Westview Press, Boulder, CO.

Meadowcroft, J. (1996), 'Taking Issue with UNCED's Critics', *New Political Economy*, Vol. 1(3), pp. 408–12.

Melamed, D. (1990), 'Congress Gets Tough on Heavy Polluters', *New Scientist*, Vol. 128(1741), 3 November, p. 20.

Mendes, C. (1989), *Fight for the Forest: Chico Mendes in his Own Words*, Latin American Bureau, London.

Merrills J.G. (1996) in A.E Boyle and M.R. Anderson (eds), *Human Rights Approaches to Environmental Protection*, Clarendon Press, Oxford.

Methyl Bromide Alternatives Network (1998), 'A First Class Poison', *Corporate Watch*, http://www.corpwatch.org/trac/feature/bromide/poison.html.

Metress, S. (1996), 'The Great Starvation and British Imperialism in Ireland', *The Irish People*, 10 January, http://www.vms.utexas.edu/~jdana/iphunger.html.

Mill, J.S. (1994) in G. Dworkin (ed.), *Morality, Harm and the Law*, Westview Press, Boulder.

Miller, M. (1995), *The Third World in Global Environmental Politics*, Lynne Rienner, Boulder, CO.

Miller, S. (1998), 'For Arms Industry, Pondering Morality Can Seem a Costly Extra', *The Guardian* (debt supplement), 15 May, p. 6.

Milliken, R. (1998), 'Aborigine Fury Erupts over Land Bill', *The Independent*, 7 July, p. 11.

Mills, S. (1998), 'UN Report on Nigerian Human Rights Calls for Investigation of Shell', 7 May, received via email from *The Sierra Club*.

Mills, S. (1998), 'Russia: Government Admits 'Serious' Radiation Near Norway', *National Journal's Greenwire*, 11 May, received via email from *The Sierra Club*.

Milne, A.J.M. (1968), *Freedom and Rights*, Humanities Press, London.

Mishan, E.J. (1993), *The Costs of Economic Growth*, Weidenfeld and Nicolson, London.

Miskel, J. (1997), 'The Debate about Foreign Aid', *Journal of Humanitarian Assistance*, 17 January, http://www-jha.sps.cam.ac.uk/a/a013.htm.

Mitra, A. (1987), 'The Empire Strikes Back', *The New Internationalist*, No 167, January, pp. 8–10.

Mittelman, J.H. (1996) in J.H. Mittelman (ed.), *Globalisation: Critical Reflections*, Lynne Rienner, Boulder, CO.

Mittelman, J.H. (1998), 'Coxian Historicism as an Alternative Perspective in International Studies', *Alternatives*, Vol. 23(1), pp. 63–92.

Moghadam, V. (1996), 'Comments on Warren Wagar', *Journal of World Systems Research*, Vol. 2(2), http://csf.colorado.edu/wsystems/jwsr.html.

Mokhiber, R. (1995), 'Names in the News', *Multinational Monitor*, Vol. 16(1,2), January/February, http://www.essential.org/monitor/hyper/mm0195.html.

Mokhiber, R. (1996), 'The Ten Worst Corporations of 1996', *Multinational Monitor*, Vol. 17(12), December 1996, http://www.essential.org/monior/hyper/mm1296.04. html.

Monbiot, G. (1996), 'The Land is Ours', Schumacher Lecture, 19 October, Bristol, http://www.oneworld.org/schumachersoc/lectures96/monbiot.html.

Monbiot, G. (2000), 'The Seas Rise, The Glaciers Disappear', *The Guardian*, 27 January, p. 20.

Montagu, P. (1989a), 'How to Achieve Pollution Control?', *Rachel's Environment and Health Weekly*, Issue 154, 7 November 1989, http://www.monitor.net/rachel/r154.html.

Montagu, P. (1989b), 'Some Good News: We Could Give Up Oil', *Rachel's Environment and Health Weekly*, Issue 154, 7 November, http://www.monitor.net/ rachel/r252.html.

Montagu, P. (1989c), 'Invisible Killers: Fine Particles', *Rachel's Environment and Health Weekly*, Issue 154, 7 November 1989, http://www.monitor.net/rachel/r373.html.

Montagu, P. (1991), 'International Waste Trade Part 2: The Struggle to Ban the Waste Trade', *Rachel's Hazardous Waste News*, Issue 257, 30 October, http://xp0. rtknet.org/E3615T132.html.

Montagu, P. (1997), 'Kyoto', *Rachel's Environment and Health Weekly*, Issue 577, 18 December, http://www.monitor.net/rachel/r577.html.

Morales, P. (1996), in P. Morales (ed.), *Towards Global Human Rights*, International Centre for Human and Public Affairs, Tilburg, Netherlands.

Morita-Lou, H. (1999), 'Right to the Environment in the Context of Agenda 21 and its Implementation', paper presented at the Seminar of Experts on the Right to the Environment, Bilbao, Spain, 10–13 February.

Morriss, P. (1987), *Power: A Philosophical Analysis*, Manchester University Press, Manchester.

Mortishead, C. (1997), 'Beleaguered Shell Takes Stand on Human Rights', *The Times*, 17 March, p. 45.

Morton, P. 'Top US Investment Dealer Endorses Single Currency for North America', *National Post*, 7 June 1999, p. A8.

Mosca G. (1970) in M.E. Olson (ed.), *Power in Societies*, Macmillan, London.

Multinational Monitor (1994), 'Putting Environment Last', *Multinational Monitor*, Vol. 15(9), September 1994, http://www.essential.org/monitor/hyper/mm0994.html.

Multinational Monitor (1995a), 'Nigeria's Drilling Fields', *Multinational Monitor*, Vol. 16(1, 2), January/February, http://www.essential.org/monitor/hyper/mm0195. html.

Multinational Monitor (1995b) 'Mapuche Put Earth First', *Multinational Monitor*, Vol. 16(11), November 1995, http://www.essential.org/monitor/hyper/mm1195.09.html.

Multinational Monitor (1996), 'Behind the Lines', *Multinational Monitor*, Vol. 17(11), November, http://www.essential.org/monitor/hyper/mm1196.01.html.

Multinational Monitor (1997), 'The Lawrence Summers Memorial Award', *Multinational Monitor*, Vol. 18(5), November, http://www.essential.org/monitor/hyper/mm1197.04.html.

Murphy, C.N and Watson, Jr, T.J. (1998), 'Egalitarian Social Movements and New World Orders', paper presented at the British International Studies Association Annual Conference, University of Sussex, 14–16 December.

Muzaffer, C. (1993), 'Double Standards in the West', *World Press Review*, September.

Mwingira, M.J. (1999), 'Gender, Poverty and Sustainable Environment: A Challenge of our Times', paper presented at the Seminar of Experts on the Right to the Environment, Bilbao, Spain, 10–13 February.

Naess, A. (1973), 'The Shallow and the Deep, Long-Range Ecology Movement. A Summary', *Inquiry*, Vol. 16, pp. 95–100.

Naess, A. (1997), 'Deep Ecology', http://www.envirolink.org/elib/enviroethics/deepindex. html.

Nagel, T. (1994) in G. Dworkin (ed.), *Morality, Harm and the Law*, Westview Press, Boulder.

Nagy, A. (1995), 'Welcome Greenwash', *The Bulletin*, Winter, http://www.rec.hu/REC/Bulletin/Bull54/media.html.

Natali, S. (1993), 'The Political Agenda of the Wise Use Movement', June, http://www.ewg.org/pub/home/clear/on_wise/AFTE.html.

Nettheim G. (1992) in J. Crawford (ed.), *The Rights of People*, Clarendon Press, Oxford.

New Internationalist, The (1987), 'This Singing Land', *The New Internationalist*, No 177, November, pp. 12–3

New Internationalist, The (1991), 'To Bomb Greenpeace and be Made a Knight', *The New Internationalist*, No 226, December, p. 30.

New Scientist (1994a), 'Legal Air Pollution May Also Kill', *New Scientist*, Vol. 145(1), 1 January, p. 15.

New Scientist (1994b), 'Cars That Kill', *New Scientist*, Vol. 143(1945), 1 October, p. 3.

New Scientist (1995), 'Britain's Last Gasp', *New Scientist*, Vol. 146(1977), 13 May, p. 3.

New Scientist (1996), 'Death in the City', *New Scientist*, Vol. 150(2025), 13 April, p. 10.

Norman, R. (1983), *The Moral Philosophers*, Clarendon Press, Oxford.

Nusser, N. and Haurwitz, R.K.M. (1998), 'Toxic Waste Pollution One of Border Region's Worst Problems', *Cox News Service*, http://www.latinolink.com/news/bort1223.html.

Nuttall, N. (1995), 'Campaign Launched to Save Madagascan Forests From Mining', *The Times*, 19 January, p. 7.

O'Brien, R. (1997), 'Complex Multilateralism: The Global Economic Institutions – Global Social Movements Nexus', British International Studies Association conference paper.

O'Connell, P. (1999), 'WTO Boss: Protesters Harm the Poor', *BBC News*, 1 December, http://news.bbc.co.uk/hi/english/business/newsid_544000/544543.stm.

O'Connor, J. (1997), *Natural Causes*, Guilford Press, London.

Ogden, J.M. and Williams, R.H. (1989), *Solar Hydrogen: Moving Beyond Fossil Fuels*, World Resources Institute, Washington DC.

Ohm, B. (1997), 'Principles of Takings Law in Wisconsin', *Downstream*, Fall/Winter, http://www.geocities.com/Rainforest/8073/down1.html.

Olsen, M.E. (1970) in M.E. Olsen (ed.), *Power in Societies*, Macmillan, London.

Opschoor H. (1994) in W. Zweers and J. Boersema (eds), *Ecology, Technology and Culture: Essays in Environmental Philosophy*, White Horse Press, Cambridge.

Ostrom, E. (1990), *Governing the Commons*, Cambridge University Press, Cambridge.

Ostrom, E. and Schlager, E. (1996) in S. Hanna, C. Folke and K.G. Maler (eds), *Rights to Nature: Ecological, Economic, Cultural and Political Principles of Institutions for the Environment*, Island Press, Washington DC.

Ould-Mey, M. (1994), 'Global Adjustment: Implications for Peripheral States', *Third World Quarterly*, Vol. 15(2), pp. 319–36.

Pacenza, M. (1996), 'A People Damned: The Chixoy Dam, Guatemalan Massacres and the World Bank', *Multinational Monitor*, Vol. 17(7, 8), July/August, http://www. essential.org/monitor/hyper/mm0796.04.html.

Paine, T. (1987), *Thomas Paine Reader*, Penguin, London.

Painter, J. (1987), 'Country for Sale', *The New Internationalist*, No 177, November, pp. 9–10.

Parekh, B. (1973) in B. Parekh (ed.), *Bentham's Political Thought*, Croom Helm, London.

Park, P. (1991), 'Great Lakes Pollution Linked to Fertility', *New Scientist*, Vol. 131(1788), 28 September, p. 18.

Park, P. (1992), 'Canadian Cree Take Quebec's Hydro Scheme to Tribunal', *New Scientist*, Vol. 133(1806), 1 February, p. 15.

Patel, T. (1994), 'Killer Smog Stalks the Boulevards', *New Scientist*, Vol. 144(1947), 15 October, p. 8.

Patel, T. (1996), 'French Smog Smothers Hundreds', *New Scientist*, Vol. 149(2017), 17 February, p. 7.

Paterson, L. (1998), 'Famine Economist Wins Nobel Prize', *The Independent*, 15 October, p. 4.

Paterson, M. (1996a), 'UNCED in the Context of Globalisation', *New Political Economy*, Vol. 1(3), pp. 401–404.

Paterson, M. (1996b), *Global Warming and Global Politics*, Routledge, London.

Paterson, M. (2000), 'Car Culture and Global Environmental Politics', *Review of International Studies*, Vol. 26(2), pp. 253–70.

Paul, T.V. and Hall J.A. (1999) in T.V. Paul, and J.A. Hall (eds), *International Order and the Future of World Politics*, Cambridge University Press, Cambridge.

Payer, C. (1991), *Lent and Lost*, Zed Books, London.

Pearce, D. and Moran, D. (1993), 'Letters: Cash Concerns', *New Scientist*, Vol. 140(1894), 9 October, p. 52.

Pearce, D. and Turner, R K. (1990), *Economics of Natural Resources and the Environment*, Harvester Wheatsheaf, London.

Pearce, F. (1990), 'Hit and Run in Sarawak', *New Scientist*, Vol. 126(1716), 12 May, pp. 46–9.

Pearce, F. (1992a), 'No Southern Comfort at Rio?', *New Scientist*, Vol. 134(1821), 16 May, pp. 38–41.

Pearce, F. (1992b), 'Soils Spoilt by Farming and Industry', *New Scientist*, Vol. 134(1821), 16 May, p. 7.

Pearce, F. (1992c), 'Back to the Days of the Deadly Smogs', *New Scientist*, Vol. 136(1850), 5 December, pp. 24–8.

Pearce, F. (1993), 'Letters: New is Old', *New Scientist*, Vol. 139(1880), 3 July, p. 47.

Pearce, F. (1994a), 'Mounting Evidence Ties Asthma to Car Fumes', *New Scientist,* Vol. 143(1945), 1 October, p. 4.

Pearce, F. (1994b), 'Gummer Buries List of Poisoned Land', *New Scientist,* Vol. 144(1954), 3 December, p. 6.

Pender, J. (1995), 'You May As Well Kill Me Now', *Living Marxism*, Issue 83, October, http://www.informie.co.uk/LM/LM83/LM83Africa.html.

Penttinen, E. (2000) in H. Goverde, P. Cerny, M. Haugaard and H. Lentner (eds), *Power in Contemporary Politics*, Sage, London.

Perera, J. (1994), 'Tragedy of Muslimova', *New Scientist*, Vol. 141(1917), 19 March, pp. 40–43.

Permanent Peoples' Tribunal (1993), 'Charter on Industrial Hazards and Human Rights', *The Corporate Planet*, http://www.corwatch.org/trac/corner/altvision/charter.html.

Permanent Sovereignty Over Natural Resources (1962), General Assembly Resolution 1803 (XVII), 17 United Nations GAOR Supp. at 15, UN Doc A/5217, http://www.umn.edu/humanrts/instree/c2psnr.htm.

Perry, M.J. (1997), 'Are Human Rights Universal? The Relativist Challenge and Related Matters', *Human Rights Quarterly*, Vol. 19(3), pp. 461–509.

Pertman, A. (1994), 'Wise Use Foot Soldiers on the March', *Boston Globe*, 3 October, p. 25, http://www.cdfe.org/globe.html.

Phillips, J. (1997) in B.R. Johnston (ed.), *Human Rights and the Environment at the End of the Millennium*, Alta Mira, Walnut Creek.

Pi-Sunyer, O. and Thomas, R.B. (1997) in B.R. Johnston (ed.), *Human Rights and the Environment at the End of the Millennium*, Alta Mira, Walnut Creek.

Pickering, K. and Owen, L. (1994), *Global Environmental Issues*, Routledge, London.

Pilger, J. (1998), 'Hidden Agendas', *New Statesman and Society*, 15 May, p. 12.

Pinter, H. (1998), 'A State of War with Unlimited Duck in Lime Sauce for the Victor', *The Guardian* (debt supplement), 15 May, p. 7.

Polonsky, M.J. (1994), 'An Introduction to Green Marketing', *Electronic Green Journal*, Vol. 1(2), November, http://www.lib.uidaho.edu:70/docs/egj02/polon01. html.

Pomeroy, W. (1995), 'New US Attempts to Control World Economy', *People's Weekly World*, 28 January, http://www.hartford-hwp.com/archives/25a/011.html.

Pope, C.A. and Kanner, R.E. (1993), 'Acute Effects of PM 10 Pollution on Pulmonary Function of Smokers with Mild to Moderate Chronic Obstructive Pulmonary Disease', *American Review of Respiratory Disease*, Vol. 147, pp. 1336–40.

Pope, C.A., Schwartz, J. and Ransome, M.R. (1992), 'Daily Mortality and PM 10 Pollution in the Utah Valley', *Archive of Environmental Health*, Vol. 47, pp. 211–7.

Pope, C.A., Dockery, D.W., Spengler, J.D. and Raizenne, M.E. (1991), 'Respiratory Health and PM 10 Pollution: A Daily Time Series Analysis', *American Review of Respiratory Disease*, Vol. 144, pp. 668–74.

Porter, G. and Welsh Brown, J. (1991), *Global Environmental Politics*, Westview Press, Boulder, CO.

Postema, G. (1994) in G. Dworkin (ed.), *Morality, Harm and the Law*, Westview Press, Boulder, p.78.

Pozzolini, A. (1970), *Antonio Gramsci: An Introduction to his Thought*, Pluto Press, London.

Prakash, S. (1995), 'The Right to the Environment, Emerging Implications in Theory and Praxis', *Netherlands Quarterly of Human Rights*, Vol. 13(1), pp. 403–33.

Project International (1997), 'Occidental and Shell Threaten U'wa of Colombia', 19 October, http://www.alphacdc.com/ien/uwa.html.

Project Underground (1997a), 'Mind the Gap Between Shell's Rhetoric and Reality', *Drillbits and Tailings*, 21 May, p. 1, http://www.moles.org/ProjectUnderground/drillbits/970521/97052101.html.

Project Underground (1997b), 'Oxy and Shell Keep Pushing the U'wa of Colombia', *Drillbits and Tailings*, 7 October, p. 3, http://www.moles.org/ProjectUnderground/drillbits/971007/97100703.html.

Project Underground (1997c), 'Occidental: Supporting Suicide', 27 October, http://www.moles.org/ProjectUnderground/drillbits/motherlode/oxy.html.

Project Underground (1998), 'Mobil Operations in Sumatra (Indonesia) Investigated as Villagers Sue', *Drillbits and Tailings*, 21 December p. 1, http://www.moles.org/ProjectUnderground/drillbits/981221/98122101. html.

Public Citizen (1998a), 'Another Broken NAFTA Promise: Challenge by US Corporation Leads Canada to Repeal Public Health Law', *Public Citizen*, http://www.citizen.org/pctrade/nafta/ethyl.html.

Public Citizen (1998b), 'Ethyl Corporation vs Government of Canada', *Public Citizen*, http://www.citizen.org/pctrade/nafta/Ethylbri.html.

Pye-Smith C. and Feyerabend G.B. (1995) in J. Kirkby, P. O'Keefe and L. Timberlake (eds), *The Earthscan Reader in Sustainable Development*, Earthscan, London.

Qadir, S., Clapham, C. and Gills, B. (1993), 'Sustainable Democracy: Formalism v Substance', *Third World Quarterly*, Vol. 14(3), pp. 213–26.

Radford, T. (1997a), 'A Tale of Smogmobiles and Nanofibres', *The Guardian*, 23 October, p. 3.

Radford, T. (1997b), 'Around the Corner: The 80mpg Clean Car', *The Guardian*, 23 October, p. 3.

Raghavan, C. (1995), 'New Global Order in Crisis', *Third World Network*, 4 February, http://www.hartford-hwp.com/archives/25a/001.html.

Raghavan, C. (1996), 'TNCs Control Two-Thirds of World Economy', *Third World Network*, 26 January, http://www.hartford-hwp.com/archives/25/007.html.

Raghavan, C. (1996), 'Multinationals' Spreading Tentacles', *Multinational Monitor*, Vol. 17(3), March, http://www.essential.org/monitor/hyper/mm 0396.08.html.

Ramonet, I. (1998), 'Global Authoritarian Regimes', *New Renaissance*, http://www.ru.org/artgloba.html.

Rangnes, M.S. (1998), 'Canada Slapped with NAFTA Lawsuit Against Another Environmental Law', *Public Citizen Global Trade Watch*, 24 August, http://www.ban.org/ban_news/canada_slapped.html.

Ransome, P. (1992), *Antonio Gramsci: A New Introduction*, Harvester Wheatsheaf, New York.

Raven, P. (1995), The Melinda Denton Lecture 1995, 'What is Biological Diversity and Why is it Important to Us?', *Environmental Review*, June, http://www.igc.apc.org/envreview/raven.htm.

Rawls, J. (1972), *A Theory of Justice*, Oxford University Press, Oxford.

Read, C. (1989), 'Science: Even Low Levels of Ozone in Smog Harm the Lungs', *New Scientist*, Vol. 123(1681), 9 September, p. 40.

Read, R. and Read, C. (1991) 'Breathing can be Hazardous to your Health', *New Scientist*, Vol. 129(1757), 23 February, pp. 34–7.

Regan, T. (1984) in T. Regan (ed.), *Earthbound: New Introductory Essays in Environmental Ethics*, Temple University Press, Philadelphia.

Reguly, E. (1999), 'Global Warming Skeptics: Chill Out', *Globe and Mail*, 31 July, p. B2.

Rehman, S. (1993), *Agrarian Reform and Social Transformation*, Zed Books, London.

Reid (1995) in B. Hadfield (ed.), *Judicial Review: A Thematic Approach*, Gill and Macmillan, Dublin.

Renteln, A.D. (1990), *International Human Rights: Universalism v Relativism*, Sage, London.

Rest, A. (1994), 'Implementing the Principles of Intergenerational Equity and Responsibility', *Environmental Policy and Law*, Vol. 24(6), pp. 314–20.

Rest, A. (1998), 'Improved Environmental Protection Through an Expanded Concept of Human Rights in Europe', http://www.xcom.it/icef/abstracts/rest/html.

Reuters (1999), 'Global Anti-Pollution Pact Near', *Times Colonist*, 7 September, p. A4.

Reynolds, P. (1999), 'Trade Protesters Spark Emergency', *BBC News*, 1 December, http://news.bbc.co.hi/english/world/americas/newsid_544000/544447.stm.

Rich, B. (1994), *Mortgaging the Earth*, Earthscan, London.

Richards, H. (1987), 'Dependency Theory', *The New Internationalist*, No. 167, January, p. 23.

Rifkin, J. (1992) 'Bovine Burden', *Geographical Magazine*, July, pp. 12–6.

Rizvi, H. (1995), 'Haiti Bucks Privatization', *Multinational Monitor*, Vol. 16(11), November, http://www.essential.org/monitor/hyper/mm1195.03.html.

Roberts, C. (1997), 'Both Sides: Exxon v Environment', CNN 17 August 1997 published in *Downstream*, Fall/Winter, http://www.geocities.com/Rainforest/8073/down1.html.

Robertson, B. (1995), 'Refocusing the Human Rights Debate in East Asia: A Review of Recent Writings', *Human Rights Dialogue*, Vol. 2, September, http://www.cceia.org/dialog2.html.

Robinson, F. (1995), 'Contractarianism and Rights-Based Morality: The Limits of a Human Rights Approach to International Ethics', British International Studies Association conference paper, Southampton, 18–20 December.

Roemer, W., Hoek, G. and Brunekreef, B. (1993), 'Effect of Ambient Winter Air Pollution on Respiratory Health of Children with Chronic Respiratory Symptoms', *American Review of Respiratory Disease*, Vol. 147, pp. 118–24.

Rogers, A. (1994), 'Environmental Rights', *Lancet*, Vol. 344, Issue 8938, 17 December, p. 1695.

Rolston, H. (1981), 'Values in Nature', *Environmental Ethics*, Vol. 3(2), Summer, pp. 113–28.

Root, A. (1987), 'Exporting Illusion: The New Imperialism', *The New Internationalist*, No. 167, January, pp. 4–6.

Rosenau, J. (1993) in J.N. Rosenau (ed.), *Global Voices*, Westview Press, Boulder.

Rosenbaum, A. (1980) in A. Rosenbaum (ed.), *The Philosophy of Human Rights: International Perspectives*, Aldwych Press, London.

Rosenberg, J. (1994), *The Empire of Civil Society: A Critique of the Realist Theory of International Relations*, Verso, London.

Ross, R.J.S. (1996), 'Agency and Enlightenment', *Journal of World-Systems Research*, Vol. 2(2), http://csf.colorado.edu/wsystems/jwsr.html.

Rounds, D. (1995), 'Neo-liberalism in Latin America: A Critique in the Framework of Karl Polanyi', http://psirus.sfsu.edu/IntRel/IRJournal/wi95/w95neoliberalism. html.

Rowell, A. (1996), *Green Backlash: Global Subversion of the Environmental Movement*, Routledge, New York.

Rowell, A. (1999), 'Greenwash Goes Legit', *The Guardian*, 21 July, p. 5.

Royal Dutch Shell Group (1999), advertisement, *New Statesman*, 9 April, pp. 14–5.

Roychowdhury, A. (1998), 'False Start: Pollution Control Agencies Are Toothless', *Down to Earth*, Vol. 7(4), 15 July, http://www.oneworld.org/cse/html/dte/dte 980715/dte_cross.html.

Ruhl, J.B. (1997), 'An Environmental Rights Amendment: Good Message, Bad Idea', *Natural Resources and the Environment*, Vol. 11(3), pp. 46–9.

Rupert, M. (1995), *Producing Hegemony: The Politics of Mass Production and American Global Power*, Cambridge University Press, Cambridge.

Russell, B. (1948), *Power: A New Social Analysis*, George Allen and Unwin, London.

Sabir, N.Z. (1995), 'A Hazardous Existence', *Black Enterprise*, Vol. 25, Issue 8, March, pp. 25–41.

Sachs, A. (1995), *Eco-Justice: Linking Human Rights and the Environment*, Worldwatch Paper 127, Worldwatch Institute, Washington DC.

Sachs, A. (1996a), 'Dying For Oil', *World Watch*, May/June, pp. 10–21.

Sachs, A. (1996b) 'State of the World 1996', The Worldwatch Institute, http:// worldwatch. org/pubs/sow/sow96/ch08.html.

Sachs, W. (1993) in W. Sachs (ed.), *Global Ecology*, Zed Books, London.

Sagoff, M. (1984) in T. Regan (ed.), *Earthbound*, Temple University Press, Philadelphia.

Sagoff, M. (1995) in A. Brennan (ed.), *The Ethics of the Environment*, Dartmouth, London.

Sagoff, M. (1997), 'Do We Consume Too Much?', *The Atlantic Monthly*, Vol. 279(6), June, pp. 80–96, http://www.theatlantic.com/atlantic/issues/97jun/ consume.html.

Salmi, J. (1993), *Violence and Democratic Society: New Approaches to Human Rights*, Zed Books, London.

Sanderson, S.K. (1996), 'The Future of W Warren Wagar', *Journal of World-Systems Research*, Vol. 2(2), pp. 1–12.

Sattaur, O. (1991), 'Decade of Disaster Predicted for Third World', *New Scientist*, Vol. 132(1789), 5 October, p. 14.

Sattaur, O. (1994) 'Review: Hour of the Soft Revolutionaries', *New Scientist*, Vol. 141(1917), 19 March, p. 47.

Saurin J. (1993) in C. Thomas (ed.), *Rio: Unravelling the Consequences*, Frank Cass, Ilford.

Schaap, A. (2000), 'Power and Responsibility: Should we Spare the King's Head?' *Politics*, Vol. 20(3), pp. 129–36.

Schindler, D.L. (1994) in B.R. Johnston (ed.), *Who Pays the Price?*, Island Press, Washington DC.

Schmidt, K. (1996), 'The Zero Option', *New Scientist*, Vol. 150(2032), 1 June, pp. 32–7.

Schoon, N. (1997), 'US Proposes Swap Club for Emissions', *The Independent*, 10 December, p. 8.

Schwartz, J. (1994a), 'What Are People Dying of on High Pollution Days?' *Environmental Research*, Vol. 64, pp. 26–35.

Schwartz, J. (1994b), 'Air Pollution and Daily Mortality: A Review and Meta-Analysis', *Environmental Research*, Vol. 64, pp. 36–52.

Seaton, A. (1995), 'Bookshelf', *The Lancet*, Vol. 346(8977), 16 September, p. 759.

Seaton, A., MacNee, W., Donaldson, K. and Godden, D. (1995), 'Particulate Air Pollution and Acute Health Effects', *Lancet*, Vol. 345(8943), 21 January, pp. 176–8.

Secrett, C. (1993), 'Fight for Your Rights', *Earth Matters*, Issue 20, Winter, p. 1.

Sen, A. (1983) in A. Gauer (ed.) *South – South Strategy*, Third World Foundation, Penang.

Sen, A. (1996), 'Thinking About Human Rights and Asian Values', *Human Rights Dialogue*, Vol. 4, March, http://www.cceia.org/dialog4.html.

Sennott, C. (1996), 'The $150 Billion Welfare Recipients: US Corporations', *Boston Globe*, 7 July, p. 1.

Sessions, G. and Naess, A. (1991) in J. Davis (ed.), *The Earth First! Reader*, Gibbs Smith, Layton, UT, pp. 157–60.

Sharon, H. (1994), 'Forum: Convergent We Stand, Divided We Fall', *New Scientist*, Vol. 142(1919), 2 April, pp. 39–40.

Shelton, D. (1991), 'Human Rights, Environmental Rights and the Right to Environment', *Stanford Journal of International Law*, Vol. 28(1), pp. 103–38.

Shiva, V. (1991), *The Violence of the Green Revolution: Third World Agriculture, Ecology and Politics*, Third World Network, Penang.

Shiva, V. (1996), 'Seeds of Discontent', *Multinational Monitor*, Vol. 17(6), June, http://www.essential.org/monitor/hyper/mm0696.08.html.

Shiva, V. (1998), 'Creative Principles: Fighting Capitalism and Patriarchy on a World Scale', http://tdg.uoguelph.ca/~kwakely/rhizone/twt/shiva_creative.html.

Shue, H. (1980), *Basic Rights: Subsistence, Affluence and United States Foreign Policy*, Princeton University Press, Princeton.

Shute, S. and Hurley, S. (1993) in S. Shute and S. Hurley (eds), *On Human Rights: The Oxford Amnesty Lectures 1993*, Harper Collins.

Shute, S. and Hurley, S. (1994) in S. Shute and S. Hurley (eds), *On Human Rights*, Basic Books, London.

Silverstein, K. (1996), 'Defending Corporate Welfare', *Multinational Monitor*, Vol. 17(12), December, http://www.essential.org/monitor/hyper/mm1296.09.html.

Simpkins, J. and William, J.J. (1992), *Advanced Biology*, Collins, London.

Singer, P. (1990), *Animal Liberation*, Thorsons, London.

Sloep, P. and Blowes, A. (1996) in P. Sloep and A. Blowes (eds), *Environmental Policy in an International Context*, Arnold, London.

Smith, D.M. (1981), *Where the Grass is Greener*, Penguin, Harmondsworth.

Smith, G. (1996), *Pluralism, Deliberative Democracy and Environmental Values*, PhD Thesis, University of Southampton, Southampton.

Smith, L. (1992), 'Indigenous Rights', *Race and Class*, Vol. 33(3), p. 104.

Smith, M.J. (1986), *Realist Thought From Weber to Kissinger*, Louisiana State University Press, Baton Rouge.

Smith, M.J. (1998), *Social Science in Question*, Sage, London.

Smith, S., Booth K. and Zalewski, M. (1996) in S. Smith, K. Booth and M. Zalewski (eds), *International Theory: Positivism and Beyond*, Cambridge University Press, Cambridge.

Solis, O. (1996), 'Defending the State, Empowering the People', *Multinational Monitor*, Vol. 17(9), September, http://www.essential.org/monitor/hyper/mm 0996.06.html.

Sorenson, G. (1993) in G. Sorenson (ed.), *Political Conditionality*, Frank Cass, London.

South and Meso American Indian Rights Center (SAIIC) (1998), 'Urgent Action: International Day of Action in Support of the Indigenous People and Land of Nicaragua's Atlantic Coast', http://www.nativeweb.org/saiic/actions/urgent12up. html.

South West Organising Project (1998), 'Community Environmental Bill of Rights', *The Corporate Planet*, http://www.corwatch.org/trac/feature/hitech/swopbill. html.

Sponzel, L. (1994) in B.R. Johnston (ed.), *Who Pays the Price?*, Island Press, Washington DC.

Stammers, N. (1983), 'Human Rights and Power', *Political Studies*, Vol. XLI, pp. 70–82.

Stammers, N. (1995), 'A Critique of Social Approaches to Human Rights', *Human Rights Quarterly*, Vol. 17, pp. 488–508.

Stammers, N. (1999), 'Social Movements and the Social Construction of Human Rights', *Human Rights Quarterly*, Vol. 21(4), pp. 980–1008.

Stanford, J. (1993), 'Free Trade and the Imaginary Worlds of Economic Modelers', 5 April, gopher://csf.colorado.edu:70/00ipe/Th...ade_Imaginery_Worlds_Economic _Modelers.

Stansel, D. (1997), 'Corporate Welfare', *CATO Handbook for Congress*, http://www.cato.org/pubs/handbook/hb105–9.html.

Stea, D., Elguea, S. and Bustillo, C.R. (1997) in B.R. Johnston (ed.), *Human Rights and the Environment at the End of the Millennium*, Alta Mira, Walnut Creek.

Steele, J. (1997), 'Bloody Deeds Raised Against People's Struggle to Control Their Resources', *The Guardian*, 11 November, p. 3.

Steiner, H. (1994), *An Essay on Rights*, Blackwell, Oxford.

Stephens, J.F. (1994) in G. Dworkin (ed.), *Morality, Harm and the Law*, Westview Press, Boulder.

Stiglitz, J. (1998), 'That Elusive Blueprint for Debt Relief', *The Guardian*, 18 May, p. 19.

Stonich, S.C. (1994) in B.R. Johnston (ed.), *Who Pays the Price?*, Island Press, Washington DC.

Strider, R. (1995), 'Blood in the Pipeline', *Multinational Monitor*, Vol. 16(1, 2), January/February, http://www.essential.org/monitor/hyper/mm0195.html.

Sturnot, L. (1997), 'Coalition for Fair Regulation', *Downstream*, Fall/Winter, http://www.geocities.com/Rainforest/8073/down1.html.

Sumner, C. (1979), *Reading Ideologies*, Academic Press, London.

Sweatshop Watch (1998), 'The Garment Industry', http://www.sweatshopwatch.org/ indur.html.

Swope, L., Swain, M.B., Yang, F. and Ives, J.D. (1997) in B.R. Johnston (ed.), *Human Rights and the Environment at the End of the Millennium*, Alta Mira, Walnut Creek.

Symonides, J. (1999), 'Address to the Seminar of Experts on the Right to the Environment', Bilbao, Spain, 10–13 February.

Tan, K.Y.L. (1996), 'What Asians Think About the West's Response to the Human Rights Debate', *Human Rights Dialogue*, Vol. 4, March, http://www.cceia.org/dialog4.html.

Tandon, Y. (1993) in W. Sachs (ed.), *Global Ecology*, Zed Books, London.

Tansey, S.D. (1995), *Politics*, Routledge, London.

Tarlock, D. (1988), 'Earth and Other Ethics: The Institutional Issues', *Tennessee Law Review*, Vol. 56, pp. 43–76.

Taylor, A. (1998), 'The Significance of Non-governmental Organisations in the Development of International Environmental Policy: The Case of Trade and Environment', PhD thesis, Southampton University, Southampton.

Taylor, A. and Thomas C. (1999) in A. Taylor and C. Thomas (eds), *Global Trade and Global Social Issues*, Routledge, London.

Taylor C. (1986) in D.C. Hoy (ed.), *Foucault: A Critical Reader*, Blackwell, Oxford.

Taylor, P.W. (1986) *Respect for Nature*, Princeton University Press, Princeton.

Tetreault, M.A. (1988), 'Regimes and Liberal World Orders', *Alternatives*, Vol. XIII, pp. 1–27.

Third World Resurgence editors (1994) (untitled), *Third World Resurgence*, No. 50, October, p. 18.

Thomas, C. (1993a), 'Beyond UNCED: An Introduction', *Environmental Politics*, Vol. 2(4), pp. 1–27.

Thomas, C. (1993b) in C. Thomas (ed.), *Rio: Unravelling the Consequences*, Frank Cass, Ilford.

Thomas, C. (1995), 'Market Forces Put Pressure on Traditions', *The Times*, 15 August, p. 18.

Thomas, C. (1996), 'Unsustainable Development?', *New Political Economy*, Vol. 1(3), pp. 404–408.

Thomas, C. (1999), 'Where is the Third World Now?', *Review of International Studies*, December, Vol. 25, pp. 225–44.

Thomas C. and Weber, M. (1999) in A. Taylor and C. Thomas (eds), *Global Trade and Global Social Issues*, Routledge, London.

Thoreau, H.D. (1993), *Walden and Civil Disobedience*, Penguin, New York.

Timberlake, L. (1985), *Africa in Crisis*, Earthscan, London.

Timberlake, L. and Thomas, L. (1990), *When the Bough Breaks*, Earthscan, London.

Timberlake, M. (1996), 'Book Review', *Journal of World-Systems Research*, Vol. 2(5), http://csf.colorado.edu/wsystems/jwsr.html.

Tinder, G. (1979), *Political Thinking: The Perennial Questions*, Little, Brown and Company, Boston.

Tomasevski, K. (1993), *Development Aid and Human Rights Revisited*, Pinter Publishers, London.

Tully, J. (1999), 'An Ecological Ethics for the Present' (transcript), p. 21, since published in B. Gleeson and N. Low (eds), *Government for the Environment*, Macmillan, London.

UNESCO (1995), 'Fact File', *United Nations Economic and Social Council Courier*, March, p. 30.

United Nations Development Programme (1999), 'Habitat and UNEP Welcome the Weekend Car Ban in Italy', 8 February, http://www.unep.org/Documents/Default. asp.html.

Universal Declaration on the Eradication of Hunger and Malnutrition (1974), adopted by the World Food Conference, Rome, UN Doc E/CONF. 65/20, at 1, http://www.umn.edu/humanrts/instree/q1uddehm.htm.

Vaughan, C. and Cross, M. (1990), 'Streetwise to the Dangers of Ozone', *New Scientist*, Vol. 126(1718), 26 May, pp. 56–9.

Vaux, T. (1987), 'Cast-off Colonies', *The New Internationalist*, No. 167, January, p. 21.

Vidal, J. (1998), 'A Dirty Business Bogged Down in a Moral and Political Mire', *The Guardian*, 15 August, p. 5.

Vincent, R.J. (1986), *Human Rights and International Relations*, Cambridge University Press, Cambridge.

Vogler, J. (1995), *The Global Commons: A Regime Analysis*, John Wiley and Sons, Chichester.

Wagar, W. (1996), 'Toward a Praxis of World Integration', *Journal of World-Systems Research*, Vol. 2(2), http://csf.colorado.edu/jwsr.html.

Waks, L.J. (1996), 'Environmental Claims and Citizen Rights', *Environmental Ethics*, Vol. 18(2), pp. 133–48.

Waldron, J. (1984) in J. Waldron (ed.), *Theories of Rights*, Oxford University Press, Oxford.

Waligorski, C.P. (1990), *The Political Theory of Conservative Economics*, University Press of Kansas, Kansas.

Walker, R. (1990), 'Security, Sovereignty and the Challenge of World Politics', *Alternatives*, Vol. 15(1), pp. 12–25.

Walker, R. (1993), *Inside/Outside: International Relations as Political Theory*, Cambridge University Press, Cambridge.

Walker, R. (1996), 'Book Reviews', *The Professional Geographer*, Vol. 48(1), February, pp. 117–8.

Wallerstein, I. (1979), *The Capitalist World Economy*, Cambridge University Press, Cambridge.

Wallerstein, I. (1983), *Historical Capitalism*, Verso, London.

Wallerstein, I. (1991) in R. Little and M. Smith (eds), *Perspectives on World Politics*, Second Edition, Routledge, London.

Wallerstein, I. (1995), 'The Modern World System and Evolution', *Journal of World-Systems Research*, Vol. 1(19), http://csf.colorado.edu/wsystems/ jwsr.html.

Walton, J. and Seddon, D. (1994) in J. Walton, and D. Seddon (eds), *Free Markets and Food Riots: The Politics of Global Adjustment*, Blackwell, Cambridge.

Ward, S. (1996), 'UK Local Authorities and Local Agenda 21', *New Political Economy*, Vol. 1(3), pp. 412–6.

Warren, B. (1980), *Imperialism: Pioneer of Capitalism*, Verso, London.

Watson, J.S. (1979), 'Legal Theory, Efficacy and Validity in the Development of Human Rights Norms in International Law', *University of Illinois Law Forum*, Vol. 3, pp. 609–41.

Weale, A. (1998) in P. Kelly (ed.), *Impartiality, Neutrality and Justice*, Edinburgh University Press, Edinburgh.

Weber, H. (1999), 'Global Finance, Development Finance Institutions and the Microcredit Approach to Poverty', paper presented at the International Studies Association Annual Conference, Washington.

Weinberg, P. (1998), 'Selling Myth of Powerlessness in Global Economy', *Inter Press Service*, 18 April, http://www.oneworld.org/ips2/apr98/04_25_006.html.

Weissman, R. (1996), 'The WTO Strikes', *Multinational Monitor*, Vol. 17(1, 2), January/February, p. 5.

Weissman, R. (1996), 'A Tailings Tall Tale', *Multinational Monitor*, Vol. 17(3), March, http://www.essential.org/monitor/hyper /mm0396.03.html.

Weissman, R. (1996), 'Book Review: Breakfast of Biodiversity', *Multinational Monitor*, Vol. 17(4), April, http://www.essential.org/monitor/hyper/mm0496.11. html.

Weissman, R. (1996a), 'Waiting to Export: Africa Embraces Export Processing Zones', *Multinational Monitor*, Vol. 17(7, 8), July/August, http:www.essential. org/monitor/ hyper/ mm0796.05.html.

Weissman, R. (1996b), 'Another NAFTA Nightmare', *Multinational Monitor*, Vol. 17(10), October, http://www.essential.org/monitor/hyper/mm1096.03.html.

Weissman, R. (1997), 'Book Notes', *Multinational Monitor*, Vol. 18(5), May, http:/ /www.essential.org/monitor/hyper/mm0597.12.html.

Werksman, J. (1996) in J. Werksman (ed.), *Greening International Institutions*, Earthscan, London.

Wesselius, E. (1995), 'Corporate Lobbying by the International Chamber of Commerce', 23 October, http://www.hartford-hwp.com/archives/25a/009.html.

Westlund, M. (1998), 'Central African Rainforests', received 12 February as email from *The Sierra Club*.

Wheat, A. (1995) 'Exporting Repression', *Multinational Monitor*, Vol. 16(1,2), January/February, http://www.essential.org/monitor/hyper/mm0195.html.

Wheat, A. (1996), 'Troubled NAFTA Waters', *Multinational Monitor*, Vol. 17(4), April, http://www.essential.org/monitor/hyper/mm0496.08.html.

Wheeler, D. (1993) in L. Harrison (ed.), *Environmental Auditing Handbook*, McGraw Hill, New York.

Wheeler, T. (1996), 'The Global Pillage: Whose World Economy is it Anyway?', *People's Weekly World*, 9 November, http://www.hartford-hwp.com/archives/25/020.html.

Wignaraja, P. (1993), *New Social Movements in the South*, Zed Books, London.

Wilkin, P. (1995), 'New Myths for the South: Globalisation and the Conflict Between Private Power and Freedom', British International Studies Association Conference Paper, Southampton, 20 December.

Williams, H. (1991), *Autogeddon*, Jonathan Cape, London.

Williams, H., Wright, M. and Evans, T. (1993), *A Reader in International Relations and Political Theory*, Open University Press, Buckingham.

Williams M. (1993) in C. Thomas (ed.), *Rio: Unravelling the Consequences*, Frank Cass, Ilford.

Williams, M. (1994), *International Economic Organisation and the Third World*, Harvester Wheatsheaf, Hemel Hempstead.

Williams, R.H. (1989), *Solar Hydrogen: Moving Beyond Fossil Fuels*, World Resources Institute, Washington DC.

Wisner, B. (1995), 'The Reconstructing of Environmental Rights in Urban South Africa', *Human Ecology*, Vol. 23(2), June, pp. 259–84.

Wiwa, K.S. (1995), 'Nigeria in Crisis', *Review of African Political Economy*, Vol. 22(64), June, pp. 234–56.

Wiwa, O. (1996), 'A Call to End the Shelling of Nigeria', *Multinational Monitor*, Vol. 17(7, 8), July/August, http:www.essentialorg/monitor/hyper/mm0796.05.html.

Wood, N. (1984), *John Locke and Agrarian Capitalism*, University of California Press, Berkeley.

Woollacott, M. (1995), 'A World Forced to Keep Bad Company', *The Guardian*, 18 November, p. 8.

World Bank (1995), *Mainstreaming the Environment*, World Bank, Washington DC.

World Health (1993), 'Air Pollution', *World Health*, Vol. 141(22), September/October, pp. 18–9.

World Rainforest Movement and Forests Monitor Ltd. (1998), *High Stakes: The Need to Control Transnational Logging Companies*, World Forest Movement, Montevideo.

World Wide Fund for Nature (1990), *WWF Handbook*, Macdonald and Company, London.

Worldwatch Institute (1995), 'Worldwide Repression of Peaceful Environmental Protestors Spurs new Coalitions with Human Rights Activists', 9 December, http://www.antenna.nl/news/women/180days/mn 00161.html.

Wright, D. (1998), 'Greenhouse Effect ... Or Not?', *Geography Review*, Vol. 12(1), September, pp. 10–13.

Wright, S. (1997), 'U'wa Indigenous Leader Beaten and Threatened', *Rainforest Action Network*, 20 October, http://www.alphacdc.com/ien/uwa.html.

Yamin, K. (1998), 'Freer Trade May Quicken Pace of Logging', *Inter Press Service*, 5 January, http://www.oneworld.org/ips2/jan98/indonesia2.html.

Yates, A. (1998), 'Rio Tinto Faces Wrath of Investors', *The Independent*, 14 May, p. 20.

Young, C.M. (1992), 'Noam Chomsky: Anarchy in the USA', *Rolling Stone*, Issue 631, 28 May, pp. 42–51.

Ziman, J.E. (1997), 'The Social and Environmental Costs of Oil Company Divestment From US Refineries', *Multinational Monitor*, May, Vol. 18(5), http://www. essential.org/monitor/hyper/mm0597.12.html.

Zimbabwe Trust, Department of National Parks and Wildlife Management and the CAMPFIRE Association (1990), *People, Wildlife and Natural Resources – The CAMPFIRE Approach to Rural Development in Zimbabwe*, Zimbabwe Trust, Harare.

Zinn, C. (1998), 'Aboriginals Win Title to the Sea', *The Guardian*, 7 July, p. 15.

Zweers, W. and Boersema, J. (1994) in W. Zweers and J. Boersema (ed.), *Ecology, Technology and Culture: Essays in Environmental Philosophy*, White Horse Press, Cambridge.

Index